The need to read Scripture in its context is vital if we are to understand it properly, but grasping that whole context is not always easy for those without professional training. In this useful book, Dr. Leschert provides the reader with valuable help in seeing how the New Testament writers develop their themes and teaching. He provides a clear summary of what each book is saying and traces the flow of the writing chapter by chapter. A helpful overview together with a more detailed outline of each book is also supplied. Comments are kept to a minimum and the text is allowed to speak for itself. A fine help to all who want to dig deeper into the books of the New Testament.

Dr. Paul Gardner
Vicar of Hartford

Dale Leschert has produced a fine book which has as its sole purpose the assisting of readers in acquiring a basic knowledge of the content of the New Testament. Rather than being another book about the New Testament, this book focuses on what the New Testament itself says, with a minimum of interpretation. Very helpful, detailed outlines are provided for each book and they serve as the foundation for carefully written expositions that unfailingly take the reader to the heart of the matter. From working through this book, readers will acquire a sense of the flow of the New Testament, just as the title suggests. I know of no book that accomplishes this task as effectively as Dr. Leschert's and I am happy to recommend it.

Donald A. Hagner
George Eldon Ladd Professor of New Testament
Fuller Theological Seminary

Dale Leschert combines the insights of a scholar with the communicative skills of a pastor-teacher as he guides us through the unfolding message of the New Testament. In so doing, he provides a tool that takes the reader from overview, through detailed outline to a comprehensive, flowing summary of each New Testament book. Here is a study guide which will prove to be a true asset to anyone who wants to engage in serious Bible study, or who is looking for help in preparing to teach the New Testament to others.

Mark G. Johnston
Grove Chapel, London

I am most happy to commend *The Flow of the New Testament*. I know of no other title which covers the ground occupied by Dr. Leschert's work. The summaries, as indeed the whole book, are pleasingly clear and straightforward. The text reads smoothly and admirably accomplishes its goal of providing a summary of the entire New Testament. Dr. Leschert wisely avoids unhelpful controversies and keeps the main thread constantly in view.

At a time when so many people, young and old, are coming into a living faith without any previous Biblical knowledge, this book should prove a godsend in giving them a readable, comprehensive summary of the contents of the New Testament. But it will also have a ministry to those whose knowledge of the New Testament books is confined to certain well-worn passages and lacks the sense of the larger context of the book as a whole. I commend *The Flow of the New Testament* most heartily. May the Lord be pleased to use it widely to the good of his people.

Dr. Bruce Milne
First Baptist Church, Vancouver

The wonderful goal of our earliest translators of the Bible into English was to enable ordinary Christians to read the Bible for themselves, in their own English language, in their own copies. Dale Leschert's book continues this same heritage. His desire is to empower ordinary Christians to understand the New Testament. While the modern era has seen the production of many significant interpretative commentaries and other tools for interpreting the New Testament, most of these are too technical and detailed for the average Christian who lacks special training. This situation cannot be consistent with God's purpose of communicating his glorious truth with all people everywhere. Dale Leschert's book is needed to fill a niche where every Christian can begin to understand God's marvellous word, and go on from there, if desired, to more comprehensive sources for interpretation. Dale's outlines and accompanying comments are detailed and comprehensive enough to illumine the meaning of the text, but do not encumber the reader with the research or technical matters which underlie his interpretations. The vulgar translations in our heritage must be accompanied by vulgar tools for interpretation.

James B. De Young
Professor of New Testament Language and Literature,
Western Seminary, Portland, Oregon

THE FLOW OF THE NEW TESTAMENT

DALE LESCHERT

MENTOR

This book is dedicated in memory of my father,
Paul Leschert,
who first introduced me to the sacred Scriptures
that are able to make one wise unto salvation.

© Dale F. Leschert
ISBN 1 857 92 501 7

Published in 2002 by
Christian Focus Publications,
Geanies House, Fearn, Ross-shire,
IV20 1TW, Great Britain

www.christianfocus.com

Cover design by Owen Daily

Contents

THE PAULINE EPISTLES

THE MISSIONARY EPISTLES

THE PRISON EPISTLES

THE PASTORAL EPISTLES

THE GENERAL EPISTLES

PROPHECY

Information Boxes

Maps

PREFACE

This preface is intended for readers who want to know what this book is about and how to derive the maximum benefit from it. Those who are impatient and are confident that the plan of the book is self-evident may plunge right in, but they will likely miss some valuable insights and stumble over questions along the way that could have been answered by spending a few minutes here at the outset. The choice between reading the preface or skipping it is similar to the choice facing a person who purchases a new computer program or a gadget that needs to be assembled. Some people meticulously read the manual first; others, who couldn't be bothered, prefer to learn by trial and error. Both methods can work, but they are not always equally efficient. Sometimes intuition is rewarded; other times deliberate patience can produce superior results more quickly. Reading this preface is not required, but it is recommended for those who have any doubts.

What this Book is About
Although the Reformation goal of placing the Bible in the hands of every ploughboy to read and understand for himself has been with us for almost five hundred years, this aspiration has not yet been fully realized. Thankfully, Scripture is now readily available for anyone to read in almost every major language across the face of the globe; but even in the "Christianized" western world, the majority of lay people still have only a superficial acquaintance with the actual contents of the Bible. Even though excellent scholarly commentaries and biblical studies are being published at an unprecedented rate, it seems that the average person in the pew lacks either the inclination, the time, or the technical expertise to take full advantage of these valuable resources.

The Flow of the New Testament attempts to make the most important book in the world accessible to ordinary people without becoming light and fluffy. Although it respects the best in scholarship, it seeks to transcend the narrow interests of professional scholars in order to serve the more basic need of lay people to understand the Scriptures for themselves. It provides the reader with an efficient and exegetically accurate tool for opening up the contents of the whole New Testament. To achieve this end it builds upon a series of expository outlines that unfold the literary structure and logical development of each New Testament book in a highly concentrated and comprehensive manner. The substance of these outlines has then been recast into essay format in order to facilitate reading ease and make important transitions and connections clear.

Without in any way demeaning the important work of careful exegesis, *The Flow of the New Testament* purposely looks past the minutia and seeks to elucidate the New Testament as a whole. An artist paints the delicate petals of a flower with a fine brush, but he uses broader strokes to sketch the mountains in the background. This book paints the mountains and sky rather than individual flowers. Rather than examining a tiny fragment of Scripture under a microscope, it projects the contents of the entire New Testament onto a giant screen so that the reader can gaze at the breathtaking panorama of the whole range of scriptural mountains and valleys, forests and meadows, lakes and streams.

As recent discussions of the hermeneutical circle have shown, it is critically important to gain a correct understanding of the whole in order to interpret the parts accurately. The task of interpretation always involves an ongoing interchange between analysis and synthesis. Scripture needs to be broken up into little parts in order to examine the intricacies of its grammar and syntax, but it also needs to be put back together.

The Flow of the New Testament builds upon the fruits of scholarship that have helped to define the parameters of our study, and it prepares the way, in turn, for more careful exegesis to bring the fine details that have been overlooked into clear focus. Although it lies beyond the scope of our immediate objective here, all of these steps in the interpretive process are preliminary to the final goal of personally applying Scripture to ourselves so that by bringing our lives into conformity with the will of God we might glorify him.

How this Book Differs from Other Books

The Flow of the New Testament is unique in that it uses detailed expository outlines and essays to unfold the literary structure and logical development of each New Testament book in a way that makes the fruits of careful scholarship readily accessible to ordinary people without sacrificing either exegetical accuracy or literary quality. Some books on the New Testament may bear a superficial resemblance to this book, but their true essence is not the same. Others touch upon our concerns, but either they do so incidentally on the way to another goal or they do not treat the entire New Testament in a thorough manner.

The singular focus of this book upon the contents of the New Testament allows readers to proceed directly to the heart of the matter without becoming lost in peripheral issues, as can easily happen in standard New Testament introductions or surveys. Some excellent New Testament introductions are available, but their critical purpose requires technical discussions of authorship, destination, and sources that would side-track beginning students whose primary interest lies in the contents of the New Testament itself. *The Flow of the New Testament* is not an introduction in the traditional sense; it focuses, rather, on content and structure and holds critical questions at a distance. *The Flow of the New Testament* also differs from the standard New Testament surveys, in that it offers more detailed and useful outlines and avoids detailed discussions of historical and cultural backgrounds. Although a few older surveys of the entire Bible contain reasonably full outlines, they tend to be more homiletical than exegetical and do not always accurately reflect the structure of the biblical writers. The recent popularity of applying linguistic principles to Scripture has produced a number of studies in discourse, or structural, analysis, but so far they only treat individual books and not the entire New Testament.

Most commentaries include an outline (or, in the British tradition, an analysis) of the book under consideration, but they are generally disappointing. With a few exceptions, they are usually rather sketchy. Their headings are often ambiguous and lack descriptiveness; at times they are not even exegetically accurate. Even the outlines in the most scholarly commentaries often suffer from poor literary quality. Their headings are seldom grammatically parallel, and they often fail to maintain logical coherence or proper subordination between points. New Testament commentaries generally do better at exegeting the meaning of their texts than they do at outlining the structure of an entire book, and The Flow of the New Testament is not intended to take their place in exegesis. Rather, it grows out of original exegesis and is a first step towards engaging the reader in the same interpretive process. After working through this book to gain a clearer understanding of the New Testament as a whole, the reader should go back and study its parts in greater detail with the assistance of several good commentaries.

How this Book could be Useful

The general usefulness of *The Flow of the New Testament* could vary slightly from one New Testament book to another, and a variety of readers could find it particularly useful for attaining different objectives. The existence of different literary genres in the New Testament means that different books require slightly different approaches and our structural analysis of them will serve slightly different ends.

The historical books of the New Testament would not be intelligible to us as an endless list of isolated incidents or as a loose assortment of unrelated literary fragments. Even in the Synoptic Gospels, which form criticism has unfortunately stylized as a broken string of pearls, the narrative follows an orderly progression, and the freedom that Matthew or Luke show in departing from the Markan chronology is instructive of their peculiar literary or thematic purposes. As The Flow of the New Testament charts the structure of the biblical narrative through the Gospels and Acts, it helps the reader to place the events that they recount to into a historically and theologically meaningful sequence of connected words and deeds.

The New Testament epistles often develop abstract theological concepts by means of logical argumentation. In a book like Romans, for example, it is easy for someone without a map to lose sight of the forest for the trees. At times Paul leaves a premise, an inference, or a transition unexpressed; these omissions can make it difficult to grasp the meaning of isolated verses without prior comprehension of the surrounding argument. A good outline can help to make these connections clear. It can provide readers with a view of the whole to make the parts intelligible and with signposts along the way to guide them through the forest.

Revelation is a highly structured book. It is not possible to understand its mysterious apocalyptic visions without grasping their orderly sequence. Here again, a good outline is invaluable for interpreting the parts within the framework of the whole.

Various kinds of readers, including lay people, college and seminary students, and pastors, could each use *The Flow of the New Testament* for their own purposes. The book could readily serve as a textbook for an introductory college course in New Testament. It could also function as a study-guide for lay people who are looking for an introduction to the New Testament, whether they choose to study on their own, in a small group, or a Sunday School class. Furthermore, it could serve as a handbook for busy pastors and seminary students who need a readily accessible reference tool to help them place their sermon text or exegetical assignment within its literary context in the New Testament. Scholars are welcome to read this book if they wish, but it was intended for common people who shun the pretentious erudition that scholars highly esteem.

How the Book is Constructed

A few words on the way that the book is constructed will help the reader understand the methodology by which it attempts to accomplish its goals and the organizational scheme that it follows. Upon completing the book, a clever reader could figure out most of what will be said here, but the following explanation should spare the needless bother and give direction from the outset.

The Method of Development

Each New Testament book is introduced with some brief notes on its authorship and historical background to help the reader understand it within its most probable setting. Major differences of scholarly opinion on critical matters are noted, but the arguments have, for the most part, been left to other books specializing in introductory issues. It would not be possible to deal adequately here with the complex issues that are involved without seriously detracting from our central focus.

A number of information boxes have been interspersed throughout the book to address various additional points of special interest. Included here are notes on literary structure and style, comparative literary and theological analyses, quotations from the Old Testament and quotations of historical significance, biographical summaries and anecdotes, chronological charts, archeological discoveries, and more detailed discussions of a few particular critical issues and historical backgrounds. Several maps have also been included to help place the New Testament books and events in their geographic setting.

Each book is also introduced by a simple, one line statement of its theme and a key verse which comes as close as possible to summarizing the theme. Accompanying these summaries, the reader will find a condensed overview consisting of the higher level headings of the main outline that follows. This overview will enable the reader to see the central structure of a book at a glance before examining it in somewhat greater depth.

Following the overview for each book, the reader will find its literary flow in essay format. The literary flows have been constructed from more the detailed outlines that follow, and they say essentially the same thing as the outlines, only they translate the headings into sentences and spell out necessary transitions and connections between points. Although the outlines are logically prior, it will probably be most advantageous for the reader to follow the order as printed here. Reading the essay for a New Testament book at one sitting should provide an overall impression of its literary flow, which will be helpful before studying the detailed outline to analyze how all the pieces fit together. The reader may choose, however, to examine either the essay or the outline for a particular book separately, or study both of them side by side. Each has its own value: the essays should read more smoothly and include more information, but the outlines should make it easier to visualize the structure of a book.

At the heart of this book lies its expository outlines, which unfold the literary structure and logical development of each New Testament book. These outlines are sufficiently detailed to reference each main point in the text. Usually the headings correspond to the natural paragraph divisions, but at times they need to represent individual sentences or clauses.

The methodology used for constructing these outlines has taken into consideration both the grammatical structure of the text and the logical development of its ideas. Unfortunately, English translations can obscure the Greek grammatical structure. The NIV, for example, tends to break up long Greek sentences into shorter ones that are more manageable in English; and it frequently omits Greek conjunctions or inserts its own transitions. Although standard English translations have been consulted, the outlines are based upon the Greek text as found in the 27th edition of the Nestle-Aland text and the 4th edition of the United Bible Societies. Even here, there are disagreements over paragraph divisions and punctuation that force one to make a choice.

Once the grammatical structure of the text has been determined, it is still necessary to reckon with the fact that it does not always perfectly reflect the logical development. Points that are subordinated on the grammatical level may be more prominent on the notional level, or vice versa. In such cases a decision has to be made whether to follow the grammar or the idea.

Every attempt has been made to keep the headings as descriptive as possible while at the same time remaining accurate to the biblical text. As much as possible, points on the same level have been kept grammatically and logically parallel, with the same grammatical elements persisting in the same order throughout a series of parallel points (e.g., 1. Paul's boldness; 2. Paul's gentleness; rather than 1. Paul's boldness; 2. The gentleness of Paul). Ideas have been kept logically subordinated so that each subpoint is a subdivision of its main point, and each main point encompasses all of its subpoints. The practical value of an outline lies in its ability to exhibit a clear, simple, and orderly structure that the mind can easily grasp. To succeed here, however, may mean risking the danger of imposing greater structure on the text than what actually exists. At times one is caught in a tension between exegetical accuracy and homiletical artistry where the best one can do is to strike a careful balance between following the biblical writer in departing from a strict literary structure and imposing a slightly artificial form on his work. Since an outline must by its very nature emphasize certain elements to the exclusion of others, some distortion is inevitable; but our goal has been to create a minimum of distortion and bring out a maximum of form.

At times when the text is ambiguous it has been necessary to make interpretive judgments. There is a danger here, similar to that inherent in a paraphrase, that our interpretations could be mistaken for the inspired text. All that can be done is to stick as closely to the text as possible; to make as few interpretations as possible; and, where they are necessary, to base them upon the best evidence and reasoning possible. Although this author has his own theological biases, as does everyone else, a conscious attempt has been made to push them into the background wherever they could be detected intruding upon the text so that we may hear the voice of the inspired writer as clearly as possible rather than the theology of the interpreter.

Since much of the value of the book derives from its ability to say as much as possible as concisely as possible, footnotes have been kept to a bare minimum, and bibliography has been eliminated altogether. Essentially, the work results from an inductive study that has been checked against many different sources, but these sources have influenced the text in such minor and indirect ways, such as suggesting alternative wordings or weighing exegetical options, that it would be impossible to document them all. Brevity, however, has not been allowed to override concerns for accuracy; rather, the need to be concise has impregnated every word with meaning.

The Organization of the New Testament Books

The Canonical Arrangement of the New Testament Books
Before explaining the organization of this book, we must comment on the canonical arrangement of the New Testament books. The church fathers who gradually gave the canon its shape over time had their own reasons for choosing the order that they did, but their rationale is not always obvious. At its most basic level, the New Testament is divided into three general sections dealing with history, doctrine, and prophecy.

There are five historical books. The first four are called Gospels because they focus on the public ministry and teachings of Jesus from a decidedly evangelistic perspective, and the first three Gospels are known as synoptics because they view the events surrounding Christ from a similar perspective. Rather than repeating what they say, the Fourth Gospel, which is attributed to John, adds other details and brings out the theological significance of these events. The Acts of the Apostles, which is the final historical book, records the deeds of the risen Jesus performed through the apostles by the power of the Holy Spirit.

The doctrine of the early church is developed in a series of epistles written to various churches or individuals, usually in response to a local situation. The largest group of epistles are those of the Apostle Paul, which are placed first in the canon in order of length from the longest to the shortest, with the paired epistles grouped together. Hebrews strictly belongs to neither the Pauline Epistles nor to the General Epistles. Its placement after the Pauline Epistles reflects early doubts that it was written by Paul, and its address to a very specific situation distinguishes it from the General Epistles. These so called General, or Catholic, Epistles were loosely grouped together because they were supposedly universal in their intended readership. Some of them, such as 2 and 3 John, are, in fact, addressed to specific audiences, but it was convenient to lump these shorter epistles together with the rest of them.

Finally, the canon closes with an apocalyptic book of prophecy that unveils Jesus' final victory over evil. Revelation, or the Apocalypse, carries a warning about adding any words to it, which, whether appropriately or not, has been taken by some as designating the close of the canon.

Our Thematic, Chronological Arrangement of the New Testament Books

The Flow of the New Testament departs from the canonical order at times in order to place the New Testament books into chronological order within their broader thematic arrangement so that their historical and logical flow will become more evident. The Synoptic Gospels are placed in their presumed order of writing, beginning with Mark's Gospel (probably before A.D. 60), which was probable used by Matthew (before A.D. 70) and Luke (before A.D. 61 or 62). John's Gospel fittingly follows the Synoptics because it gives a theological interpretation of the events that the Synoptics record. The logical connection between John and the other Gospels has been allowed to override its literary attachment to the other Johannine writings and break a strict chronological sequence, which would place it near the end of the canon (A.D. 80-95). Although Acts (A.D. 61 or 62) is linked to Luke's Gospel by common authorship, it has been placed after the Gospels because it carries the story beyond the things that Jesus began to do and teach to the things that he continued to do by the Holy Spirit after his ascension.

Paul's epistles have been rearranged in chronological order and set against their historical background in Acts wherever that is possible. For the sake of convenience, they have been placed into three groups: the Missionary Epistles, the Prison Epistles, and the Pastorals. The Missionary Epistles are those written during Paul's three missionary journeys that are recorded in Acts. The first missionary journey, which started from Antioch in Syria, took Paul and Barnabas through Cyprus, Southern Galatia and back to Antioch before they attended the first Jerusalem church council (Acts 12:25—15:35). Galatians has been moved to the head of the Pauline Epistles because it was likely written during this period, just prior to the convening of the church council in 49 A.D.

After the council, Paul embarked upon a second journey (Acts 15:36—18:22) to deliver its decrees to the churches that he had established on his first trip. He quickly passed through Asia Minor because the Spirit was compelling him on to Macedonia, where he founded churches at Phillipi and Thessalonica. Jealous Jews soon forced Paul to leave Thessalonica, but when he arrived in Corinth, he encouraged this very young church with two epistles, 1 and 2 Thessalonians (A.D. 50 or 51).

After returning to his home base in Antioch, Paul set out on a third journey (Acts 18:23—21:16). Initially, he spent about three years at Ephesus, from where he wrote 1 Corinthians (c. A.D. 55). On the return trip, Paul determined to take up a collection for the poor in Jerusalem. While he was travelling through Macedonia to raise money, he wrote 2 Corinthians (c. A.D. 56). He arrived in Corinth shortly after this epistle and spent about three months there. During this time he wrote his epistle to the Romans (A.D. 57 or 56), which was intended to prepare the way for a proposed visit to the imperial capital and a future trip to Spain.

About three years later, providence eventually brought Paul to Rome, but under different circumstances than he had anticipated (Acts 21:17—28:31). Shortly after his arrival in Jerusalem, some orthodox Jews tried to lynch him for supposedly bringing a Gentile into the temple. Although the Roman commander rescued him from the mob, he was detained, first in Jerusalem and then in Caesarea, while awaiting his trial, which was postponed indefinitely for political expediency. Finally, an appeal to be heard before Caesar's tribunal started him on the way to Rome, but he was shipwrecked along the way and had to spent two more years under house arrest before his case was decided (A.D. 60-61).

During that time, Paul wrote four Prison Epistles. We cannot be sure of their order, but three of them are closely tied together. Paul probably wrote Colossians first to combat a heresy that was invading the church. Along with this letter, he sent a personal correspondence to Philemon, a member of the church at Colossae. At the same time, he revised and expanded Colossians into a circular letter for distribution to Ephesus and the other churches of Asia Minor. Philippians probably stands alone as the last of the Prison Epistles to be written.

Paul was probably released and visited Spain, as he had planned, and also embarked upon further missionary journeys. The Pastoral Epistles fit into this period following the close of the Book of Acts. These epistles contain pastoral instructions to Timothy and Titus, two of Paul's most trusted assistants, who were left in charge of the churches at Ephesus and Crete. Paul wrote 1 Timothy and Titus at about the same time (A.D. 63-66), but he tailored each letter to its local situation. When he wrote 2 Timothy (A.D. 65-67), Paul was a prisoner at Rome again, only this time he was expecting his imprisonment to end in martyrdom.

Hebrews has been left to stand between the Pauline Epistles and the General Epistles. It was probably written to Jewish Christians living at Rome shortly before the outbreak of the Neronian persecutions in A.D. 64.

The General Epistles are treated in roughly canonical order with a couple minor changes. James is placed at their head, both because of its canonical order and its date, which may be the earliest of any New Testament book (possibly as early as the mid 40's). Peter's two epistles follow in canonical order. First Peter was probably written to Northern Asia Minor shortly before the Neronian persecutions in Rome spilled over to that distant corner of the empire (A.D. 60-68). Jude has been shifted out of canonical order so that it may stand next to 2 Peter, to which it bears a close literary connection, but it has not been allowed to split the Petrine Epistles, even though 2 Peter (A.D. 64-68) may follow it chronologically. Shifting Jude out of its canonical order also allows the Johannine Epistles to stand next to Revelation, which shares the same author. All of the Johannine Epistles probably fall into the range of A.D. 90-95, but we cannot be sure of their dates relative to each other so it is best to leave them in canonical order.

It is fitting that the last book in the New Testament should be a prophetic unveiling, literally, a revelation or an apocalypse, of God's final victory over evil. Revelation is also likely the last book in the New Testament that was written (c. A.D. 96).

May the reader enjoy and through this tool come to a better understanding of the flow of the inspired New Testament writings. This book has no value in itself; it only derives worth insofar as it is a faithful distillation of these sacred Scriptures that have proven their wisdom over the course of history and unfold God's new covenant with all who will accept its message of redemption.

Dale Leschert

THE
HISTORICAL
BOOKS

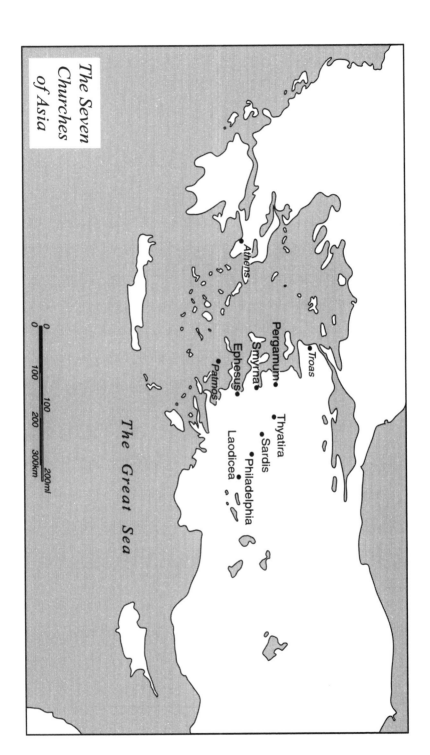

The Seven
Churches
of Asia

The Great Sea

Troas

Pergamum

Smyrna

Ephesus

Patmos

Thyatira

Sardis

Philadelphia

Laodicea

Athens

0
0
100
100
200
200
300km
200ml

The Four Faces of the Gospels

Earlier Christians commonly drew a correlation between the four Gospels and the four living creatures of Ezekiel and Revelation (cf. Ezek 1:10; Rev 4:7). They did not always identify the same Gospel with the same living creature, but church fathers and popular artists alike believed that there was a genuine correspondence between them. Irenaeus even argued that this correspondence was inevitable:

> It is not possible that the Gospels can be either more or fewer in number than they are. For, since there are four zones of the world in which we live, and four principal winds, . . . it is fitting that she [the church] should have four pillars, breathing out immortality on every side, and vivifying men afresh. . . . the Word, . . . who was manifested to men, has given us the Gospel under four aspects, but bound together by one Spirit. . . . the cherubim, too, were four-faced, and their faces were images of the dispensation of the Son of God. For, [as the Scripture] says, "The first living creature was like a lion," symbolizing His effectual working, His leadership, and royal power; the second [living creature] was like a calf, signifying [His] sacrificial and sacerdotal order; but "the third had, as it were, the face as of a man," — an evident description of His advent as a human being; "the fourth was like a flying eagle," pointing out the gift of the Spirit hovering with His wings over the Church. (Irenaeus, Against Heresies, *3.11.8, in* The Ante-Nicene Fathers, *Alexander Roberts et al., eds. vol 1:* The Apostolic Fathers, *trans. A. Cleveland Coxe [Grand Rapids: Wm. B. Eerdmans Pub. Co., 1975], 1:428.)*

Perspectives of the Four Gospels				
Gospel	Matthew	Mark	Luke	John
Perspective of the author	prophetical	practical	historical	spiritual
Audience	Jews	Romans	the world	the church, potential believers
Portrayal of Christ	mighty king lion	lowly servant ox	ideal human man	divine Son eagle

The Four Source Theory of the Synoptic Gospels

The four source theory is the most widely accepted explanation of the literary relationships between the synoptic Gospels. It holds that Mark wrote first, and both Matthew and Luke used Mark plus a sayings source known as Q that they shared in common. Matthew and Luke also added material from a source, or sources, that were peculiar to them, known respectively as M and L.

As can be seen from the diagram, Mark contains 661 verses, 610 of which are duplicated in either Matthew or Luke. 500 of the verses in Mark appear in Matthew, and 320 of them appear in Luke. Matthew and Luke share 250 verses in common that are not found in Mark. To explain the origin of this material, which consists primarily of sayings, a hypothetical document called Q has been postulated. Matthew has 318 verses that are peculiar to him, and Luke has 579 peculiar verses of his own.

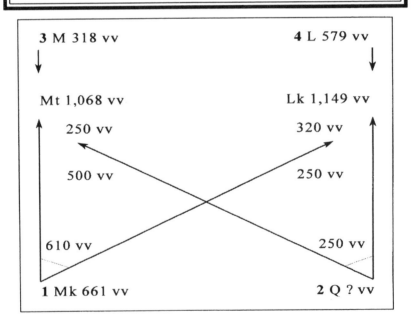

3 M 318 vv

4 L 579 vv

Mt 1,068 vv

Lk 1,149 vv

250 vv

320 vv

500 vv

250 vv

610 vv

250 vv

1 Mk 661 vv

2 Q ? vv

The Matthean priority theory, which is sometimes known as the Griesbach Hypothesis, is the most common alternative to the four source theory of the synoptic Gospels. It holds that Matthew wrote first. Luke then used Matthew, and Mark used both Matthew and Luke.

MARK

OVERVIEW OF MARK

Theme: Jesus, the lowly servant who came to die for us.

Key Verse: Mark 10:45, 'For even the Son of Man did not come to be served, but to serve, and to give His life a ransom for many' (NASB).

HISTORICAL BACKGROUND

According to tradition dating back to Papias, the Bishop of Hierapolis (c. A.D. 130), the *third* Gospel was written by John Mark, in close consultation with Simon Peter. This apostolic connection explains the book's ready acceptance into the canon even though Mark was not one of the original twelve disciples. Mark probably picked up his pen in answer to the church's need for a written record of the ministry and teachings of Jesus after he had departed, but Mark had an evangelistic thrust as well, which is evident in his abbreviation of historical details and teaching material so that nothing can hinder the rapid movement of his action-packed Gospel towards its climax in the cross.

The high number of Latinisms in this Gospel suggests that Mark wrote for a Roman audience during his stay in the imperial capital (1 Pet 5:13). Judging from the literary simplicity of his rough, but vivid, account and the priority given by the other synoptic writers to his chronology, he was probably the first to produce a Gospel, which was used later by Matthew and Luke. Assuming the possibility of predictive prophecy, Mark wrote before the fall of Jerusalem in A.D. 70, and possibly as early as A.D. 45. If Luke used Mark as a source and completed his own Gospel during Paul's first Roman imprisonment, the latest possible date for Mark would be pushed back to about A.D. 60.

The Authority Behind Mark's Gospel

The universal acceptance of Mark's Gospel into the canon even though its author was not himself an apostle can be easily explained by the strong identification of Peter as the authority behind its composition. Eusebius, the early church historian, takes this tradition back to Papias, whose writings are now lost to us:

> Mark, having become the interpreter of Peter, wrote down accurately, though not indeed in order, whatsoever he remembered of the things done or said by Christ. For he neither heard the Lord nor followed him, but afterward, as I said, he followed Peter, who adapted his teaching to the needs of his hearers, but with no intention of giving a connected account of the Lord's discourses, so that Mark committed no error while he thus wrote some things as he remembered them. For he was careful of one thing, not to omit any of the things which he had heard, and not to state any of them falsely. (Papias; as cited by Eusebius, *Church History*, 3.39.15, *t*rans. Arthur Cushman McGiffert, in *The Nicene and Post-Nicene Fathers*, 2nd Series, Philip Schaff, ed., vol. 1: Eusebius, *Church History* (Grand Rapids: Wm. B. Eerdmans Pub. Co., 1976), 172.

The Occasion for Mark's Gospel

Eusebius cites an earlier tradition identifying the occasion for Mark's Gospel as the popular demand to have Peter's oral teachings about Jesus in writing.

> . . . so greatly did the splendor of piety illumine the minds of Peter's hearers that they were not satisfied with hearing once only, and were not content with the unwritten teaching of the divine Gospel, but with all sorts of entreaties they besought Mark, a follower of Peter, and the one whose Gospel is extant, that he would leave them a written monument of the doctrine which had been orally communicated to them. Nor did they cease until they had prevailed with the man, and had thus become the occasion of the written Gospel which bears the name of Mark.
>
> (Eusebius, *Church History*, 2.15.1-2, trans. Arthur Cushman McGiffert, in *The Nicene and Post-Nicene Fathers*, 2nd Series, Philip Schaff, ed., vol. 1: Eusebius, *Church History* [Grand Rapids: Wm. B. Eerdmans Pub. Co., 1976], 116).

THE FLOW OF MARK

The first verse of Mark stands alone as a superscription over the entire gospel: 'The beginning of the gospel of Jesus Christ, the Son of God' (1:1). The Gospel proper opens with a brief prelude to Jesus' public ministry (2-13), which commences with an account

---

The Quotation from Malachi 3:1 and Isaiah 40:3 in Mark 1:2-3

Malachi 3:1: 'Behold, I am going to send My messenger, and he will clear the way before Me. *And the Lord, whom you seek, will suddenly come to His temple; and the messenger of the covenant, in whom you delight, behold, He is coming,' says the Lord of hosts. (NASB)*

Isaiah 40:3-5: A voice is calling, 'Clear the way for the Lord in the wilderness; Make smooth in the desert a highway for our God. *Let every valley be lifted up, And every mountain and hill be made low; And let the rough ground become a plain, And the rugged terrain a broad valley; Then the glory of the Lord will be revealed, And all flesh will see [it] together; For the mouth of the Lord has spoken.'* (NASB)

---

of the preparations that John the Baptist made for the Messiah (2-8). In accordance with Isaiah's prophecy, John appeared in the wilderness proclaiming a baptism of repentance, and many people responded by being baptized and confessing their sins (2-6). John also prepared the way by announcing the coming of one mightier than himself who would baptize with the Holy Spirit (7-8).

Mark connects John's prophecy directly with Jesus' entrance into public ministry, which he summarizes tersely (9-13). While John was baptizing in the Jordan River, Jesus came to him and was baptized; in response the Spirit descended upon Jesus, and the Father spoke approvingly from heaven (9-11). Immediately after his baptism, Jesus was driven out into the wilderness by the Spirit, where he was tempted by Satan (12-13).

Having set the stage, Mark moves directly to Jesus' proclamation of the coming kingdom of God, which will be the central thrust throughout the first half of his Gospel (1:14–8:30). He locates Jesus' proclamation of the kingdom primarily in Galilee,[1] but he also records its extension into Gentile regions.[2]

Although Mark introduces the kingdom theme in a Galilean setting (1:14-20), his introduction covers all of Jesus' kingdom preaching. He creates a formal announcement of this theme by summarizing Jesus' preaching in Galilee: 'The kingdom of God has come near; repent and believe in the gospel' (14-15). Mark then follows this announcement with a picture of Jesus preparing for the task of proclaiming the kingdom by calling four fishermen, Simon, Andrew, James and John, to help him (16-20).

In the initial phase of the Galilean ministry, Jesus repeatedly demonstrates his divine authority over any challenge that might call it into question (1:21–3:6). The first challenge to be answered comes from demons and sickness (1:21-45).

Mark begins to disclose Jesus' authority over these spiritual forces within the context of a typical day's ministry, which finds Jesus busily ministering at Capernaum (21-34). The day begins with the exorcism of a demon-possessed man, which is described in greater detail than the subsequent miracles on that day (21-28). While Jesus was teaching in the synagogue on the Sabbath (21-22), he was confronted by a man with an unclean spirit, which he commanded to come out (23-26). The crowd was amazed at the authority behind Jesus' teaching and spread the news about him everywhere (27-28). Immediately after leaving the synagogue, Jesus entered the home of Simon Peter and Andrew, where he healed Peter's mother-in-law of a fever (29-31). After the sun had gone down, the whole city gathered around the door of the house, and Jesus healed many people who were ill or demon-possessed (32-34).

Early the next morning before the sun had risen, Jesus withdrew to a deserted place for prayer because it was difficult to escape the crowds (35-38). When his disciples found him, Jesus led them away on a preaching tour through the surrounding Galilean towns (39-45). After giving a general summary of Jesus' itinerary and activities (39), Mark reports one example of Jesus' healing (40-

---

1. Mark 1:14–7:23.
2. Mark 7:24–8:30.

45). A leper came to Jesus and, falling down on his knees, begged him to make him clean (40). Jesus was moved with compassion for the man, and reaching out his hand, he touched the leper and cleansed him (41-42). Although Jesus warned him to say nothing to anyone, the cleansed man spread the news freely with the result that Jesus could not enter a city publicly because of the crowds thronging about him (43-45).

The second challenge to Jesus' authority comes from sin and the law (**2**:1–3:6). Jesus demonstrated his authority to forgive sin on two occasions in Mark (2:1-17); the first is the healing of a paralyzed man (2:1-12). When the friends of the paralytic brought him for healing, Jesus responded by pronouncing that his sins were forgiven (1-5). Reasoning that only God can forgive sin, the scribes who were sitting around concluded that Jesus was guilty of blasphemy (6-7). Jesus, however, authenticated his authority to forgive sin by ordering the man to pick up his mat and go home (8-12).

The second occasion on which we see Jesus' forgiveness of sin is the call of Levi, who is also known as Matthew (13-17). Levi was sitting in the tax office when Jesus passed by and called him to follow him (13-14). Levi upset the Pharisees by inviting many tax collectors and sinners to a banquet with Jesus, but Jesus proclaimed that his mission was to call sinners (15-17).

Jesus went on to demonstrate his authority over the law, both in the oral form of religious rituals enshrined by tradition (18-22) and the Mosaic Law itself (2:23–3:6). The Pharisees expected Jesus' disciples to fast, but Jesus replied they could not fast as long as he, the bridegroom of the feast, was with them (18-20). Jesus used two illustrations to show the incompatibility of the new form of religion he was bringing with the outworn rituals of Judaism (21-22). No one sews an unshrunken patch of cloth on an old garment; otherwise the patch will shrink and tear the garment (21). And no one puts new wine into old wineskins; otherwise the expansion of the fermenting wine will burst the skins (22).

The primary point of conflict in Jesus' authority over the Mosaic Law was the Sabbath (2:23–3:6). On one Sabbath Jesus was walking with his disciples through some grainfields while they were plucking heads of grain along the way (2:23-28). The Pharisees accused them of violating the Sabbath (23-24), but Jesus rebutted the charge by citing the precedent of David's eating consecrated bread when the preservation of life was at stake (25-26). Jesus concluded by asserting that he was Lord over the Sabbath (27-28).

On a subsequent Sabbath, Jesus healed the withered hand of a man in the synagogue (3:1-6). He performed this act of mercy in open defiance of the Pharisees who were standing around watching (1-5); and they, in response, conspired to kill him (6).

This decision to kill Jesus, which occurs very early in the narrative, marks the transition to the central period in Jesus' Galilean ministry (3:7–6:6a), which differs from the initial period, not in a change of geography, but in a change of mood as the strong opinions and emotions that Jesus aroused in people increasingly built in conviction and intensity on both sides with the result that any chance for him to present his claims to a neutral audience gradually disappeared (3:7-35). The news of Jesus' healings stirred up a great commotion and attracted such large crowds from all over Palestine that Jesus was in danger of being trampled in the excitement and was scarcely able to restrain the evil spirits from revealing his identity (7-12). In the wake of this overwhelming popularity, Jesus retreated to a mountain, where he called twelve apostles to learn from him and share his mission with him (13-19).

At the same time, controversies arose about Jesus' character (20-35). When Jesus returned home, the crowds imposed such unreasonable demands upon his time that his personal acquaintances came to take custody of him out of fear that he had lost his sanity (20-21). The scribes added to the controversy by accusing Jesus of casting out demons by the prince of demons (22). He replied that their accusation made no logical sense because it implied that Satan was opposed to himself (23-27). He further warned that their accusation placed them in serious peril of committing the unpardonable sin of blaspheming the Holy Spirit (28-30). When the relatives of Jesus came searching for him on another occasion, he looked around at the surrounding crowd and declared his spiritual kindred to be those who do God's will, thereby forcing the crowd to make a decision about him (31-35).

In this context of great outward popularity, accompanied by the genuine faith of a few followers and the strong opposition of the religious leaders, Jesus began to teach the crowds in parables (4:1-34). He started with a parable about a sower who scattered his seed on a variety of soils with results that varied in correspondence with the quality of the soil (1-9). Jesus explained to his inner circle of followers, who were puzzled by his use of parables, that parables provided a means of disclosing truth about the kingdom to those who were predisposed to accepting it while at the same time concealing it from those who rejected it (10-12). He then interpreted the parable of the soils for them as a model for interpreting other parables (13-20). To this parable, which he explained in terms of the varying responses of different kinds of people to the Word, he added other parables about hiding a light under a bushel basket (21-25), about the way that seed grows spontaneously until the time for harvest comes (26-29), and about the phenomenal growth of a tiny mustard seed to a disproportionately large plant (30-32). Mark summarizes Jesus' use of parables by telling us that Jesus spoke many other parables to the crowds, but he explained everything privately to the disciples (33-34).

Mark follows the parables with a series of signs which attest to Jesus' authority over various forces (4:35–5:43). The calming of a storm while Jesus and his disciples were crossing over the Sea of Galilee attests to his authority over nature (4:35-41), and the healing of the Gerasene demoniac attests to his authority over the spirit world (5:1-20). When Jesus and his disciples reached the eastern shore, they were met by a fierce, demon-possessed man whom no one was able to subdue (1-10). Jesus cast many demons out of the man and permitted them to enter into a herd of swine, which stampeded over a precipice into the sea and about two thousand of them were drowned (11-13). When the news reached the people of the surrounding community, they became frightened and requested Jesus to leave, but the man who was healed stayed behind and proclaimed throughout the entire region what Jesus had done for him (14-20).

Jesus' authority over sickness and death is attested by two miracles which are intertwined (21-43). A crowd was waiting for Jesus when the boat landed, and a synagogue official named Jairus stepped forward to entreat Jesus on behalf of his young daughter who was dying (21-24a). So many people were seeking to be healed that another miracle happened while Jesus was still on the way: a woman who had suffered from a hemorrhage for twelve years was cured simply by touching Jesus' garments (24b-34). While Jesus

---

Mark's Candid Portrayal of the Disciples' Weaknesses

Mark portrays the disciples' weaknesses more candidly than the other synoptic writers. In the case of the calming of the storm, for example, each of the synoptic writers records Jesus' reproof of the disciples' unbelief in his own paraphrase, but Mark uses stronger wording than the others. Mark has Jesus ask the disciples, "Why are you so timid? How is it that you have no faith?" (Mk 4:40). Here they appear to have no faith at all. Matthew softens the question to, "Why are you timid, you men of little faith?" (Matt 8:26). He grants them a modicum of faith, but it is not very much. In Luke, Jesus asks, "Where is your faith?" (Lk 8:25). Luke allows that the disciples may actually have had faith, even though they were not exercising it on this occasion.

---

was still speaking with the woman, messengers arrived with the disheartening news that Jairus' daughter had already died, but Jesus continued to the house and, taking the little girl by the hand, raised her back to life (35-43).

From there Jesus returned to his home town, but his own townsfolk could not fit together the reports of miracles with what they knew of the boy who had grown up among them. Their unbelief amazed Jesus and prevented him from doing any notable miracles there (6:1-6a).

Leaving them, Jesus embarked upon the final campaign in his Galilean ministry, which was characterized by increasing conflict (6:6b–7:23). Mark begins with a cursory summary of Jesus' teaching tour (6:6b), and then he reports the commissioning of the twelve to go out in pairs and multiply Jesus' preaching and healing ministry (7-13).

The news about Jesus made a significant impact upon Herod Antipas (14-29). His explanation for all the miraculous occurrences was that John the Baptist had come back to life (14-16). Having mentioned John's death, Mark explains in retrospect that the conscience of Herod was uneasy because he had beheaded John (17-29). This calamity fell upon John because he had rebuked Herod for his adulterous relationship with his sister in-law, Herodias (17-20). She had designs upon John's head and readily demanded it when Herod rashly promised to grant her daughter whatever she wished (21-25). Although Herod was upset by Herodias' request, he acquiesced to the girl's wish and sent an executioner (26-28). John's disciples claimed the body and buried it in a tomb (29).

Mark follows the report of John's horrible death with one of Jesus' greatest miracles: the feeding of the five thousand (30-44). It is set in a remote place across the Sea of Galilee where Jesus and the disciples had withdrawn for some much needed rest after their return from an exhausting preaching tour, but their retreat also provides the reader with a needed psychological break after learning the distressing news about such a great man as John (30-32).

Unfortunately, Jesus and the disciples had no chance to relax. The crowds, seeing them crossing over in the boat, outran them along the shore on foot; and Jesus, feeling compassion on the people who had gathered, began to teach them many things (33-34). As evening approached, the disciples became concerned about the practical impossibility of providing for such a large crowd in that remote place (35-37); but Jesus, taking the five loaves and two fish the people had among them, multiplied their meagre provisions to feed the entire crowd of over five thousand (38-44).

Jesus sent the disciples away in the boat while he dismissed the crowd, but seeing them straining at the oars late at night, he came to them walking on the water (45-52). When they arrived at Gennesaret, the people immediately recognized Jesus and brought to him their sick from throughout the entire region (53-56).

Some of the Pharisees and scribes, who had come up from Jerusalem, started to dispute with Jesus over the issue of ceremonial

---

The Pivotal Point in Mark's Gospel

Peter's confession, "You are the Christ" (Mk 8:29), is the pivotal point in Mark's Gospel. In the opening chapters of Mark, Jesus came preaching, 'the kingdom of God has come near; repent and believe in the gospel" (Mk 1:14), but after this point he shifts his attention away from preaching to the crowds to preparing his disciples for his imminent suffering and death.

---

defilement (7:1-23). They accused the disciples of violating the tradition of the elders by eating without washing their hands (1-5). Jesus countered their hypocrisy by showing how they used the traditions of men to invalidate the commandments of God (6-13). After the Pharisees left, Jesus explained the meaning of true defilement (14-23). He enunciated the general principle to the crowd that a person is not defiled by what enters from the outside but by what proceeds from within (14-15 [some MSS add 16]), and he gave a more detailed explanation to the disciples later because they failed to grasp the point (17-23). He denied that food, which enters the body, defiles a person (17-19); he affirmed, rather, that sin, which proceeds from the heart, defiles the person (20-23).

Jesus had already made a few brief excursions into Gentile territory across the Sea of Galilee, but at this point he began an extended ministry into Gentile regions (7:24–8:30). In the vicinity of Tyre, he met a Syrophoenician woman who pleaded with him on behalf of her demon-possessed daughter; because of her persistent faith, he answered her request (7:24-30). Some people in the region of the Decapolis brought a deaf mute to Jesus, and he healed him also (31-37). After listening to Jesus' teaching for three days at a desolate place across the Sea of Galilee, the crowd became hungry, and Jesus satisfied their need by multiplying seven loaves to feed all four thousand of them (**8**:1-10).

When Jesus and his disciples returned to the western shore, the Pharisees began demanding a sign, but Jesus, being deeply grieved, refused to grant a sign and went back across the water (11-13). On the way, the disciples became concerned that they had forgotten to take sufficient food along; realizing that they were more concerned about physical than spiritual matters, Jesus rebuked them for their failure to understand that he, who had fed five thousand on one occasion and four thousand on another, could easily handle this trivial problem (14-21). At Bethsaida Jesus healed a blind man by spitting on his eyes and laying his hands on him (22-26). As Jesus and the disciples proceeded north to Caesarea Philippi, he posed the crucial question to them, 'Who do you say I am?' and Peter answered correctly, 'You are the Christ' (27-30).

Peter's recognition of Jesus' messiahship is the pivotal point in Mark's Gospel; from this time onward Jesus began to prepare for his sufferings in Jerusalem (8:31–13:37). Many of his initial preparations focused on the psychological readiness of the disciples and took place while they were gradually working their way towards Jerusalem (8:31–10:52). Jesus began by attempting to impress upon the disciples the necessity of suffering (8:31–9:1). His first prediction of his passion came immediately after Peter's great confession, but evidently Peter did not fully understand yet, for Jesus had to rebuke him severely for trying to dissuade him from accomplishing God's purposes through death (8:31-33). The announcement of his passion becomes a fitting occasion for Jesus to make all his would-be disciples aware that they also have an inescapable obligation to bear their own cross (8:34–9:1).

Six days after predicting his death, Jesus allowed three of his disciples a foretaste of the coming kingdom to enable them to see beyond the seemingly tragic events that were impending (9:2-29). He took them up a high mountain, where his appearance was transfigured before them into a blaze of radiant glory while he talked with Moses and Elijah (2-8). During their descent from the mountain, the disciples had a deep discussion about two issues they could not understand (9-13): the rising of the Son of Man from the dead (9-10), and the coming of Elijah to restore all things (11-13).

When they rejoined the other disciples at the base of the mountain, they were met by a crowd gathered around a demon-possessed boy, who was then turned over to Jesus (14-29). The disciples who had remained behind had been unable to cast the demon out (14-18). Consequently, the boy's father was a bit doubtful that Jesus could help, but Jesus elicited from him the willingness to believe (19-24). He commanded the demon to come out, and it was constrained to obey (25-29).

Jesus began to pass through Galilee, but he did not want anyone to know because he was concentrating on teaching the disciples (30-50). He predicted his passion a second time, but they still did not understand (30-32). Because they had been arguing about which one of them was the greatest, Jesus found it necessary to teach them about humility (33-37). He also taught them that the people who were working towards the kingdom included more than just their little circle (38-41), and he warned them about various stumbling blocks to entering the kingdom (42-50).

From Galilee, Jesus travelled through Judea and Perea on the east side of the Jordan, where he continued to teach (**10**:1-31). After a brief geographical transition (1), Mark records Jesus' teaching on divorce (2-12). In response to the Pharisees' question, Jesus taught that although Moses permitted divorce because of the hardness of people's hearts, God's intention from creation was that a husband and his wife should inseparably become one flesh (2-9). In response to the further questions of the disciples, Jesus taught that whoever divorces his spouse and marries another commits adultery (10-12).

When Jesus saw the disciples rebuking some people who were bringing little children to him, he became indignant. Welcoming the children into his arms, he blessed them (13-16).

As Jesus was starting out on a journey, an incident arose which evoked some extended teaching on wealth (17-31). A rich man ran up to Jesus and asked how to inherit eternal life; but when Jesus told him to sell all he had and give to the poor, he went away deeply grieved because he was bound by his possessions (17-22). When Jesus drove home the point that riches are a peril to entering the kingdom, the disciples were astonished (23-27). Peter, speaking for the rest of them, boasted that they had left everything to follow him; and Jesus replied that they would be amply rewarded, both in the present age and the one to come (28-31).

We see the tension rise as Jesus set out on the final stage of his journey along the road to Jerusalem (32-52). For a third time, he took the disciples aside and tried to prepare them by telling them exactly what was going to happen at Jerusalem (32-34). It appears, however, that they failed to grasp the significance of his words because he was immediately thrust into settling a dispute arising from their ambitious pride (35-45). James and John requested that Jesus grant them the chief positions of honour in the kingdom (35-40). Jesus tried to correct their self-seeking and calm the indignation of the other disciples by teaching that the way to true greatness lies in service, following his own example (41-45). As they were leaving Jericho, Jesus healed a blind beggar named Bartimaeus, who was sitting beside the road (46-52).

When they arrived in Jerusalem, Jesus shifted his focus from preparing the disciples for what was about to happen to preparing more directly for the passion itself (11:1–13:37). Jesus orchestrated his entry into the city as a public presentation of himself as the Messiah (11:1-25). He entered triumphally (1-10) mounted upon a colt, which two of the disciples had fetched for him (1-6); and the crowds welcomed him, spreading leafy branches on the road and crying, 'Hosanna!' (7-10). After looking around the temple, Jesus departed for Bethany that evening (11).

On the way back into the city on the next day, Jesus paused to eat from a fig tree; but when he saw that it had only leaves and no fruit, he cursed it (12-14). Upon entering the temple, he drove out those who were exchanging money and selling merchandise (15-17). When the religious leaders heard what he had done, they conspired to find a way to kill him (18). Again, Jesus retired from the city in the evening (19).

When he re-entered the city in the morning with the disciples, Jesus drew a lesson from the fig tree which he had cursed the previous day (20-25). The disciples were somewhat surprised when they noticed that the fig tree had withered (20-21); but Jesus exhorted them to have faith in God, and their prayers would be answered (22-25 [some MSS add verse 26]).

The religious leaders were waiting for Jesus in the temple with a series of loaded questions to trap him (11:27–12:44). The chief priests, scribes and elders questioned Jesus concerning the authority by which he acted, but he cleverly exposed their hypocritical unwillingness to accept that authority (11:27-33). Jesus went on further to expose their evil intentions by telling a parable about some wicked tenant farmers who treacherously killed the landlord's son when he came to collect the share of the crop that they owed (12:1-12).

The Pharisees and Herodians took a turn at trying to trap Jesus by asking if they should pay tribute to Caesar, but Jesus responded with the general principle to render to Caesar what belonged to Caesar and to God what belonged to God (13-17). Next the Sadducees used an invented scenario about a woman who had survived seven husbands to ridicule Jesus' belief in the resurrection of the dead, but Jesus dismissed their story as irrelevant to the issue at hand and affirmed from Scripture that the dead are in fact raised (18-27). One of the scribes took his turn to ask Jesus which was the greatest commandment, but he was impressed with Jesus' summarization of the law under the double duty of love for God and neighbour (28-34).

Seeing that the religious leaders had no more questions, Jesus asked them a question of his own about how the Messiah could be David's son since David called him 'Lord' (35-37). Jesus further took the offensive by warning the crowds about the hypocrisy of the scribes, who loved people's respect but devoured widow's houses (38-40). In contrast with their greed, a poor widow walked up to the temple treasury and dropped in two small coins, which represented her whole livelihood (41-44).

In an extended teaching section, known as the Olivet Discourse, Jesus helped the disciples to put the coming events into global perspective by prophetically taking them past his passion to a description of last things (**13**:1-37). Mark introduces the discourse by placing it in its setting (1-4). As Jesus was leaving the temple, one of the disciples remarked on its impressive appearance, but Jesus prophesied that it would be completely destroyed (1-2). When they had walked across to the Mount of Olives and sat down at a vantage point overlooking the temple, some of the disciples questioned Jesus about when these events would take place and what sign would precede them (3-4).

The substance of the discourse which follows is the answer to their questions (4-37). Jesus warned them not to be misled by the many political upheavals and natural catastrophes that would occur, because these tumultuous events would only signal the beginning of birth pains before the end (5-8). To a warning that they would be persecuted from all sides, he added the encouragement that 'the one who endures to the end will be saved' (9-13). He predicted the coming of a time of great tribulation, in which they should flee from Judea (14-23). As a sign, he told them that when they saw the 'abomination of desolation' standing where it ought not to be they should flee immediately (14-17) because the severity of the tribulation in those days would be without precedent since creation and would never be equalled again (18-20). He also warned them not to be led astray because many false Christs would appear performing deceptive signs and wonders (21-23).

He prophesied that there would be a cataclysmic upheaval of the heavens just before the coming of the Son of Man with great power and glory (24-27), and he gave the budding of the fig tree as a sign to indicate the nearness of the end (28-31). Finally, he warned that since no one knows the precise time, they should be alert at all times lest they be caught unprepared (32-37).

From the preparations leading up to Jesus' sufferings, Mark moves us along to the events directly associated with the passion itself (**14:1–15:47**). He begins by reporting the preliminary arrangements for Jesus' death, which swiftly build to their climax (14:1-52). The chief priests were seeking how to seize Jesus stealthily and kill him, for they were afraid to make an open attempt during Passover lest they stir up a riot among the people (1-2). In contrast with the sinister plotting of the priests, a woman of pure devotion came up to Jesus while he was dining with friends and anointed him with expensive perfume in symbolic preparation for his burial (3-9). Judas, who was present at the dinner, went away to make a deal with the chief priests to betray Jesus to them at an opportune time (10-11).

Before his death, Jesus ate one last meal with his disciples (12-26). First, he sent two of them into the city to prepare for the

Passover feast (12-16). While they were eating the Passover meal that evening, Jesus announced that he would be betrayed by one of the twelve, whom he identified as 'the one who dipped with him into the bowl' (17-21). Jesus concluded the meal by giving new symbolic meaning to the bread as his body and to the cup as his blood poured out on behalf of many (22-26).

As they proceeded to the Mount of Olives, Jesus predicted that Peter would deny him three times that very night (27-31). When they reached a place called Gethsemane, Jesus knelt down three times and prayed earnestly that if possible the bitter cup of death might pass from him (32-42).

As soon as Jesus had finished praying, a mob sent by the Sanhedrin came to arrest him (43-52). Judas, who was leading the mob, identified Jesus to the rest of them by walking up to him and kissing him (43-45). The mob seized Jesus and led him away while all the disciples fled (46-50). The mob also seized an unidentified young man who was wearing a linen sheet; but leaving the sheet behind, he fled away naked (51-52).

Now that a mob of wicked men had Jesus in their possession, the final stages of his passion were set (14:53–15:47). His trial took place in two major stages (14:53–15:15). First, he was subjected to a religious trial before the Sanhedrin (14:53-72). The mob led Jesus to the high priest's residence, where the Sanhedrin had gathered, and Peter followed from a distance up to the courtyard (53-54). Mark briefly summarizes the proceedings for us (55-65). Although the Sanhedrin tried desperately to find testimony against Jesus, they were unable to convict him because the witnesses were not consistent (55-59). Finally, the high priest charged Jesus with blasphemy for claiming to be the Son of God (60-65). As predicted, Peter denied Jesus three times before he remembered his Lord's words and wept in bitter remorse (66-72).

In addition to being tried before the Sanhedrin, Jesus was also subjected to a civil trial before Pilate (15:1-15). Early in the morning, the Sanhedrin met and decided to transfer Jesus to Pilate (1). Pilate interrogated him, but Jesus remained silent to the charges brought against him (2-5). Pilate vacillated for a while before sentencing Jesus to crucifixion (6-15). Although he tried to release

Jesus, the crowd demanded that he crucify him and release Barabbas instead (6-14). Because Pilate wanted to please the crowd, he complied with their wishes (15).

Following the trial, Mark recounts the death of Jesus (16-41). The soldiers took Jesus to the governor's palace where they mocked and beat him (16-20a). Then, compelling a passer-by named Simon to bear Jesus' cross, they led him out to Golgotha, the place of crucifixion (20b-22). There they crucified him, while they cast lots for his garments (23-26). The other men who were being crucified with Jesus joined together with the people passing by and the chief priests and scribes in mocking Jesus for his apparent inability to save himself (27-32). Darkness covered the land for three hours as Jesus hung on the cross, until he cried out, 'My God, My God, Why have You forsaken Me?' and uttering a loud cry, breathed his last (33-39). All the while, the women who used to minister to Jesus and had followed him from Galilee kept watch from a distance (40-41).

Mark concludes the passion with a brief account of the burial of Jesus (42-47). Joseph of Arimathea, a sympathetic member of the Sanhedrin, obtained permission from Pilate to take down Jesus' body from the cross (42-45). He wrapped it in a linen sheet, placed it in a tomb, and rolled a stone against the entrance (46-47).

But Jesus' body did not remain in the tomb; Mark closes with the report of witnesses to the resurrection of Jesus (**16**:1-8 [9-20]). Here we need to consider a couple of textual variants. The traditional ending of Mark's Gospel, which is probably the authentic one, ends in an abrupt and unembellished way at Mark 16:1-8. Very early on the first day of the week the women went to the tomb to anoint Jesus' body; but they discovered that the stone had been rolled away, and a young man dressed in white was sitting there (1-5). When the angel told them that Jesus had risen and would met them in Galilee, they ran away terrified and astonished (6-8).

The abruptness of ending at verse 8 is the probable reason that gave rise to a couple of supplementary endings to Mark. The longer ending (9-20) reflects ancient tradition, but it is lacking in the older manuscripts and is probably not original. This reading includes a series of post-resurrection appearances of Jesus to his followers (9-18). He appeared first to Mary Magdalene (9-11), then to two disciples who were out walking in the country, (12-13), and afterwards to the eleven disciples, who had not believed the reports of the others (14-18). Finally, the longer ending includes a note about Jesus' ascension to the Father's right hand (19-20). Some later manuscripts round out verse 8 with a shorter ending which summarizes the missionary response of the disciples to the resurrection.

Three Portraits of Jesus: Matthew, Mark and Luke

The portraits which Matthew, Mark, and Luke paint of Jesus are remarkably similar. They cover essentially the same subject matter, hold the same fundamental theological convictions about him, follow the same general arrangement of events in his life, and often they agree precisely in the wording of their accounts. Because they see the Gospel events together from a common perspective, they have come to be known as the Synoptic Gospels.

But in the divine process of inspiration, the Holy Spirit worked through the individual personalities of the biblical writers and the circumstances of their particular audiences in such a way that allowed room for special theological emphases, peculiar literary characteristics, and a unique personal flavour to emerge from each Gospel. Although this individuality presents problems for understanding the literary relationship between these documents and harmonizing their differences, it expands our field of vision and reassures us of the independent historical value of each Gospel witness.

A Brief Chronology of the New Testament

Birth of Jesus	6-4 B.C.
Death of Herod the Great	4 B.C.
The public ministry of Jesus	c. A.D. 28-30
Conversion of Paul	c. A.D. 33
The Jerusalem Church Council (Acts 15)	A.D. 49
The Decree of Claudius expelling the Jews from Rome	A.D. 49
Gallio becomes proconsul of Achaia	A.D. 51
Reign of the Emperor Nero	A.D. 54-68
Paul's first imprisonment in Rome	A.D. 61-63
The great fire at Rome and start of the Neronian persecutions	A.D. 64
Martyrdom of Peter and Paul	c. A.D. 64-68
Fall of Jerusalem	A.D. 70
John's release from exile on Patmos	A.D. 96

A Reconstruction of the Events
Surrounding Jesus' Passion

Saturday	The symbolic anointing of Jesus at Bethany (Mark 14:3-9; Matthew 26:6-13; John 12:1-8)[1]
Sunday	The triumphal entry (Mark 11:1-11; Matthew 21:1-11; Luke 19:28-44; John 12:12-19)
Monday	The cursing of the unproductive fig tree (Mark 11:12-14; Matthew 21:18-19)
	The cleansing of the temple (Mark 11:15-17; Matthew 21:12-17; Luke 19:45-46)
	The request of some Greeks to see Jesus (John 12:20-36a)
	The plot to kill Jesus (Mark 11:18-19; Luke 19:47-48)
Tuesday	Lessons from the withered fig tree (Mark 11:20-[26]; Matthew 21:20-22)
	The religious leaders' attempts to entrap Jesus (Mark 11:27–12:44; Matthew 21:23–23:39; Luke 20:1–21:4)
	The Olivet Discourse (Mark 13:1-37; Matthew 24:1–25:46; Luke 21:5-38)
Wednesday	The chief priests' quiet conspiracy against Jesus (Mark 14:1-2; Matthew 26:1-5; Luke 22:1-2)
	Judas' treacherous agreement with the chief priests (Mark 14:10-11; Matthew 26:14-16; Luke 22:3-6)
Thursday[2]	Jesus' last supper with the disciples (Mark 14:12-31; Matthew 26:17-35; Luke 22:7-34; John 13:1–17:26)

---

1. Mark and Matthew have probably arranged the anointing thematically in order to contrast it with the chief priests' plot against Jesus and Judas' agreement to betray him.

2. The Passover lambs were slaughtered on Nisan 14th and eaten that evening, which would be the 15th by Jewish reckoning (Ex 12:1-14; Lev 23:5; Num 9:1-3; Deut 16:1-2).

Thursday Continued	Jesus' agonizing struggle in Gethsemane (Mark 14:32-42; Matthew 26:36-46; Luke 22:39-46; John 18:1)
	Jesus' arrest by the mob (Mark 14:43-52; Matthew 26:47-56; Luke 22:47-53; John 18:2-11)
Friday[3]	The religious trial at night before the Sanhedrin (Mark 14:53-72; Matthew 26:57-75; Luke 22:54-65; John 18:12-27)
	The religious trial in the morning before the Sanhedrin (Matthew 27:1-2; Luke 22:66-71)
	The death of Judas (Matthew 27:3-10)
	The Roman civil trial before Herod and Pilate (Mark 15:1-15; Matthew 27:11-26; Luke 23:1-25; John 18:28–19:16a)
	Jesus' death (Mark 15:16-41; Matthew 27:27-56; Luke 23:26-49; John 19:16b-37)
	Jesus' burial (Mark 15:42-47; Matthew 27:57-66; Luke 23:50-56a; John 19:38-42)
	The setting of a guard over the tomb (Matthew 27:62-66)
Saturday	Rest (Luke 22:56b)
Sunday	Resurrection appearances of Jesus (Mark 16:1-8, [9-20]; Matthew 28:1-10; Luke 24:1-49; John 20:1-18)
	The chief priest's fraudulent cover-up for the missing body (Matthew 28:11-15)

---

3. By the traditional reckoning, Good Friday was the first day of the Feast of Unleavened Bread (Ex 12:15-20; Lev 23:6-8; Deut 16:3-8) and the day of preparation for the Sabbath of Passover week that year (John 19:14, 31).

OUTLINE OF MARK

The superscription to Mark's Gospel   1:1

I. The prelude to the public ministry of Jesus   1:2-13

A. The preparations of John the Baptist for the Messiah   1:2-8
1. John's baptism of repentance   1:2-6
2. John's preaching about the Messiah   1:7-8

B. The entrance of Jesus Christ into public ministry   1:9-13
1. Jesus' baptism by John   1:9-11
2. Jesus' temptation by Satan   1:12-13

II. The proclamation of the coming kingdom of God   1:14–8:30

A. Introduction   1:14-20
1. The announcement of Jesus' theme   1:14-15
2. The call of four fishermen   1:16-20

B. The initial phase of the Galilean ministry   1:21–3:6
1. The demonstration of Jesus' authority over demons
  and sickness   1:21-45
    a. A day's ministry at Capernaum   1:21-34
      (1) The exorcism of a demon-possessed man   1:21-28
        (a) The setting in the synagogue   1:21-22
        (b) The confrontation with the demon   1:23-26
        (c) The response of the crowd   1:27-28
      (2) The healing of Peter's mother-in-law   1:29-31
      (3) The healing of some inhabitants   1:32-34
    b. A prayer-retreat at a quiet place   1:35-38
    c. A preaching tour through Galilee   1:39-45
      (1) A summary of the itinerary   1:39
      (2) An incident of healing   1:40-45
        (a) The plea of a leper   1:40
        (b) The compassion of Jesus   1:41-42
        (c) The throng of the crowds   1:43-45
2. The demonstration of Jesus' authority over sin and the law   2:1–3:6
    a. The authority to forgive sin   2:1-17
      (1) The healing of a paralytic   2:1-12
        (a) Jesus' forgiveness of the paralytic   2:1-5
        (b) The scribes' implications of blasphemy   2:6-7
        (c) Jesus' authentication by healing   2:8-12

---

1. Verse 16 is not found in the oldest manuscripts.

2. Verse 26 is not found in the oldest manuscripts.

---

3. The oldest manuscripts end at Mark 16:8 with the astonishment of the women. Because of the seeming abruptness of this ending, other supplemental endings have been associated with Mark's Gospel from ancient times. The so called 'longer ending' (vv 9-20) is considered to be authentic by the KJV, and the 'shorter ending' is included in a footnote in many of the modern versions.

MATTHEW

OVERVIEW OF MATTHEW

Theme: Jesus Christ, the Davidic King

Key Verse: Matthew 1:1, 'The book of ... Jesus Christ, the son of David' (NASB).

I. Jesus' humble entrance into history	1:1–4:11
A. The birth of the Messiah	1:1–2:23
B. Preparations for ministry	3:1–4:1
II. Jesus' early ministry to Israel	4:12–16:20
A. Introduction to Jesus' proclamation of the kingdom	4:12-25
B. Teaching about the principles of the kingdom	
(FIRST DISCOURSE: The Sermon on the Mount)	5:1–7:29
C. Manifestations of the power of the kingdom	8:1–11:1
Instructions to the twelve (SECOND DISCOURSE)	10:5–11:1
D. Various responses to the mystery of the kingdom	11:2–12:50
E. Jesus' clarification of the kingdom for the disciples	
(THIRD DISCOURSE: seven parables about the	
kingdom)	13:1-53
F. The widening rift between followers and detractors	13:54–16:20

HISTORICAL BACKGROUND

Tradition uniformly ascribes the first Gospel to Matthew, who was transformed from his despised occupation as a tax collector into one of Jesus' twelve disciples. He is also called Levi in Mark and Luke. Matthew was intent on showing that Jesus was the Messiah promised by the Old Testament and the legal heir to David's throne. The arrangement of his material around five major teaching discourses and his frequent use of pneumonic devices suggest that Matthew intended his Gospel to be used as a manual for instructing Christian converts.

The geographic location of Matthew's first readers remains uncertain, but judging from the strong Jewish flavour of this Gospel, they were probably of Jewish descent. The whereabouts of Matthew at the time of writing is also a matter of speculation, but our best guesses would place him either somewhere in Palestine or else Syria.

Although there have been various advocates of Matthean priority, it is more likely that Matthew expanded Mark than it is that Mark condensed Matthew. In addition to Mark and his own peculiar sources, Matthew probably used a sayings source called Q, which he shared in common with Luke. He probably wrote sometime between the completion of Mark and the fall of Jerusalem in A.D. 70.

Numerical Groupings of Material in Matthew

Matthew arranges his material into convenient numerical groupings, which were probably intended to serve as memory aids. Jesus' genealogy, for example, is broken down into three groups of fourteen, which happens to be the numerical value of David's name in Hebrew:

1.) From Abraham to David	1:2-6a
2.) From David to the exile	1:6b-11
3.) From the exile to Christ	1:12-16

The general teaching of Matthew's Gospel is structured around five major discourses, which may have been intended as counterparts to the five books of Moses:

1.) The Sermon on the Mount	5:1–7:29
2.) Instructions to the twelve	10:5–11:1
3.) Parables about the kingdom	13:1-53
4.) Teaching on community relationships	18:1–19:2
5.) The Olivet Discourse	24:1–25:46

Each of these discourses ends with some variation on the formula, 'it came about that when Jesus had finished these words' such and such happened. Matthew contains a sixth discourse denouncing the scribes and Pharisees (Matt 23:1-39), but its omission of the formula implies that it is not to be counted with the others.

Jesus' teaching about the kingdom often comes in a parable with the introductory formula, 'the kingdom of heaven is like....' Matthew gathers together seven of these kingdom parables in chapter 13:

1.) The parable of the soils	13:3-23
2.) The parable of the weeds	13:24-30, 36-43
3.) The parable of the mustard seed	13:31-32
4.) The parable of the yeast	13:33
5.) The parable of the hidden treasure	13:4
6.) The parable of the costly pearl	13:45-46
7.) The parable of the dragnet	13:47-50

He concludes the discourse with an eighth parable about a householder disbursing goods from his storeroom as a description of the newness and continuity of these parables with previous teaching about the kingdom (Matt 13:51-52).

THE FLOW OF MATTHEW

Matthew's Gospel begins by describing the humble entrance of Jesus into history (1:1–4:11). Although Jesus' birth lacked the pomp befitting royalty, Matthew presents it as the fulfilment of the promised Davidic Messiah (**1:1–2:23**). To substantiate this claim to messiahship, he records Jesus' royal lineage (1:2-17), which he introduces with a superscription declaring Jesus to be the son of David, the son of Abraham (1). First, he traces Jesus' genealogy from Abraham to David (2-6a), then from David to the Babylonian exile (1:6b-11), and finally, from the exile to Jesus' birth (12-16). He provides his readers with a mnemonic device by noting that the genealogy is neatly divided into three groups of fourteen generations each (17).

Matthew also puts forward the supernatural conception of Jesus as a confirmation of his messiahship (18-25). He remarks that when Joseph learned that Mary was pregnant, he wanted to break off their betrothal quietly (18-19), but an angel explained to him that she had conceived the promised Saviour through the Holy Spirit (20-21). Matthew comments that these events took place in fulfilment of Isaiah's prophecy (22-23),[1] and he appends the note that Joseph took Mary as his wife but did not have sexual relations with her until after Jesus was born (24-25).

Matthew also relates a few providential events in the early childhood of Jesus which reinforce his claim to messiahship (**2:1-23**). A group of wise men from the East came to pay homage to the Christ-child (1-12). After searching in Jerusalem for this newborn king of the Jews (1-6), they eventually found him in Bethlehem and bowed down in worship (7-12). When they had departed, an angel warned Joseph to take his family and flee to Egypt because King Herod would seek to kill the child (13-15). Herod, in fact, slaughtered all the male infants in the surrounding area of Bethlehem in his attempt to destroy Jesus (16-18). Joseph and his family returned to Israel (19-23) when an angel confirmed that it

---

1. Isaiah 7:14.

The Death of Herod the Great

[1] [Herod] fell ill and made a will, giving the kingdom to his youngest son [Antipas] because of his hatred of both Archelaus and Philip.... But having given up hope of recovering...he became quite savage and treated everyone with uncontrolled anger and harshness. The cause of this was his belief that he was despised and that the nation took pleasure in his misfortunes....

[5] But Herod's illness became more and more acute.... The fever that he had...produced internal damage.... There was also an ulceration of the bowels and intestinal pains that were particularly terrible.... And he suffered similarly from an abdominal alignment, as well as from a gangrene of his privy parts that produced worms. His breathing was marked by an extreme tension...and constant gasping. He also had convulsions in every limb.... Accordingly it was said by the men of God...that all this was the penalty that God was exacting of the king for his great impiety.... A black mood seized him and made him so bitter at everyone that though he was at the point of death, he devised the following plan. The notable Jews were commanded to come to him from all parts of the entire nation... and the king...had them all shut up in the hippodrome. He then sent for his sister Salome and her husband Alexas, and told them that he would be dead before long...but that he should have to go without the lamentation and mourning that are customary when a king dies was an extremely painful thought to him.... Accordingly, when they saw that he had breathed his last, they were to post soldiers around the hippodrome...and order them to shoot down those imprisoned there, for...they could not fail to make him happy over...his being honoured by conspicuous mourning.

(Josephus, *Antiquities, 17.6.1, 5* [# 146, 148, 168-70, 173-75, 178], trans. Ralph Marcus. Loeb Classical Library [Cambridge: Harvard University Press, 1969], 8:439, 449-455

---

was safe (19-21), and eventually they settled in Nazareth (22-23).

Without any mention of the intervening years, Matthew moves directly from the birth and early childhood of Jesus to the preparations for his public ministry that thrust him onto the center stage of world-history (**3**:1–4:11). To prepare the way for the Messiah, John the Baptist came preaching that the kingdom of heaven was near (3:1-12). He called people to repent of their sins and be baptized (1-6). In response, many of the religious leaders came to be baptized, but sensing that they were not sincere, John rebuked them sharply (7-10). John announced that one far greater than he was coming who would baptize with the Holy Spirit and fire (11-12). Then Jesus arrived to be baptized by John; as he went up out of the water, the Father spoke approvingly from heaven and the Spirit descended upon him as a dove (13-17).

Following his baptism, Jesus was tempted by the devil (4:1-11). The Spirit led him away into the wilderness, where he fasted for forty days (1-2). Then the devil came and tempted him to satisfy his hunger by turning stones into bread (3-4). Not succeeding at this temptation, he further tempted Jesus to test God's providential care by jumping down from the temple (5-7). Finally, he tempted Jesus to grasp all the world's kingdoms, which he promised to give him if only he would bow down and worship him (8-10). Having failed three times, the devil left Jesus (11).

The early ministry of Jesus to Israel (4:12–16:20) is introduced by his proclamation of the kingdom (4:12-25). When John was taken into custody, Jesus withdrew into Galilee where he began to preach, 'Repent, for the kingdom of heaven is at hand' (12-17). Jesus called two pairs of brothers, Peter and Andrew, and James and John, to leave their fishing nets and follow him (18-22). Then he went on a tour throughout Galilee (23-25). He taught in the synagogues, proclaimed the kingdom, and healed the sick (23). People with all kinds of diseases thronged to him, and great multitudes followed him from all over Palestine (24-25).

As the first of five extended discourses, Matthew includes The Sermon on the Mount, in which Jesus sets forth principles of the kingdom (5:1–7:29).[2] The setting for the sermon is on a mountainside where Jesus sat down and taught his disciples (5:1-2). He began by defining the character of true discipleship (3-16). He pronounced spiritual blessings upon his followers in ways that contradict the normal expectations of the world (3-12), and he described them as a preservative (13) and illuminating force in the world (14-16).

Next, Jesus spoke about his relationship to the Old Testament

---

2. Cf. Matthew 10:5–11:1; 13:1-53; 18:1–19:2; 24:1–25:46.

law as its fulfilment (17-48). He denied that he had come to abolish the law, even in its minutest details, but to fulfil it (17-20). Using the formula, 'You have heard it said, ... but I say unto you,' Jesus took up six points of the interpretation of the law, and in each case used his own personal authority to supersede the rabbis' external and legalistic interpretation of the law with its true intention (21-48). He denounced not only murder but also hatred (21-26). He made not only adultery sin but also lust (27-30). He went beyond the legal requirement of writing out a certificate of divorce, to prohibit divorce except for adultery (31-32). He also went beyond the requirement to fulfil one's vows, to argue that one should speak plainly without taking an oath at all to affirm one's intention (33-37). He argued that, rather than retaliating, we should do good to those who do evil to us (38-42). Rather than simply loving those who love us, he required that we love our enemies as well (43-48).

Jesus also spoke about the piety of authentic disciples (6:1-18). After stating the general principle that we should practise our piety as a private observance before God rather than as a public display to win the approval of people (1), he derived three specific precepts from this principle. We are not to give publicly (2-4) or to pray publicly so as to be honoured and respected by people (5-15). To illustrate the second precept about not praying to win people's respect, Jesus cited the practice of the hypocrites who pray long and meaningless prayers on the street corners (5-8); and he contrasted their prayers with 'the Lord's prayer' as a positive model of simplicity and humility (9-15). In the third precept he taught that we are not to appear gloomy when we fast so as to be noticed for our spirituality, but to fast secretly before God (16-18).

Jesus also delineated the proper attitude towards material goods (19-34). We are not to hoard treasures on earth but to store up treasures in heaven (19-21). We are to guard the desires that we allow to enter through our eyes so that we will be single-minded and full of light rather than darkness (22-23). We are to be undivided in our loyalty without trying to serve God and riches at the same time (24); and we are not to be anxious about the necessities of life, knowing that God will take care of us (25-34).

The last major subject Jesus addresses is our proper relationships to others (7:1-12). In relation to a brother, we are not to judge harshly (1-5). In relation to the ungodly, we are not to encourage their profaneness by casting our pearls before swine (6). In relation to God, we are to pray persistently (7-11). Jesus extended the invitation for us to ask (7-8); and he left the assurance that our heavenly Father is much more willing to answer than are earthly fathers (9-11). In relation to everyone, we are to do the good to them that we would want them to do to us (12).

At this point, Jesus left off his universal ethical instructions and began to apply the sermon personally to his listeners (13-27). First, he gave them warnings about the seriousness of rejecting his teaching (13-23). He warned that the road leading to destruction is broad; whereas, the way leading to life is narrow (13-14). He further warned that false prophets will come whose outward appearance is not consistent with their true character; although they might appear dressed in sheep's clothing, inwardly they will be ravenous wolves (15-20). Finally, Jesus warned that there are many who will be damned because they do not know him, even though they profess his name and perform miracles (21-23). To these warnings, Jesus added an encouragement for his listeners to build their lives upon the solid foundation of his words (24-27). The sermon ends with Matthew's typical concluding formula, 'when Jesus had finished [these words] ...,' followed by a comment about the amazement of the crowd at the authority of Jesus' teaching (28-29).

From Jesus' teaching about the kingdom, Matthew moves to various manifestations of the power of the kingdom (8:1–11:1). Its power was demonstrated in the triumph of Jesus' mighty works over disease, nature, demons and sin (8:1–9:8). Matthew includes four examples of Jesus' power to heal diseases (8:1-17). When Jesus came down from the mountain, he cleansed a leper (1-4). At Capernaum, he healed a centurion's paralysed servant *in absentia*, simply by speaking the word (5-13). In addition to healing Peter's mother-in-law from a fever (14-15), he healed numerous sick and demon-possessed people who gathered around that evening (16-17).

Matthew provides a transition to the next demonstration of

Jesus' mighty works by recording some reactions to such a person who had the power to heal diseases. In a setting of great popularity where crowds were pressing in upon him and ready to follow, Jesus put them off by demanding that his would-be disciples forsake everything to follow him (18-22). A certain scribe wanted to follow Jesus, but Jesus warned that he would have to forego creature comforts to be his disciple (18-20). Another man wanted to follow Jesus after he had buried his father, but Jesus insisted that he would have to relinquish family relationships (21-22).

In the face of this tide of popularity, Jesus withdrew with his disciples. While they were crossing over to the other side of the Sea of Galilee by boat, a storm arose which gave Jesus opportunity to demonstrate his power over nature. He simply spoke to the storm, and it became calm (23-27). When they landed, they were met by two fierce, demon possessed men who provided an occasion for Jesus to demonstrate his power over demons (28-34). When Jesus and the disciples crossed back over again, they encountered a paralytic; this time Jesus used the incident to demonstrate his authority to forgive sin by telling the man to take up his bed and walk (**9:1-8**).

Monetary References in Matthew

Matthew was a tax collector when Jesus called him to be a disciple (Matt 9:9), and, as might be expected, his financial background has left its imprint upon his gospel. Only Matthew mentions the two-drachma temple tax (Matt 17:24), and only he has the parable of the unforgiving servant who owed 10,000 talents (Matt 18:21-35). Although Luke has a similar parable to Matthew's parable of the master who entrusted his wealth to his servants while he went on a journey, Luke gives each servant a mina (Lk 19:11-27); whereas, Matthew varies the amount entrusted to each according to his ability—the first receives five talents, the second two talents, and the third one (Matt 25:14-30). Luke records that when Jesus sent out the twelve, he instructed them to take no money (Lk 9:3). Mark adds the detail that they were not to take any money in their belts (Mk 6:8), but Matthew specifies the various kinds of metal used for currency that they were not to take in their belts: 'no gold, or silver, or copper' (Matt 10:9). Matthew is the only Gospel writer to use the expression 'to settle accounts' (Matt 18:23, 24; 25:19) and the only one to refer to bankers (Matt 25:27) and debt (Matt 18:32).

The power of the kingdom was manifested not only by Jesus' mighty acts, but also by Jesus' impact upon people (9-34). Jesus made such a great impact upon Matthew himself that he quit his lucrative and disreputable job to become a disciple (9-13). Matthew was sitting in the tax office when Jesus called him to follow him (9). He hosted a banquet and invited his acquaintances from dubious backgrounds so that he might introduce them to Jesus (10-13). Some of John's disciples complained that Jesus' disciples didn't fast, but Jesus replied that as long as he was with them it was impossible to keep them from celebrating (14-17). Those who were healed by Jesus created widespread publicity for him even though he wanted to keep a low profile (18-34). When Jesus restored a twelve year old girl to life, 'this news went out into all that land' (18-26). When he restored the sight of two blind men, they 'spread the news about him in all that land' (27-31). When he restored speech to a dumb demoniac, the multitudes marvelled, saying, 'Nothing like this was ever seen in Israel' (32-34).

We also see the power of the kingdom manifested in the mission of the twelve disciples (9:35–11:1). Matthew gives an introduction to their mission (9:35–10:4), in which Jesus requested them to pray for workers because he could not attend personally to all the needy people who were flocking to him (9:35-38). Presumably, the immediate answer to that prayer comes in Jesus' authorization of the twelve to cast out demons and heal the sick (**10**:1). Their authorization for this task provides Matthew with a suitable opportunity for naming the disciples (2-4).

Rather than describing the actual work of the twelve, Matthew records Jesus' instructions to them just prior to their going out, which form the substance of the second discourse (10:5–11:1). Jesus began by defining their task: they were to go to the lost Jews, heal the sick, raise the dead, cast out demons and preach, 'the kingdom of heaven is at hand' (10:5-15). He warned that some people would meet them with hostility (16-25), but he encouraged them not to be afraid because even though their enemies might kill their bodies, they could not harm their souls; furthermore, God would providentially watch over them (26-33). Jesus also warned that one of the repercussions of being his disciple might be the creation of conflict, even within one's own home (34-36). Jesus laid down stiff conditions for discipleship that disqualified anyone who would put one's own life or family first, as well as anyone who was unwilling to bear one's cross (37-39). To offset the high cost of discipleship, Jesus offered spiritual rewards along with the assurance that his disciples were acting on his behalf (40-42). Matthew concludes the discourse with his usual formula and notes the continuation of Jesus' preaching tour (**11**:1).

Having presented the power of the kingdom, Matthew now records various responses to the mystery of the kingdom in Jesus Christ, most of which tend to be either uncertain or negative (11:2–12:50). At this time John the Baptist was in prison, and even he was having some doubts about whether Jesus was the Messiah (11:2-19). John sent a delegation to Jesus (2-6) to ask him if he was the one they had expected (2-3), and Jesus responded simply by listing the miracles that were taking place (4-6). As the delegation was leaving, Jesus turned to bear witness to the greatness of John (7-19). He identified John as the greatest and last in the long line of Old Testament prophets (7-15), but he noted that though John's style was very different from his own, the people had rejected both of them (16-19).

The Galilean cities in which Jesus performed most of his miracles did not repent, so Jesus condemned them to a worse judgment than that of Sodom (20-24). Ironically, the wise and intelligent did not understand who Jesus was, but the Father gave this insight to little children (25-27). Those who were weary and burdened down, Jesus invited to come to him for rest (28-30).

The strongest opposition to Jesus came from the religious leaders (**12**:1-45). The Pharisees were especially upset about Jesus' supposed violations of the Sabbath (1-14). They protested the disciples' plucking heads of grain as they walked through the fields on the Sabbath (1-8), and they plotted to kill Jesus when he healed a man with a withered hand on the Sabbath (9-14). Knowing of their plots, Jesus withdrew from that region (15-21).

In addition to charging Jesus with violating the Sabbath, the Pharisees also accused him of collusion with Satan (22-37). Jesus cast a demon out of a dumb man, but the Pharisees accused him of casting out demons by the ruler of demons (22-24).[3] He calmly pointed out the inconsistency of pitting Satan against Satan (25-30). Furthermore, he warned them that blaspheming against the Holy Spirit is an unpardonable sin (31-37).

Some scribes and Pharisees came to Jesus demanding a sign (38-45). Recognizing their insincerity, he refused to give a sign, other than the sign of Jonah who spent three days in the belly of a great fish (38-42). He also warned that when a demon is cast out, it is dangerous to leave a spiritual vacuum by not replacing it with something positive (43-45).

While Jesus was still speaking to the crowd, his family came seeking to speak to him; but pointing to a higher allegiance, he replied that his true family was spiritual (46-50).

Against this backdrop of general uncertainty about the coming of the kingdom in Christ, Matthew presents Jesus' third discourse, which uses seven parables about the kingdom to clarify its meaning for the disciples (**13**:1-53). These parables, which are usually introduced by the phrase 'the kingdom of heaven is like ...,' may be divided into two groups: the first four parables were spoken to the crowds by the sea, and the last three were explained to the disciples in the house. There is an eighth concluding parable, but it is distinct from the first seven in that it speaks about the disciples' understanding of the kingdom parables rather than describing the kingdom itself.

Matthew introduces the parables spoken to the crowds by the sea (1-35) by describing their setting with Jesus sitting in a boat and teaching the large crowd gathered around him on the beach (1-2). The first parable is about a man who sowed seed on four different kinds of soil, but only the seed sown on the good soil produced a harvest (3-23). First, we have the narration of the parable (3-9). It is followed by an aside in which Jesus explained to the disciples that his rationale for speaking in parables was to make the mysteries of the kingdom clear to those who were predisposed to understand and at the same time leave the meaning obscure for those who were not favourably disposed (10-17). Jesus interpreted the parable of the soils for the disciples as referring to four different

---

3. Cf. Matthew 9:34.

kinds of people who respond to the message of the kingdom in four different ways (18-23).

Jesus went on to tell another parable about weeds that were allowed to grow up with the wheat until harvest because it was too difficult to separate them (24-30). He also told a parable about mustard seed, which is smaller than all other seeds but grows into a tree large enough for birds to nest in (31-32). In the fourth parable, he told about some yeast which a woman hid in three measures of flour until the whole batch was leavened (33). Matthew comments that Jesus' speaking in parables was a fulfilment of Psalm 78:2, in which the psalmist promised to open his mouth in parables and utter hidden things (34-35).

At that point Jesus left the crowds and went inside the house, where he gave further explanation to the disciples (36-52). With regard to the second parable, Jesus explained that the weeds are sons of the evil one who are allowed to grow together with the sons of the kingdom until the judgment (36-43). Jesus also compared the kingdom of heaven to a hidden treasure which a man found in a field; to gain the treasure he sold all that he had and bought the field (44). Again, Jesus compared the kingdom of heaven to a merchant who discovered a costly pearl and sold everything that he had to buy the pearl (45-46). He went on to compare the kingdom of heaven to a dragnet which brought up all kinds of fish, good and bad, which had to be separated later (47-50). Jesus drew his teaching to a close by likening the disciples' understanding of the parables to a householder who brings new things as well as old ones out of his storeroom (51-52). Matthew concludes the discourse with his typical formula: 'when Jesus had finished these parables he departed' (53).

As the issues regarding Jesus become more clearly set, we see the rift between his followers and his detractors widening (13:54–16:20). The people of his home town didn't believe in Jesus because they could not reconcile his miraculous powers with their knowledge of the boy who had grown up among them (13:54-58). Herod was confused about Jesus' identity (**14**:1-12); he supposed that Jesus must be John the Baptist risen from the dead (1-2). Herod made this association because he had previously executed John to satisfy his wife Herodias (3-12). As Matthew makes clear, the underlying reason for the execution of John was that he had rebuked Herod and Herodias for their adulterous marriage (3-5). The immediate occasion for John's execution came when Herodias' daughter danced for Herod at his birthday party, and he foolishly promised to give her whatever she asked; her mother told her to ask for the head of John the Baptist (6-12).

Although not everyone accepted Jesus, large crowds of people in Galilee were attracted to him (13-36). Jesus wanted to be alone to grieve John's death, but he felt compassion on the crowds that intruded upon his solitude (13-14). After spending the day with Jesus in a desolate place, the people became hungry so he multiplied five loaves and two fish to feed over five thousand of them (15-21). After the meal Jesus dismissed the crowd (22-33). While the disciples got into a boat and crossed over to the other side, he went away by himself to a mountain to pray (22-23). Early in the morning he came to them walking on the water in the midst of a fierce storm; after rescuing Peter from an aborted attempt to accomplish the same feat, Jesus got into the boat and the storm stopped, to the disciples' amazement (24-33). When they came to land at Gennesaret on the other side, the people from all the surrounding region thronged to Jesus with their sick (34-36).

But some Pharisees and scribes came from Jerusalem to stir up opposition against Jesus (**15**:1-20). They got into a dispute with Jesus because his disciples didn't wash their hands before eating (1-11). Jesus responded by teaching the disciples that defilement comes from inward thoughts and attitudes rather than external observances (12-20).

In the region of Tyre and Sidon, Jesus met a Canaanite woman who incessantly pleaded with him to heal her demon-possessed daughter, which he did because of her great faith (21-28). When he returned to Galilee, the crowds were amazed and glorified God as they saw their acquaintances with infirmities restored to health (29-31). After a crowd of over four thousand spent three days with Jesus in a deserted location, they became hungry, but Jesus satisfied their hunger by multiplying seven loaves and a few small fish to feed all of them (32-39).

The Pharisees and Sadducees came to Jesus to test him by asking for a sign (**16**:1-12), but he rejected their request both because their motives were evil and they should have been able to discern the times without a sign (1-4). Instead, he warned his disciples of the permeating effect of the false teaching of the Pharisees and Sadducees (5-12). The widening rift between those who rejected Jesus and those who followed him culminates in Simon Peter's confession of Jesus' true identity as the Messiah, the Son of the living God (13-20).

From this point on, the direction of the Gospel changes as Jesus steadily moves towards the passion he is about to undergo in Jerusalem (16:21–25:46). This change in direction probably comes about both from the growing evidence that, although the crowds will follow Jesus because of his miracles, the nation as a whole will not accept him as divine, and from the outworking of the redemptive implications necessarily involved in Messiahship, now that the disciples have correctly understood Jesus' true identity. With these considerations in the background, Jesus began to prepare the disciples for what would soon take place (16:21–19:2). Here we have the first of several times that Jesus predicts his passion to the disciples (16:21-28).[4] In direct opposition to Peter's rebuke, Jesus unswervingly maintained that it was absolutely necessary for him to suffer (21-23). Furthermore, he insisted that anyone who wanted to be his disciple would have to deny himself and bear his own cross (24-28).

But Jesus projected the disciples beyond the pain of the cross to a foretaste of the kingdom's glory on the other side (**17**:1-27). Six days later, he took three of them up a high mountain where his appearance was transfigured before them into a dazzling white (1-8). On the way down the mountain, the disciples discussed the prophecy that Elijah would come before the Messiah (9-13). At the base of the mountain, they were met by a father with his epileptic son, whom the disciples had not been able to heal (14-21). Jesus healed the boy before the crowd that had gathered (14-18), and explained to the disciples privately that the reason they couldn't heal the boy was that they lacked faith (19-21).

---

4. Cf. Matthew 17:22-23; 20:17-19.

While the disciples were gathering together in Galilee, Jesus clearly predicted a second time that he would suffer (22-23). When some officials came to Peter asking for payment of the temple tax, Jesus told him to throw a hook into the sea and he would find a coin worth the right amount to pay for both Peter and himself (24-27).

At this point Matthew draws together a fourth teaching discourse, which deals with various community relationships and is addressed to the disciples (**18**:1–19:2). In response to the disciples' question about who would be the greatest in the kingdom of heaven, Jesus attempted to remove any rivalry (1-14) by pointing out the greatness of childlike humility (1-5). He reinforced this point by drawing attention to the peril of stumbling stones, whether it be a child or an adult that is caused to stumble (6-9), and he again emphasized the value of a child by comparing it to the value of a lost sheep (10-14).

Jesus also includes a lesson on securing forgiveness between brothers (15-35). He approaches the subject from both directions; first he tells us how to reprove a brother who has offended us (15-20). The proper procedure is to go and speak to the offending brother in private first, and then if there is no resolution to take along two or three witnesses; and finally, as a last resort, to present the case to the church (15-17). Jesus gave the disciples the full authority of heaven to judge in such cases, and he also promised to do anything that two or three believers agreed upon in his name (18-20).

Jesus also tells how to forgive a brother who desires mercy (21-35). He prohibited keeping records of how often a brother sins against us or setting limits on how many times we will forgive him (21-22). Jesus used a parable about the judgment of an unmerciful servant to illustrate that we are indebted to show mercy to others because God has forgiven us far more than we are ever called upon to forgive them (23-35). Matthew concludes the discourse with the formula, 'when Jesus had finished these words, he departed from Galilee ...' (**19**:1-2).

The next section describes Jesus' ministry as he slowly made his way to Jerusalem (19:3–20:34). This ministry, which was primarily concerned with teaching, either by word or by example, begins with Jesus' teaching on divorce and celibacy (19:3-12). In response to the Pharisees' question, Jesus affirmed that God's intention was the indissoluble union of man and wife and that the only permissible grounds for divorce was adultery (3-9). To the disciples' comment that it would be better for people who would seek divorce not to marry, Jesus replied that some people have remained celibate for the sake of the kingdom (10-12).

Jesus taught the value of children in the kingdom of heaven by receiving them to himself and blessing them (13-15). He also used an incident that arose to teach concerning eternal rewards (19:16–20:16). A young man came to Jesus asking about how to inherit eternal life, but he was unwilling to accept the condition of giving up his wealth (19:16-22). Out of this incident flowed a discussion with the disciples about the rewards for following Jesus (23-30). Jesus commented, to the disciples' surprise, that it is humanly impossible for a rich person to enter the kingdom of heaven (23-26). In reply to Peter's remark that they had left everything they had to follow him, Jesus promised that they would be rewarded abundantly (27-30). Jesus illustrated the abundance of God's rewards with a parable about a generous landowner who paid the labourers hired at the last hour the same as those who worked all day in his vineyard (**20**:1-16).

Jesus took the disciples aside and told them a third time that they were going up to Jerusalem, where he would be put to death and rise again (17-19). He was barely finished when another incident arose that again made it necessary for him to reprove the selfish ambition of the disciples (20-28). The mother of James and John came to Jesus with a request that in the kingdom her sons be given special positions of honour on either side of him, but Jesus denied the request, leaving it up to the Father to decide (20-23). Instead, he admonished all the disciples to seek greatness by following his example in becoming a servant (24-28).

To the teaching which was the primary focus on Jesus' journey to Jerusalem, Matthew adds one case of healing. As they were passing through Jericho, Jesus healed two blind men who were crying out, 'Have mercy on us, Son of David!' (29-34).

The arrival of Jesus in Jerusalem presented one final opportunity for him to minister before the passion drew his earthly work to a close (**21**:1–25:46). During this final period of his ministry, Jesus directly challenged the Jews (21:1–23:39), first of all by publicly presenting himself to the nation as the Messianic King (21:1-17). He symbolically made this claim by triumphantly riding into the city upon a donkey to the cheers of the popular crowds (1-11), and he even more directly affronted the religious establishment by walking into the temple and driving out those who were selling merchandise (12-17).

These actions precipitated open confrontation between Jesus and the religious establishment (21:18–23:39). Jesus prefaced his further verbal confrontations with the Jews with a symbolic action that set the stage for and interpreted his succeeding relations with them (21:18-22). The next morning as Jesus was walking into the city, he saw a fig tree beside the road, but not finding any fruit on it, he cursed it with barrenness, and immediately it withered (18-19). The disciples were astonished, but Jesus replied that even greater miracles were possible through faith (20-22).

First of all, the chief priests and elders came into conflict with Jesus (21:23–22:14). They demanded to know by what authority he did 'these things', among which cleansing the temple must have been foremost in their minds, but Jesus unmasked their insincerity by showing that they were unwilling to accept the authority of John the Baptist even though everyone recognized that he was sent from God (21:23-27). Jesus drove home their evil rejection of divine authority even further by means of three parables (21:28–22:14). The first parable was about two sons: the first of whom promised to go to work in his father's vineyard but didn't go; the second refused to go but later changed his mind and went (21:28-32). The second parable was about some wicked tenant farmers who beat up all the servants that the landlord sent to collect his share of the crop until finally they killed the landlord's own son (33-46). The third parable was about some guests whom a king invited to his son's wedding, but they all made excuses so he sent his slaves out into the streets to invite everyone they found (**22**:1-14).

The Pharisees and Sadducees were upset because they correctly perceived that Jesus' parables were about them, and they set traps to try to catch Jesus in something that he said (15-46). The Pharisees asked Jesus if they should pay taxes to Caesar, but he avoided either going against national sentiment or the ruling government by stating the general principle, 'Give to Caesar the things that are Caesar's and to God the things that are God's' (15-22). Next the Sadducees, who denied the resurrection, tried to make Jesus' teaching look absurd by presenting the case of a woman who outlived seven husbands and obviously couldn't be married to all of them in heaven. Jesus replied that marriage is not an issue in heaven, and he presented the counter-cases of Abraham, Isaac and Jacob who are spoken of in Scripture as having a relationship with God long after they had died (23-33). A lawyer asked Jesus which is the greatest commandment, and Jesus neatly summarized the whole law under love for God and one's neighbour (34-40). When the religious leaders had finished asking their questions, Jesus went on the offensive by asking them how the Messiah could be David's son when in Psalm 110 David calls the Messiah his Lord (41-46).

Jesus then proceeded to denounce the scribes and Pharisees (**23**:1-39).[5] His denunciation is aimed in two directions. First he warned the crowds about the scribes and Pharisees on three grounds (1-12): their hypocrisy (1-4), their vanity (5-7), and their lack of humility such as is fitting for a servant (8-12). Then Jesus turned from the crowds to the scribes and Pharisees to pronounce seven woes upon them (13-36). Woe for shutting up the kingdom and not entering it themselves (13, [14]). Woe for discipling hellions who turn out even more evil than they are themselves (15). Woe for taking deceptive oaths rather than speaking honestly (16-22). Woe for neglecting the most important matters of the law, namely justice, mercy and faithfulness (23-24). Woe for putting on external appearances (25-26); and conversely, woe for concealing inward corruption (27-28). Woe for sharing ancestral blood-guiltiness for the deaths of prophets in the past, as well as for other prophets yet

---

5. Although some scholars consider ch. 23 to be another extended discourse, for a total of six, it lacks Matthew's characteristic formula and is part of a larger narrative whole.

to come (29-36). After all of these woes, Jesus broke into a lament over Jerusalem (37-39).

When he was done contending with the religious leaders, Jesus turned to the disciples and encouraged them by providing prophetic insights into God's sovereign plan for the unfolding of history. This prophetic section forms the fifth discourse in Matthew's Gospel, which is often referred to as the Olivet Discourse after the location where Jesus spoke it (**24**:1–25:46). The discourse originated on the way out of the temple as the disciples were pointing out its grandeur to Jesus (24:1-3). He replied prophetically that not one stone of the temple would be left standing (1-2). When they sat down on the Mount of Olives, the disciples asked Jesus when these things would take place and what would be the sign of his coming and the end of the age (3). The body of the discourse that follows contains Jesus' answers to these questions (24:4–25:46).

Jesus began by concentrating on the question of timing (24:4-36). He predicted that a number of global signs, such as wars, famines and earthquakes, will lead up to the end (4-8) and that the time before the end will be marked by persecution, false prophets, lawlessness and a lack of love, but the Gospel will be preached to the whole world under these conditions (9-14). Jesus warned that after the abomination of desolation, which Daniel prophesied, those in Judea ought to flee to the mountains because there will be a time of great tribulation such as has not occurred since the beginning of the world (15-22). He also warned that the last days will be characterized by false messiahs and false prophets who will be very adept at leading people astray (23-28). Jesus predicted that the coming of the Son of Man will be heralded by cosmic upheavals: the sun and moon will be darkened and the stars will fall from the sky (29-31). As a sign of the imminence of the consummation, he gave the budding of the fig tree (32-36).

In addition to providing the disciples with signs about the timing of the end, Jesus exhorted them, and us as well, to watchfulness using three illustrations (37-51). We should be alert at all times because, just as the flood was not expected by Noah's generation, so the coming of the Son of Man will come unexpectedly (37-42).

The Christians' Flight to Pella

Eusebius reports that the Christians living in Jerusalem heeded a prophetic warning to flee the city and managed to escape before it was destroyed. He apparently is not referring directly to Christ's warning recorded in the Gospels (Matt 24:15-18; Mark 13:14-15; Luke 21:20-22) but to a subsequent warning repeating its substance.

'But... the church in Jerusalem had been commanded by a revelation, vouchsafed to approved men there before the war, to leave the city and to dwell in a certain town of Perea called Pella. And when those that believed in Christ had come thither from Jerusalem, then, as if the royal city of the Jews...were entirely destitute of holy men, the judgment of God... overtook those who had committed such outrages against Christ and his apostles, and totally destroyed that generation of impious men. But the number of calamities which every where fell upon the nation at that time; the extreme misfortunes to which the inhabitants of Judea were especially subjected, the thousands of men, as well as women and children, that perished by the sword, by famine, and by other forms of death innumerable, – all these things, as well as the many great sieges which were carried on..., and the excessive sufferings endured by those that fled to Jerusalem itself, as to a city of perfect safety, and...the...course of the whole war,...and how at last the abomination of desolation...stood in the very temple of God,...which was now awaiting its total and final destruction by fire, – all these things...[are] accurately described in the history written by Josephus.'

(Eusebius, *Church History*, 3.5.3-4, trans. Arthur Cushman McGiffert, in *The Nicene and Post-Nicene Fathers*, 2nd Series, Philip Schaff, ed., vol. 1: Eusebius, *Church History* [Grand Rapids: Wm. B. Eerdmans Pub. Co., 1976], 138; cf. Josephus, *Jewish Wars*, Bks. 5, 6.)

We should be prepared because the Son of Man will come at an hour no one is expecting, just as a thief breaks into a house at an hour when the householder is not expecting (43-44). We should serve responsibly as a slave who will be rewarded or punished according to his faithfulness in caring for the household of his master in his absence (45-51).

The discourse also contains three warnings about judgment (**25**:1-46). Jesus told a parable about ten virgins, five of whom foolishly forgot to take enough oil for their lamps and were shut out of the wedding feast when the bridegroom arrived (1-13). He told another parable about investing one's resources (14-30). A man went away on a journey and entrusted his possessions to his slaves in varying amounts of talents according to their ability (14-18). When he returned, he asked for an accounting of how they used their talents and rewarded or punished them accordingly (19-30). Finally, he depicted the judgment of the nations (31-46) as a shepherd separating his sheep from the goats (31-33). The sheep on his right will be commended for the compassionate way they treated Christ incarnated in other people (34-40). The goats on his left will be condemned for the inconsiderate way that they treated other people, as if they were acting towards Christ (41-46).

At the conclusion of the Olivet Discourse, Matthew picks up the narrative which he had interrupted to present this long section of teaching. The confrontation between Jesus and the religious leaders eventually resulted in his bitter passion for us (**26**:1–27:66), and Matthew builds up to this climax by relating a series of events that increase the tension and add suspense (26:1-46). First, he shows the plot thickening through the actions of people who are either desperately seeking to kill Jesus or who innocently foreshadow his death by actions which have symbolic meaning (1-16). Rather than finishing the previous section with a concluding formula, Matthew introduces the new section with a transitional formula which indicates that the discourse is over and we are now moving into the passion (1-2).

The Sanhedrin met behind closed doors to plot how to kill Jesus, but they were afraid to seize him publicly (3-5). While he was eating at a home in Bethany, a woman upset the disciples by anointing Jesus with a vial of very costly perfume, but Jesus quieted them by remarking that she had symbolically prepared his body for burial (6-13). After the meal, Judas went to the chief priests and offered to betray Jesus at an opportune time for a sum of money (14-16).

The second way that Matthew builds tension in the series of climactic events leading up to the passion is by giving us a glimpse of Jesus on that fateful night as he prepared the disciples and himself for what was about to happen (17-46). Matthew allows us to look in on the last meal of Jesus with his disciples on the night before his death (17-30). Jesus sent the disciples ahead into the city to prepare for the Passover (17-19). During the meal, he identified the one who would betray him as the one who dipped his hand with him in the bowl, but apparently none of the disciples except Judas understood to whom he was referring (20-25). Jesus transformed the Passover meal into the Lord's Supper by declaring the bread to be his body and the wine to be his blood of the covenant (26:26-29). After singing a final hymn they went out to the Mount of Olives (30).

On the way, Jesus told his disciples that they would all desert him that evening, which Peter and all the rest of them denied (31-35). When they came to a place called Gethsemane, Jesus agonized in prayer that if possible the Father would remove the cup of death from him (36-46); but each time when he returned to check on the disciples, once (36-41), twice (42-43), and a third time (44-46), he found them sleeping.

From this point of surrender to the Father's will, actions quickly follow which culminate in Jesus' death (26:47–27:66). While Jesus was still speaking with the disciples, a mob came to apprehend him in the garden (26:47-56). This mob, sent by the chief priests and elders, was led by Judas, who betrayed Jesus with a kiss (47-50a). At that signal the mob seized him (50b). One disciple drew his sword and cut off the ear of the high priest's slave, but Jesus restrained him (51-54). Jesus rebuked the mob for arresting him as if he were a criminal rather than doing it openly while he taught in the temple (55-56a). At that point all of the disciples deserted Jesus and fled (56b).

The legal proceedings against Jesus took place in three stages (26:57–27:26). First there was a night trial before the Sanhedrin (26:57-75). They led Jesus away to Caiaphas, the high priest, and after trying unsuccessfully to procure consistent false witnesses, they finally indicted him with blasphemy (57-68). Peter, who was sitting outside in the courtyard, was accused three times of being with Jesus, and three times he denied it (69-75). In the morning, the Sanhedrin met a second time to confirm its decision to turn Jesus over to Pilate (27:1-2).

Matthew inserts a parenthesis to tell us that Judas felt remorseful for what he had done. He threw the blood money down in the temple and went away and hanged himself (3-10).

The third stage of the legal proceedings was the Roman trial before Pilate, the governor (11-26). Pilate interrogated Jesus, but was quite surprised that Jesus did nothing to defend himself (11-14). Pilate attempted to appease the crowd by offering to release Jesus in accordance with the custom at Passover, but they demanded that a notorious criminal called Barabbas be released instead (15-23). Pilate finally acquiesced to their demands and delivered Jesus up to be crucified (24-26).

Jesus was put to death in the most humiliating and painful way known to the Roman world (27-56). First, the soldiers put a crown of thorns on him and mocked and beat him, and spat upon him (27-31); then they led him away to be crucified (32-37). They forced a passer-by named Simon to carry Jesus' cross to Golgotha (32), where they offered him wine mixed with gall as a sedative, but he refused to drink it (33-34). While he hung on the cross, the soldiers cast lots for his clothing (35-36). Above his head they affixed the charge, which read, 'This is Jesus the King of the Jews' (37). Those who looked on heaped derision on Jesus because of his apparent helplessness (38-44). The taunts came from not only passers-by (38-40) and the religious leaders (41-43), but even from the robbers who were crucified along with him (44). The forces of nature, by contrast, responded to Jesus' death in ways that seemingly showed greater comprehension of the situation than did the mocking crowd (45-54). The sky grew dark, as if to hide its face in horror (45-50); and when Jesus yielded up his spirit, the earth was shaken by a powerful earthquake that split the tombs open and rent the veil of the temple from top to bottom (51-54). Many of the women who had followed Jesus from Galilee stood at a distance and observed Jesus' death (55-56).

Matthew states the considerations taken regarding the body of Jesus, both by his friends and his enemies (57-66). Joseph of Arimathea saw to the burial of Jesus' body to preserve its dignity (57-61). After obtaining permission from Pilate to remove the body (57-58), he wrapped it in a clean linen sheet and placed it in his own new tomb (59-61). The Jews, who had different motives, placed a guard in front of the tomb to ensure that the body remained there (62-66).

But the story does not end here; Matthew goes on to record Jesus' triumphant resurrection from the dead (**28**:1-20). The earliest witnesses to the resurrection were the women who came to visit the tomb at dawn on the first day of the week (1-10). They did not find the body; instead an angel appeared to them announcing that Jesus had risen from the dead (1-7). Later Jesus appeared to them in person (8-10). The chief priests fraudulently tried to cover up the disappearance of Jesus' body by bribing the guards to say that the disciples stole it while they slept (11-15). In contrast with the propagation of this lie by the religious leaders, Matthew opens the way for the advancement of the more credible explanation of Jesus' life and teachings by noting that the risen Christ appeared to the eleven disciples in Galilee and personally commissioned them to make disciples of every nation on earth (16-20).

OUTLINE OF MATTHEW

I. Jesus' humble entrance into history	1:1–4:11
A. The birth of the Messiah	1:1–2:23
1. The royal lineage of Jesus	1:2-17
a. The superscription to the genealogy	1:1
b. The genealogy from Abraham to David	1:2-6a
c. The genealogy from David to the exile	1:6b-11
d. The genealogy from the exile to Christ	1:12-16
e. A summary of the genealogy	1:17
2. The supernatural conception of Jesus	1:18-25
a. The perplexity of Joseph	1:18-19
b. The explanation of the angel	1:20-21
c. The fulfilment of prophecy	1:22-23
d. The fidelity of Joseph	1:24-25
3. The early childhood of Jesus	2:1-23
a. The visit of the magi	2:1-12
(1) Their search for the child	2:1-6
(2) Their adoration of the child	2:7-12
b. The flight to Egypt	2:13-15
c. The slaughter of the infants	2:16-18
d. The return to Israel	2:19-23
(1) The confirmation from an angel	2:19-21
(2) The settlement in Nazareth	2:22-23
B. Preparations for ministry	3:1–4:11
1. The preaching of John the Baptist concerning the kingdom	3:1-12
a. John's call to repentance	3:1-6
b. John's condemnation of the religious leaders	3:7-10
c. John's inferiority to the Coming One	3:11-12
2. The baptism of Jesus by John	3:13-17
3. The temptation of Jesus in the wilderness	4:1-11
a. The setting	4:1-2
b. First temptation – to satisfy his hunger	4:3-4
c. Second temptation – to test God's providence	4:5-7
d. Third temptation – to grasp the world's kingdoms	4:8-10
e. The conclusion	4:11

Josephus' Testimony about Jesus

'About this time there lived Jesus, a wise man, if indeed one ought to call him a man. For he was one who wrought surprising feats and was a teacher of such people as accept the truth gladly. He won over many Jews and many of the Greeks. He was the Messiah. When Pilate, upon hearing him accused by men of the highest standing amongst us, had condemned him to be crucified, those who had in the first place come to love him did not give up their affection for him. On the third day he appeared to them restored to life, for the prophets of God had prophesied these and countless other marvelous things about him. And the tribe of Christians, so called after him, has still to this day not disappeared.'

(Josephus, *Antiquities* 18.3.3 [63-64], trans. Louis H. Feldman, Loeb Classical Library [Cambridge: Harvard University Press, 1969], 9:49-51.

As a number of critics have pointed out, it is improbable that an unbelieving Jew like Josephus would affirm that Jesus was the Messiah or that he had risen from the dead. There is general consensus, however, that the substance of this text originated from him. A few simple emendations could have changed his report of what was believed about Jesus into an affirmation of faith that would only be possible for someone who was a Christian.

LUKE

OVERVIEW OF LUKE

Theme: Jesus, the ideal human who came to save the world

Key Verse: Luke 2:30-32, 'My eyes have seen your salvation, which you have prepared in the sight of all people, a light for revelation to the Gentiles and for the glory of your people Israel' (NIV).

The dedicatory preface to Theophilus   1:1-4

I. Collected narratives concerning the Saviour's
    infancy along with that of the forerunner   1:5–2:52

II. Spiritual preparations for the Messiah's public
    manifestation by the Jordan   3:1–4:13
A. John's preparation of the way for the Messiah   3:1-20

B. The Spirit's preparation of the Messiah for
    ministry   3:21–4:13

III. The opening phase of Jesus' public ministry
    in Galilee   4:14–9:50
A. The early Galilean ministry   4:14–7:50

B. The later Galilean ministry   8:1–9:50

IV. The long journey to Jesus' fateful destination
    in Jerusalem   9:51–19:44
A. The first phase of the journey   9:51–13:21

B. The second phase of the journey   13:22-17:10

C. The third phase of the journey   17:11-18:30

D. The final phase of the journey   18:31-19:27

E. The triumphal entry into Jerusalem   19:28-44

HISTORICAL BACKGROUND

The third Gospel is generally ascribed to Luke, the travelling companion of the Apostle Paul and author of the Book of Acts. Luke was a medical doctor and probably the only Gentile writer to be included in the New Testament canon (Col 4:11, 14). His education is reflected in his elevated style of writing, with a love for complicated sentences and big words, and his ethnicity comes through in his special theological concern for the salvation of the whole world.

Luke's Gospel, like Acts, is addressed to Theophilus, who may have sponsored the publication of both works, but it was probably intended to reach a wider Gentile audience as well. We do not know the geographic location of the book's recipients and are left to guess at the place of writing. Luke would have had opportunity to conduct first-hand research in Palestine during Paul's imprisonment at Caesarea. He probably made use of Mark's earlier Gospel as well as other written sources and eye-witness accounts, which he tells us he had investigated thoroughly (Luke 1:1-4). His historical reliability, though once doubted, is now widely recognized. Luke probably completed his Gospel during Paul's first imprisonment at Rome, if not sooner, since it naturally comes before its sequel, the Book of Acts, which was written at that time. Accordingly, we should date it before A.D. 61 or 62. The primary reason why some scholars date it later is the assumption that Jesus could not have predicted the fall of Jerusalem in 70 A.D. (Luke 21:6, 20).

The Authorship of the Third Gospel

. . . The third book of the Gospel is that according to Luke. Luke, the physician, when, after the ascension of Christ, Paul had taken him to himself as [travelling companion] wrote in his own name what he had been told, although he had not himself seen the Lord in the flesh. He set down the events as far as he could ascertain them, and began his narrative with the birth of John. (Muratorian Canon, 1, in Henry Bettenson, ed. *Documents of the Christian Church*, 2nd ed. [London: Oxford University Press, 1963], 28.)

Hymns of Praise in Luke's Birth Narratives

Luke's birth narratives incorporate four hymns of praise, which have inspired many well-known musical compositions.

Mary's *Magnificat*, 1:46-55
[46] My soul magnifies the Lord,
[47] And my spirit has rejoiced in God my Saviour . . . .

Zacharias' *Benedictus*, 1:67-79
[68] Blessed [be] the Lord God of Israel,
For he has visited us and accomplished redemption . . . .

The Angels' *Gloria*, 2:13-14
Glory to God in the highest,
And peace on earth among men of his good pleasure.

Simeon's *Nunc dimittis*, 2:28-31
[29] Now Lord, let your servant depart in peace . . . .

THE FLOW OF LUKE

Luke opens the first volume of his two-part work with a dedicatory preface to Theophilus, in which he states his theological reason for writing and the care with which he has investigated his historical sources (**1**:1-4).

Luke collected a series of narratives concerning the infancies of the Saviour, Jesus Christ, and his forerunner, John the Baptist (1:5–2:52). In them he tells of God's promise to a priest named Zacharias and his wife, Elizabeth, that their child would be the forerunner to the Messiah (1:5-25). Both Zacharias and Elizabeth were known for their upright character, but they were elderly and had no children (5-7). One day Zacharias received an unexpected visit from an angel (8-20). The angel Gabriel appeared to him while he was burning incense in the temple (8-12) and announced that his wife would miraculously bear a son named John, who would prepare the way for the Messiah (13-17). Because Zacharias did not believe the angel's word, he was cursed with dumbness until

---

The Holy Spirit in Luke

The Holy Spirit, who plays a prominent role in Acts, is also given special prominence in Luke's Gospel. Luke records that John the Baptist was filled with the Spirit from his mother's womb (1:15) and that the Holy Spirit was instrumental in the virginal conception (1:35). Elizabeth was filled with the Spirit when she heard the news of Mary's pregnancy (1:41), and her husband, Zacharias was also filled with the Spirit when he prophesied the significance of John's birth (1:67). Simeon's hope of seeing the Messiah was revealed by the Spirit (2:25-27). The Holy Spirit descended upon Jesus in the form of a dove at his baptism (3:22), and Jesus returned from the Jordan River full of the Spirit (4:1). He was led by the Spirit into the wilderness to be tempted (4:1), and he returned to Galilee in the power of the Spirit (4:14). At the outset of his ministry, Jesus claimed to be anointed by the Spirit in fulfillment of Isaiah's prophecy (4:18). Whereas Matthew promises that our Father in heaven will give good things to those who ask (Matt 7:11), Luke identifies the heavenly Father's supreme good gift as the Holy Spirit (11:13).

---

the prophecy was fulfilled (18-20). Luke records two different responses to the vision of Zacharias (21-25). The crowd waiting for him in the temple court was bewildered at his dumbness and had to rely upon his gestures to interpret what had happened (21-23), but Elizabeth accepted her pregnancy as from the Lord (24-25).

The angel Gabriel also appeared to Mary, a relative of Elizabeth, and announced to her that she would miraculously conceive the promised Saviour, Jesus, by the power of the Holy Spirit (26-38). Mary went to visit Elizabeth during their pregnancies (39-56). Elizabeth greeted her warmly and blessed her for believing what the Lord had spoken (39-45). Upon hearing Elizabeth's blessing, Mary broke into a hymn of praise to God for showing mercy to her in fulfilment of his promise to Abraham (46-55). At about the time that Elizabeth was due, Mary returned to her home (56).

The birth of John the Baptist took place in accordance with the angel's promise (57-80). When Zacharias indicated that the child was to be named John, his speech was immediately restored to him (57-66), and he prophesied concerning the role that the child would play in preparing the people for God's salvation (67-79). The child grew and lived in isolation in the deserts until his public appearance (80).

Jesus Christ was also born as promised (2:1-20). Luke records a remarkable convergence of historical forces that resulted in the birth of the Saviour in a humble manger in Bethlehem (1-7). Some shepherds from the fields nearby rejoiced with Mary and Joseph at this momentous birth (8-20). The shepherds had been tending their flock when an angel announced the glorious news to them (8-14). After hurrying to Bethlehem to confirm the report, the shepherds joyously proclaimed the Saviour's birth to all those around (15-20).

Soon after his birth, the child was presented to the Lord (21-38). He was circumcised on the eighth day, in accordance with Jewish custom, and given the name Jesus, as the angel had instructed (21). When the prescribed period of purification was completed, Mary and Joseph brought the baby Jesus to the temple to dedicate him to the Lord (22-24). An old man named Simeon, who had been hoping to see the promised Messiah before he died, took the child up in his arms and blessed him (25-35). An elderly widow named Anna, who constantly served in the temple by prayer and fasting, also offered her thanksgiving to God for the child (36-38).

Luke summarizes Jesus' growth as a child at Nazareth very briefly (39-40). He does, however, include one incident when the family was returning from its annual pilgrimage to Jerusalem for the Passover and forgot the boy Jesus, leaving him behind in the temple (41-52).

From the birth and early childhood of Jesus, Luke rapidly propels his readers to the spiritual preparations for Jesus' public manifestation as the Messiah (3:1–4:13). John the Baptist did much to prepare the way for the Messiah (3:1-20). Luke describes the appearance of John on the scene (1-6) in terms of both the historical setting (1-2) and the prophetic foundation for his ministry (3-6). John's preaching unabashedly called for repentance (7-9) and high standards of righteous behaviour in relation to other people (10-14). Some people were wondering if John might be the Messiah, but he clearly denied it, pointing instead to the one coming after him (15-17). When John reproved Herod for his adulterous relationship with his brother's wife, Herod locked him up in prison (18-20).

In addition to John's preparation of the way for the Messiah, the Holy Spirit prepared the Messiah himself for ministry (3:21–4:13). In preparation for his ministry, the Spirit came upon Jesus at his baptism in the bodily form of a dove (3:21-22). As a historical footnote, Luke uses the entrance of Jesus into public ministry as the occasion for listing his human ancestry (23-38). The Holy Spirit also prepared Jesus for ministry by leading him into the wilderness to be tempted by the devil (4:1-13).

Luke locates the opening phase of Jesus' public ministry in Galilee (4:14–9:50), and he distinguishes an early period within it (4:14–7:50), which began with a preaching tour of synagogues in Galilee (4:14-44). Luke introduces this preaching tour with an enthusiastic summary statement highlighting the Spirit's power manifested in Jesus (14-15); but then he notes the rejection of Jesus at Nazareth, his home town (16-30). Everyone in the synagogue there listened attentively when Jesus announced that the Spirit had anointed him to preach the

---

Luke, the Beloved Physician

In Colossians 4:14, Paul refers to Luke as 'the beloved physician'. At several places throughout his Gospel and Acts, Luke adds a physician's touch to the narrative. Matthew and Mark state that Simon's mother-in-law had a fever, but Luke specifies that it was a 'high fever' (Luke 4:38; Matt 8:14; Mark 1:30). Matthew and Mark record Jesus' cleansing of a leper, but Luke observes that the man was 'full of leprosy' (Luke 5:12; Matt 8:2; Mark 1:40).

In the case of the woman who suffered from a hemorrhage for twelve years, Mark comments that she 'had endured much at the hands of many physicians, and had spent all that she had and was not helped at all, but rather had grown worse' (Mark 5:26, NASB; cf Matt 9:20). He implies that seeing doctors was a waste of her time and money, but Luke remarks that she 'could not be healed by anyone' (8:43). For him, hers was an unusually difficult case rather than a cause for losing faith in the medical profession.

Luke's own compassion for those suffering physically comes through in the parable of the Good Samaritan. This foreigner showed compassion to a man who fell among thieves and was left half dead. He bandaged up his wounds, pouring in wine and oil to disinfect them and speed the healing; furthermore, he paid the inn-keeper out of his own pocket to take care of him (10:30, 33-35).

Luke records that after Paul miraculously healed the chief man of Malta of dysentery, the rest of the sick people on the island were coming and being cured. The change of verbs to one commonly used for a natural healing process and the inclusion of Luke in the gracious kindnesses showed by the islanders suggests that he won their affection by skillfully attending to their medical needs (Acts 28:8-10).

---

gospel to the poor in fulfilment of Isaiah's prophecy (16-21),[1] but when he likened his audience to the unbelieving Israelites in Elijah and Elisha's days, they attempted to kill him (22-30).

Jesus met with a better reception at Capernaum (31-44). Again he began his ministry in the synagogue (31-37), where he was teaching the worshippers on the Sabbath (31-32) when he was interrupted by a demon-possessed man whom he had to exorcize (33-37). From the synagogue, Jesus' ministry spread to the town (38-41). He healed

---

1. Isaiah 61:1-2.

Simon's mother-in-law, who was suffering from a high fever (38-39), and also throngs of sick people who had gathered around him that evening (40-41). The next day he departed from Capernaum (42-44). After some difficulty in withdrawing from the crowds to a desolate place (42-43), he managed to continue his journey on to other cities as well (44).

In this initial wave of popularity, Jesus called his first disciples (5:1-11). To restrain the crowds by the lake of Gennesaret from pressing in upon him, Jesus got into a fishing boat belonging to Simon and taught them from the boat (1-3). When he was finished teaching, he miraculously granted Simon and his partners a larger catch of fish than their boats could hold; then he invited them to join him in catching people (4-11).

Jesus seemed to arouse religious controversies wherever he went (5:12–6:11). The first one that Luke records here concerned his supernatural ability to heal (5:12-26). As a result of his cleansing a leper, Jesus stirred up a great commotion among the populace who wanted to be healed (12-16), but he created an even greater theological upheaval among the scribes and Pharisees by claiming that his power to heal a paralytic was evidence of his authority to forgive sin (17-26). Jesus also aroused controversies over his acceptance of social outcasts (27-32). When Jesus called a tax collector named Levi to be his disciple (27-28), Levi held a big reception for Jesus at his home (29); but the scribes and Pharisees complained about Jesus' association with tax collectors and sinners (30-32). Jesus also ran into controversies about fasting (33-39). In reply to a reproof because his disciples didn't fast, he answered that it is impossible to enforce a fast in the presence of the bridegroom (33-35); and he went on to tell two short parables showing the incompatibility of fitting the new system that he was bringing into the old structure of Judaism (36-39). Furthermore, Jesus was plagued by controversies about Sabbath observance (6:1-11). The Pharisees raised the issue over his disciples' plucking of grain as they walked through the fields one Sabbath (1-5). On the next Sabbath, they were enraged when he publicly healed a man with a withered hand (6-11).

In the midst of this busyness, Luke shows Jesus taking time to prepare authentic followers (12-49). After spending the whole night praying upon a mountain, Jesus chose twelve disciples (12-16), to whom he gave specific teaching on how to live (17-49). Luke locates the setting for this instruction 'on a level place' lower down the mountainside where a large crowd had gathered, but he notes that Jesus' words were primarily directed to the disciples (17-20a). In the following verses, Luke summarizes the contents of Jesus' sermon (20b-49). Jesus began by reversing common expectations of being blessed (20b-26); he promised blessings to the downtrodden (20b-23) and pronounced woes upon the self-satisfied (24-26). He made loving one's enemies (27-36) a moral obligation (27-30) based upon the duty to copy God's mercy (31-36). Concerning judging others (37-42), he warned that there is a reciprocal relationship between judging and being judged (37-38). He also warned that a person who guides another has a responsibility to know where they are going (39-40), and a person who offers to clean up another's life must search one's own life first (41-42). Jesus expected his followers to act consistently with their character (43-45) and to put his teaching into practice (46-49).

Although Jesus was constantly surrounded by crowds, Luke presents him as genuinely compassionate towards needy people (7:1-50). He groups together two miracles showing compassion (1-17): the healing of a centurion's servant (1-10), and the raising of a widow's only son from the dead (11-17). To these miracles, he adds two words of encouragement (18-50). The first is a word of reassurance to John the Baptist (18-35). Even John, who at this time was in prison, was perplexed, so he sent messengers to enquire about Jesus' messianic identity, but Jesus reassured them by performing many miracles (18-23). Turning towards the crowds, Jesus testified to John's greatness (24-35). He noted that there had never been a prophet greater than John (24-28), but, nonetheless, the religious leaders rejected him (29-30). Jesus attributed John's rejection to the hardness of the people rather than any fault in John because the same people rejected the Son of Man for very different reasons (31-35). Jesus also spoke a word of acceptance to an outcast woman (36-50). He was dining in a Pharisee's house when a woman of questionable character anointed his feet with costly perfume and wiped them with her hair (36-39). Jesus rebuked his host, who had been offended by her actions, for his own inhospitality (40-47), and announced to the woman that her sins were forgiven (48-50).

At this point we pass into the second half of Jesus' Galilean ministry (8:1–9:50), which commences with an itinerant preaching tour (8:1-56). In addition to the twelve, Luke lists a group of women who travelled with Jesus and supported him out of their private means (1-3). When a great crowd gathered around him, Jesus taught them in parables (4-18). The brief sampling of parables that Luke records here begins with the parable of the varied soils (4-15), which includes the narration of the parable to the crowd (4-8) along with a discussion of Jesus' reason for speaking in parables (9-10) and the interpretation of this parable for the benefit of the disciples (11-15). It is followed by the parable of the covered lamp (16-18). While Jesus was teaching, his mother and brothers came to see him, but he declared to the crowd that his true family consisted of those who practice the word of God (19-21).

About that time, Jesus performed a series of mighty works demonstrating his power (22-56), first to calm a storm while he was crossing the lake (22-25) and then to exorcize demons (26-39). On the remote side of Galilee, Jesus encountered a fierce Gerasene demoniac (26-31), from whom he cast out a legion of demons into a nearby herd of pigs, causing them to stampede into the lake and drown (32-33). The inhabitants of the surrounding region were terrified and asked Jesus to leave (34-37), but the man who had been restored to sanity remained behind to proclaim what God had done for him (38-39). Jesus also demonstrated his power to heal the sick and raise the dead (40-56). A synagogue official named Jairus came to Jesus entreating him on behalf of his twelve-year-old daughter who was dying (40-42a). On the way to see her, Jesus healed a woman who had an incurable hemorrhage (42b-48). When Jesus arrived at the house, he took the little girl by the hand and raised her back to life again (49-56).

Jesus devoted much of his later Galilean ministry to training the disciples (9:1-50). He invited them to share in his own ministry (1-17), for which he gave them a formal commission (1-6). Upon

Luke's Travellogue from Galilee to Jerusalem

Luke skillfully heightens the suspense in his narrative by allowing the reader to follow along on the fateful journey from Galilee to Jerusalem, where Jesus will be condemned and crucified. The journey starts in a remote region of Galilee with Jesus resolutely setting his face to go to Jerusalem (9:51). Luke reinforces Jesus' resolve by commenting that the first Samaritan village through which Jesus passed would not receive him because he was headed for Jerusalem (9:52-53), and he contrasts it with a story about some would-be followers whom Jesus rejected because they were looking backwards (9:57-62).

Luke slowly moves us towards the climax by inserting geographical notations along the way. 'Now as they were traveling along, he entered a certain village' (10:38). 'And he was passing through from one city and village to another, teaching, and making progress on his way to Jerusalem' (13:22). A warning of Herod's desire to kill him threatens to distract Jesus, but he summarily dismisses it because his clear sense of mission demands that he reach Jerusalem after three days of ministering and travelling (13:32-33).

In 17:11, Jesus is still somewhere in the region of Samaria and Galilee. In 18:31-33, he takes the twelve aside and warns them that they are going up to Jerusalem, where he will be killed. Suspense builds as he approaches Jericho (18:35), and Luke draws it out longer with a comment that Jesus entered and was passing through the city (19:1). Because he was near Jerusalem and the crowd that had gathered mistakenly supposed that the kingdom of God was going to appear immediately, Jesus told a parable urging faithfulness during the interim (19:11).

When he had spoken these words, Jesus went on ahead to Jerusalem, and as he approached Bethphage and Bethany, two small villages near the Mount of Olives, he sent a couple of disciples into town to fetch a colt for him to ride on into Jerusalem (19:28-30). Now there was no turning back. Although the pilgrims who travelled with him enthusiastically hailed his entrance into the city, the cold rejection of the religious officials sealed his fate and called forth a lament and a curse on the city (19:41-44).

hearing of their miracles, Herod thought that John, whom he had beheaded, had come back to life (7-9). When the apostles returned, they reported to Jesus all that they had done (10a). He then had them assist him in the miracle of the feeding of the five thousand (10b-17). A large crowd had followed Jesus to a remote area (10b-11); rather than send them away, he multiplied the five loaves and two fish they had among them and had the disciples distribute the food until everyone was filled (12-17).

At this time Jesus began to reveal his impending death on the cross to his disciples (18-50). Peter's great confession of Jesus' messiahship (18-20) is immediately followed by Jesus' prediction of his passion (21-22), and along with it comes a call for all disciples to bear their own crosses as well (23-27). About a week after Peter's confession, Jesus was transfigured on a mountain top before several selected disciples, who were granted a preview of his glory (28-36). At the foot of the mountain, Jesus delivered a demon-possessed boy, whom his disciples waiting below had been unable to deliver (37-43a). To make sure that his disciples understood, Jesus reiterated the necessity of his passion, but they couldn't grasp what he was saying (43b-45). Rather than explaining this weighty event, Jesus found it necessary to teach the disciples about humility (46-50). In response to an argument about which of them was the greatest, Jesus elevated the least to the position of the greatest (46-48). In response to their attempt to hinder a miracle-worker because he was not part of their own group, Jesus taught the disciples to recognize genuine outsiders as fellow-workers (49-50).

Now that Jesus had predicted his coming passion, he embarked upon a long journey to his fateful destination in Jerusalem (9:51–19:44). This long journey, which is an integral part of Luke's structure, is laid out in several phases, each of which is set off by a geographical marker. In the first phase (9:51–13:21), Jesus gradually commenced his journey towards Jerusalem, taking the opportunity along the way to train the disciples for ministry (9:51–11:13). He sent messengers ahead of him to a Samaritan village, but they returned disappointed (51-56). Because Jesus was on his way to Jerusalem (51), the Samaritans refused to extend hospitality to him (52-53). The disciples wanted to call down fire upon that village, but Jesus restrained them (54-56). As they were travelling, Jesus met some people who aspired to be his followers, but he had to pronounce them unfit candidates because they were not single-minded in their commitment (57-62).

Again, Jesus sent out messengers ahead of him – this time seventy-two of them were successful in their mission (**10**:1-24). In his personal commission to them (1-16), Jesus gave detailed instructions concerning their mission (1-12) and pronounced woes upon cities that had been unrepentant in the past (13-15). He also assured them of their authority to act on his behalf (16). The seventy-two returned triumphantly (17-24). They reported their victory over demons (17-20), and Jesus thanked the Father for revealing himself to his disciples (21-24).

Luke maintains his focus on the training of the disciples by following their mission with teaching that is grouped thematically around characteristics of true disciples (10:25–11:13). Jesus' mention of the first characteristic, loving one's neighbour as one's self (10:25-37), arose in response to a lawyer's enquiry about how to inherit eternal life (25-29). To illustrate the point Jesus told a parable about a good Samaritan who showed compassion to a man who had been beaten and robbed (30-37). True disciples are also characterized by listening to Jesus like Mary rather than becoming distracted by serving like Martha (38-42). Finally, true disciples know how to pray to the Father with confidence (**11**:1-13). As an example of how to pray, Jesus taught his disciples 'the Lord's prayer' (1-4), and he went on to contrast the confidence we normally have in asking human acquaintances with the confidence we may have in approaching God (5-13). We may approach God confidently because he does not give reluctantly like an inconvenienced friend who gives merely to silence the requester (5-8). Jesus encouraged the disciples to ask persistently (9-10), and he assured them that our heavenly Father is much more generous than earthly fathers (11-13).

Again Jesus came into controversy with the Jews (14-54). This time the immediate issue concerned their repudiation of his miraculous powers (14-26) in an attempt to discredit his exorcism of demons (14-23). They accused him of casting out demons by

Beelzebub, the prince of demons (14-16). Jesus responded (17-23) by pointing out the logical inconsistency of supposing that Satan opposes himself (17-20) and by noting that to triumph over a strong power it requires a stronger one (21-23). To the discussion he added a warning that if a void is left when an unclean spirit departs, it will be filled with something worse (24-26).

Rather than being conciliatory, Jesus heightened the controversy by admonishing the crowd for its spiritual insensibility (27-36). He corrected the misconception that blessedness comes from a physical relation to him, asserting instead that it comes from a spiritual relationship (27-28). He refused to grant the crowd's requests for a supernatural sign (29-32), claiming instead the sufficiency of the sign of Jonah (29-30) and the superiority of the faith of certain Gentiles who acted upon their minimal knowledge (31-32). Without relenting, he warned the crowd about the danger of foolishly extinguishing spiritual light (33-36), either by hiding the source of light (33) or by obstructing its receptacle (34-36).

Jesus furthered his offensive by denouncing the religious leaders for their hypocrisy (37-54). He denounced the Pharisees for distorting the law by replacing its true essence with a legalistic observance of trivial externals (37-44), and he denounced the lawyers for weighing down people with heavy burdens which they refused to lighten (45-52). As a result, they became very hostile towards Jesus (53-54).

In this context of widespread popularity mixed with deep-seated animosity, Jesus attempted to prepare his listeners for the coming crisis (**12**:1-13:9). He exhorted them to confess him fearlessly even in times of personal danger (12:1-12). Jesus began negatively by warning them not to be hypocritical (1-3). They should not be like the Pharisees (1) because it is impossible to conceal things done in secret (2-3). Jesus also encouraged them not to fear people (4-7); instead they should confess him openly (8-12). Confessing Christ is important because his confessing of us is conditioned upon it (8-9); conversely, blaspheming the Holy Spirit is a serious sin because it is unpardonable (10). Along with the exhortation to confess him, Jesus included a promise of the Holy Spirit's assistance in answering authorities (11-12).

Jesus also warned his listeners about the danger of accumulating possessions without regard for spiritual values (13-21). He drew this lesson from a greedy brother who wanted him to arbitrate a dispute over the family inheritance (13-15), and he reinforced the point with a parable about a rich fool who amassed more wealth than he could manage and then suddenly died (16-21). In view of eternal riches, Jesus prohibited his listeners from being anxious about earthly concerns (22-34). He reassured them that God providentially cares for the necessities of life (22-32) and that there are heavenly rewards for sacrifices made on behalf of the kingdom (33-34).

Furthermore, Jesus called his listeners to faithful vigilance in expectation of his return (35-48). He stressed the importance of being vigilant at all times because no one knows when he will return (35-40). To illustrate the unexpectedness of his return, he told a parable about slaves watching for their master to return (35-38) and another one about a householder watching for a burglar to break in (39-40). To illustrate the importance of being faithful during the interim (41-48), he told one parable about the reward of a faithful steward (41-44) and a second one about the punishment of an unfaithful slave (45-48).

Jesus predicted the coming of conflict upon the basis of present signs (49-59). He warned that his listeners should be prepared to face divisions within their own families (49-53) and asserted that they should be able to discern the signs of the times (54-56). He also encouraged them to settle legal disputes quickly before they turned into a crisis (57-59).

In view of impending judgment, Jesus called for timely repentance (**13**:1-9). He reminded his listeners of the nearness of judgment by citing recent examples of unexpected tragedies that befell innocent Jews (1-5), and he reinforced the point by telling a parable about a barren fig tree that was ready for destruction (6-9).

In addition to preparing his listeners for the coming crisis, Jesus informed them that the coming of the kingdom reverses present circumstances (10-21). He demonstrated one such reversal by restoring a woman with a crooked spine to an erect posture (10-17). He also taught that the kingdom will grow in a way that is

Parables Found only in Luke

Luke records thirty-four parables, seventeen of which are unique to his Gospel.[1] Among these are some of Jesus' best-known and loved parables.

1)	The two debtors who were forgiven	7:41-43
2)	The good Samaritan's example of loving one's neighbour	10:30-37
3)	The reluctant help of an inconvenienced friend	11:5-8
4)	The rich fool's accumulation of wealth without regard for spiritual values	12:16-21
5)	The slaves' watchfulness for the master's return	12:35-38
6)	The approaching destruction of the barren fig tree	13:6-9
7)	Choosing the places of least honour at banquets	14:7-11
8)	The unexpected participants at the kingdom feast	14:16-24
9)	The necessity of counting the cost of building a tower	14:28-30
10)	The necessity of counting the cost of waging war	14:31-32
11)	The woman searching for her lost coin	15:8-10
12)	The father welcoming his lost son	15:11-32
13)	The shrewd steward's use of worldly wealth	16:1-13
14)	The dutiful slave's fulfillment of what was expected	17:7-10
15)	The persistent widow and the unjust judge	18:1-8
16)	The humble tax-collector and the self-righteous Pharisee	18:9-14
17)	The servants' faithfulness with the master's entrusted wealth	19:11-27

[1] The story of the rich man and Lazarus (16:19-31) is not included in this enumeration because the chief character is named, contrary to Jesus' uniform practice in telling parables of leaving the characters anonymous. We are probably intended to take this story as a historic event from which Jesus drew a spiritual lesson by means of his supernatural insight.

disproportional to its tiny origins (18-21). Jesus compared the kingdom of heaven to a mustard seed which grows into a tree that birds can nest in (18-19) and again to a morsel of yeast which leavened a large batch of dough (20-21).

By introducing a geographical marker at this point, Luke gives a sense of progression to Jesus' journey towards Jerusalem, which he separates into a second phase (13:22–17:10). As he travelled, Jesus taught that the way into the kingdom is demanding (13:22-35). He exhorted the crowd to strive to enter through the narrow door (22-30). Even though some Pharisees warned Jesus that Herod was threatening to kill him, he resolved to go to Jerusalem (31-33), but he lamented the city's hardness of heart in consistently killing God's prophets (34-35).

Upon accepting an invitation to dine at the house of a leading Pharisee on the Sabbath, Jesus used the occasion to teach some incidental lessons (**14**:1-24). After introducing this setting (1), Luke records Jesus' lessons on the legality of doing good on the Sabbath (2-6) and on the kingdom-etiquette of humility at banquets (7-14). Jesus instructed the other invited guests to choose the places of least honour at banquets (7-11), and he instructed his host to invite guests of lowly status who could not repay the invitation (12-14). He also told a parable about some unexpected participants at a feast (15-24), having been set up by a comment from one of the guests on the blessing of eating in the kingdom of God (15). Everyone in the parable who had been invited to the feast made excuses (16-20) so the host invited all the social outcasts, who accepted (21-24).

As the crowds were walking along with Jesus, he taught them about the rigorous demands required of disciples (25-35). He cautioned that they would need to sacrifice (25-33) by bearing their own cross (25-27) so they ought to count the cost first (28-33). Furthermore, they would need to be people of integrity if they were to have any impact upon the world (34-35).

Jesus also taught about God's persistent mercy in reaching out to the lost (**15**:1-32). His teaching, which came in the form of three related parables, arose out of a social setting where the Pharisees and scribes were grumbling because many tax collectors and sinners were associating with him (1-2). The first parable is about a shepherd who left his flock to search for one lost sheep until he found it (3-7). The second parable is about a woman who searched her house thoroughly for one missing coin out of a set of ten (8-10). The third parable is about a father welcoming home his lost son (11-32). This prodigal son, who squandered his inheritance on loose living (11-20a), received the ready forgiveness of his merciful father (20b-24), much to the indignation of his elder brother (25-32).

The next block of teaching focuses on proper attitudes pertaining to wealth (**16**:1-31). It begins with a parable about a shrewd steward (1-13) who was about to be fired but found a way to provide for his retirement by reducing the bills of his master's debtors (1-9). From the steward's shrewd use of wealth to provide for the future, Jesus went on to draw further applications (10-13) concerning faithfulness in little things (10-12) and not serving both God and money (13). Jesus continued by rebuking the Pharisees for their greed (14-18). He contrasted their love of money with God's standards (14-15); he brought to light those who were attempting to grasp the kingdom by force (16-17) and condemned those who divorce their wives (18). He also added a story about the deaths of a rich man who awoke in the torments of Hades and a poor man named Lazarus, who was comforted in Abraham's bosom (19-31).

To the disciples Jesus gave special instructions about how to behave responsibly with respect to the community (**17**:1-10). He warned them about the seriousness of removing stumbling blocks (1-3a) and commanded them to forgive their brothers (3b-4). He told them that it was possible to increase their faith (5-6) and reminded them of their duty to serve (7-10).

Luke calls attention back to Jesus' slow, but steady, progression towards Jerusalem by introducing the third phase of the journey with another geographical marker, which places Jesus still some distance to the north in the general region of Samaria and Galilee (17:11-18:30). This section opens with the grateful response of a Samaritan who was cleansed from leprosy, in contrast with the ingratitude of nine others who were also cleansed (17:11-19).

Luke follows with Jesus' teaching to correct prevalent mistaken eschatological expectations (20-37). Jesus corrected the Pharisees' notion that the kingdom would come in a dramatically observable way by claiming that it was already present in their midst (20-21). He corrected the disciples' belief that the Son of Man would soon be revealed in glory by declaring that he would appear at a time when people do not expect (22-37). He indicated that his arrival would come suddenly, but there would be a delay first (22-25). In addition, he warned that his appearance will bring judgment on the unexpecting world (26-30) and no partiality will be shown to the unprepared, who will be taken away to judgment (31-37).

Luke groups together two parables in which Jesus used contrast to teach how to pray effectively (**18**:1-14). We should be persistent in our praying because God is far more eager to answer our requests than the unjust judge in the first parable, who finally granted a widow justice because she kept badgering him (1-8). We should be humble like the tax collector in the second parable, who was heard because he begged God for mercy, and not be self-righteous like the Pharisee, who recited to God how good he was (9-14).

The prayer of the tax collector nicely leads into two personal profiles of candidates for the kingdom of God (15-30). First, a person who is a candidate for the kingdom must enter it like a little child (15-17). Second, it is very difficult for a person who is rich to enter the kingdom (18-30). The observation about the difficulty of being rich arose out of Jesus' interaction with a rich ruler who could not give up his possessions for the kingdom (18-25). From this incident, Jesus made application for the benefit of those listeners surrounding him (26-30). He told them that divine intervention is necessary for a rich person to be saved (26-27), and he promised them that those who had sacrificed for the kingdom would receive far greater spiritual rewards (28-30).

The final phase of the journey builds tension as Jesus approaches the outskirts of Jerusalem (18:31–19:27). Jesus reminded his disciples that they were headed for Jerusalem, where he would suffer an ignoble death and rise again on the third day (18:31-34). As they came near Jericho, Jesus healed a blind beggar (35-43). While they were passing through Jericho, a chief tax collector named Zaccheus, who had climbed a tree to catch a glimpse of

Jesus, was converted (**19**:1-10). As they were nearing Jerusalem, Jesus tried to dissuade the crowd from supposing that the kingdom would appear immediately by telling them a parable about a nobleman who journeyed to a distant country and entrusted his wealth to his servants until he returned (11-27).

The journey ends with Jesus' triumphal entry into the city (28-44). Luke places Jesus on the road ascending to Jerusalem (28), and then he names the outlying towns through which Jesus passed on his final approach to the city (29-40). Just outside Jerusalem, Jesus organized a royal procession so that he could enter triumphantly, riding upon a colt (28-36). The crowd accompanying Jesus hailed him as the messianic king, while the Pharisees unsuccessfully attempted to silence them (37-40). As he overlooked the city, Jesus prophetically lamented its complete destruction because of its rejection of him (41-44).

The last days of Jesus' public ministry were centered around the temple (19:45–21:38). First, Jesus cleansed the temple of those who were selling merchandise in it (19:45-46), and then he began to teach there daily (19:47–21:38). The initial thrust of his teaching arose out of theological controversy with various representatives of the Sanhedrin (19:47–21:4). The religious leaders were plotting to kill Jesus in response to his cleansing of the temple, but they could find no opportunity because of his great popularity with the masses (19:47-48). The most they could do was to challenge his authority, but Jesus used their hypocritical rejection of divine authority to defuse their question (**20**:1-8). He then turned to expose their wickedness (9-19) by telling a parable about some tenant farmers who murder the landlord's son (9-16a). Jesus caught the religious leaders off guard by applying the parable to their rejection of him (16b-18). When they saw the connection, they were ready to kill him (19).

Their next plan of attack was to entangle Jesus in something he said (20-44). They sent out spies, who tried to trap him with a double-pronged question about paying taxes, but he responded with a general principle that could not be disputed (20-26). The Sadducees took a turn at trying to trap him with a question about the resurrection (27-40). They invented a story about a woman who survived seven husbands and asked whose husband she would be in the resurrection (27-33). Jesus dismissed the question as irrelevant to the resurrected state but went on to argue convincingly from Scripture for the truthfulness of the resurrection (34-38). When the scribes saw how well Jesus had answered, they were reticent about asking him any further questions (39-40). Having silenced them, Jesus asked a counterquestion of his own concerning the ability of the Messiah to be both David's son and David's Lord (41-44). Finally, Jesus laid bare the hypocrisy of the scribes by contrasting (20:45–21:4) their greedy self-centeredness in devouring widow's houses, while at the same time putting on pretensions of respectability (20:45-47), with the sacrificial generosity of a poor widow who willingly contributed her last two coins to the temple treasury (**21**:1-4).

Having dealt with the theological controversy arising from the religious leaders, Jesus shifted his attention to instructing the disciples about the coming of the end, which he addressed in a lengthy apocalyptic discourse (5-36). The disciples were admiring the beauty of the temple, but Jesus responded by predicting its total destruction (5-6). He went on to warn that deceptive signs would come before the end (7-11): there would be many false messiahs (7-9) and many great disasters (10-11). He encouraged them that although believers would be persecuted (12-19), they would be given supernatural wisdom to answer the legal authorities (12-15) and spiritual protection to withstand persecution from family members (16-19).

Jesus identified the surrounding of Jerusalem by armies as a sign of its impending desolation (20-24), and he foretold that the coming of the Son of Man would be preceded by cosmic disturbances (25-28). To indicate the nearness of the kingdom, he told a parable about the appearance of leaves on a fig tree (29-33), and he appealed for the disciples to be spiritually watchful at all times (34-36). Luke concludes this main section by summarizing Jesus' regular practice of teaching in the temple during the day and going out to the Mount of Olives in the evening (37-38).

He then moves directly into the momentous events which climaxed in the Saviour's death on the cross (**22**:1–23:56a). The conspiracy against Jesus (22:1-6) was able to overcome his popularity with the crowds because the Sanhedrin desperately longed to kill him (1-2) and Judas was willing to betray him quietly to them (3-6).

Before his death, Jesus had one last meal with his disciples (7-38). He sent two of them ahead to make preparations for the Paschal meal (7-13), which he instituted as the Lord's Supper (14-20). During the meal, Jesus predicted his betrayal by one of the disciples (21-23). After they had eaten, there was much conversation (24-38). Jesus had to reprove the disciples for their rivalry in seeking personal recognition (24-30). He impressed upon them the greatness of serving (24-27) and promised them great rewards for faithfulness to him (28-30). He also predicted Peter's denial of him (31-34) and warned them to take immediate precautions against the world's hostility towards them (35-38).

From the place where they had been dining, they went out to the Mount of Olives, where Jesus would be arrested (39-53). Upon arriving, he knelt down and prayed fervently three times for a way to bypass the cup he was about to drink (39-46). As soon as he was finished praying, he was arrested by a mob (47-53) that came to him led by Judas (47-51). After rebuking the religious leaders among the mob, Jesus permitted them to carry out their evil designs (52-53).

Jesus' trial took place in two stages (22:54–23:25). First, there was a religious trial (22:54-71), which commenced with a night-time hearing at the high priest's house (54-65). While Jesus was being tried, Peter, who had followed the procession, denied him three times (54-62). The guards who were holding Jesus in custody mocked and beat him (63-65). Early in the morning, the Sanhedrin reconvened in its council chamber and charged Jesus with blasphemy (66-71).

Following the religious trial, Jesus was subjected to a civil trial before the Roman authorities (**23**:1-25). The Sanhedrin brought Jesus before Pilate, who upon his first hearing declared him not guilty (1-5). Jesus also appeared before Herod (6-12). When Pilate learned that Jesus was from Galilee, he transferred him to Herod (6-7), who questioned Jesus at length and sent him back again (8-12).

Jesus' Last Words from the Cross

1) 'Father, forgive them, for they do not know what they are doing' (Luke 23:34)
2) (To Mary), 'Woman, behold, your son!' (To John) 'Behold, your mother!' (John 19:26-27).
3) (To the repentant thief), 'Truly I say to you, today you will be with me in paradise' (Luke 23:43).
4) 'I am thirsty' (John 19:28; cf. Psalm 69:21).
5) 'Eli, Eli, lama sabachthani?' that is, 'My God, my God, why have you forsaken me?' (Matt 27:46; Mark 15:34; cf. Psalm 22:1)
6) 'It is finished' (John 19:30).
7) 'Father, into your hands I commit my spirit' (Luke 23:46).

At the outset of his second hearing before Pilate (13-25), Pilate declared Jesus to be innocent (13-16) and tried to acquit him (18-23), but he eventually capitulated to the crowd's persistent demand for Jesus' crucifixion (24-25).

Luke's record of Jesus' death (26-49) begins with the journey to Calvary (26-32). A man named Simon of Cyrene, who happened to be passing by that way, was compelled to bear Jesus' cross (26). The daughters of Jerusalem followed, lamenting along the way (27-31); and two criminals, who were to be crucified with Jesus, also accompanied him (32).

When they arrived at the place of crucifixion, a series of events took place which Luke relates for us (33-49). The soldiers crucified Jesus (33-34) on the middle cross between the two criminals (33), but he forgave his executioners because they acted in ignorance (34).

The crowd that looked on derided Jesus because his apparent inability to save himself seemed inconsistent with his exalted claims (35-38). The rulers of the Jews sneered at his presumption of messiahship (35), and the Roman soldiers mocked his supposed kingship (36-38). Rather than join in the abuse, however, one of the criminals who was being crucified repented of his own sins (39-43).

As Jesus was expiring upon the cross (44-46), the sun was darkened (44-45a) and the veil of the temple was rent in two (45b). Finally, he cried out with a loud voice surrendering his spirit to the Father and died (46). Those who looked on reacted in varied ways (47-49). The centurion who had crucified Jesus confessed that he was certainly a righteous man (47). The crowd that had gathered for the spectacle dispersed, lamenting as they went (48), while Jesus' acquaintances lingered, gazing from a distance at what had happened (49).

The burial of Jesus (50-56a) was facilitated by Joseph of Arimathea, a dissenting member of the Sanhedrin, who obtained permission to remove the body and place it in a new tomb (50-54). The women who had accompanied Jesus observed where the body was laid and went home to prepare spices to embalm it (55-56a).

But that is not the end of the story; Luke records the testimonies of several people to the Lord's resurrection from the dead (23:56b–24:49). Before anyone actually saw the risen Lord, there were a couple of visits to the empty tomb (23:56b–24:12). Early on the first day of the week, the women came to the tomb bringing the spices they had prepared (23:56b–24:11). To their amazement, they found the tomb empty and were told by two angels that Jesus had risen from the dead (23:56b–**24**:7). They went and reported all that they had seen and heard to the eleven disciples and the rest (24:8-11). In response to their report, Peter ran to the tomb and also found it empty (12).

Luke follows the witnesses to the empty tomb with actual appearances of the risen Lord (13-53). The first appearance that he records was to two travellers on the road to Emmaus (13-35). As they walked, Jesus came alongside of them and conversed with them, but they did not recognize him (13-27) until he broke bread with them that evening (28-32). They hurriedly returned to Jerusalem, where the disciples were gathered, and reported what had happened on the road (33-35). While they were talking, Jesus appeared in their midst (36-50). He offered them evidence that he possessed a corporeal body (36-43) and unfolded many scriptures concerning his fulfilment of Messianic prophecy (44-49).

In a concluding summary, Luke recounts the Lord's ascension

into heaven (50-53). Jesus led the disciples out to Bethany where he was lifted up to heaven while he was blessing them (50-51). They returned to Jerusalem, where they remained in the temple, rejoicing and blessing God (52-53).

The People's Praise in Luke and Acts

The Book of Acts begins where Luke's Gospel ends—with the people in the temple praising God:

Luke 24:52: And they returned to Jerusalem with great joy, [53]and were continually in the temple, praising God.

Acts 2:46: And day by day continuing with one mind in the temple, and breaking bread from house to house, they were taking their meals together with gladness and sincerity of heart, [47]praising God, and having favor with all the people. And the Lord was adding to their number day by day those who were being saved.

OUTLINE OF LUKE

E. The death of Jesus 23:26-49
   1. The journey to Calvary 23:26-32
      a. Placing of the cross upon Simon of Cyrene 23:26
      b. Lament of the daughters of Jerusalem 23:27-31
      c. Accompaniment of Jesus by two criminals 23:32
   2. Events surrounding the cross 23:33-49
      a. The crucifixion of Jesus 23:33-34
         (1) The soldiers' placement of the cross 23:33
         (2) Jesus' forgiveness of the soldiers 23:34
      b. The derision of the crowd 22:35-38
         (1) The rulers 22:35
         (2) The soldiers 22:36-38
      c. The repentance of one criminal 23:39-43
      d. The expiration of Jesus 23:44-46
         (1) The darkening of the sun 23:44-45a
         (2) The rending of the veil 23:45b
         (3) The surrender of Jesus' spirit 23:46
      e. The reaction of the onlookers 23:47-49
         (1) The righteous confession of the centurion 23:47
         (2) The mournful dispersion of the crowd 23:48
         (3) The lingering gaze of Jesus' acquaintances 23:49

F. The burial of Jesus 23:50-56a
   1. The entombment of the body by Joseph 23:50-54
   2. The observation of the grave by the women 23:55-56a

**VII. Recorded testimonies to the Lord's resurrection
    from the dead** 23:56b–24:49

A. Visits to the empty tomb 23:56b–24:12
   1. The women's visit 23:56b–24:11
      a. The angels' announcement of the
         resurrection to the women 23:56b–24:7
      b. The women's report of the experience to
         the disciples 24:8-11
   2. Peter's visit 24:12

B. Appearances of the risen Lord 24:13-53
   1. His appearance to the two on the road to Emmaus 24:13-35
      a. Their conversation with him along the way 24:13-27
      b. Their recognition of him in the breaking
         of bread 24:28-32
      c. Their report to the disciples gathered in
         Jerusalem 24:33-35

JOHN

OVERVIEW OF JOHN'S GOSPEL

Theme: The witness of the beloved disciple concerning Jesus, the Son of God

Key Verses: John 20:30-31, 'Jesus did many other miraculous signs in the presence of his disciples, which are not recorded in this book. But these are written that you may believe that Jesus is the Christ, the Son of God, and that by believing you may have life in his name' (NIV).

The theological prologue: the human incarnation of the pre-existent Word	1:1-18
The historical narrative: the earthly ministry of the divine Son	1:19–20:31
I. The public manifestation of the Messiah	1:19–12:50
A. The period of initial openness to Jesus' manifestation as Messiah	1:19–4:54
1. The manifestation of Jesus to his disciples during his first week of ministry	1:19–2:12
(*The first sign* – changing water to wine)	2:1-11
2. The manifestation of Jesus to the wider public beginning from his *first visit to Jerusalem*	2:13–4:54
(*The second sign*) Jesus' healing of a royal official's son	4:43-54
B. The period of unsettled controversy over Jesus' claims to deity	5:1–6:71
Jesus' *second journey to Jerusalem*	5:1
(*The third sign*) The miraculous healing of the lame man	5:2-9a
(*The fourth sign*) Jesus' feeding of the 5,000 on the other side of Galilee	6:1-15
(*The fifth sign*) Jesus' walking on the water on the way back to Capernaum	6:16-21

HISTORICAL BACKGROUND

The Gospel of John was written by the "beloved disciple" (John 21:20, 24), who is traditionally identified as the Apostle John, the son of Zebedee. He is also generally held to be the author of the Johannine epistles and Revelation, although the latter has been disputed. The evangelistic purpose of this Gospel is clearly stated: it was written to persuade its readers that Jesus is the Messiah, the Son of God, so that by believing they might experience eternal life (John 20:30-31).

The destination of John's Gospel is unknown; it could very possibly have been intended for readers in Asia Minor, where John ministered, or it could have circulated over a wider area. John probably wrote from Asia Minor, and perhaps from its leading city, Ephesus. His targeted audience would have been prospective Hellenistic or Gentile converts.

John wrote independently of the Synoptics Gospels, although he probably was aware of at least some of them. He emphasizes events not mentioned in the synoptics, particularly Jesus' Judean ministry and the feasts at Jerusalem; he also draws out the theological significance of the gospel events, whereas the synoptics tend to report them with less interpretation. John most likely wrote in his old age sometime between A.D. 80 and 95, with the greater probability falling towards the end of this range. It is less likely that he wrote somewhere between A.D. 65 and 70, although this view has had some recent advocates.

The Spiritual Nature of John's Gospel

Clement of Alexandria (AD 155-220) writes that 'last of all, John, perceiving that the external facts had been made plain in the Gospel [either Mark or all of the other Gospels], being urged by his friends, and inspired by the Spirit, composed a spiritual Gospel' (As cited by Eusebius, *Church History*, 6.14.7, trans. Arthur Cushman McGiffert, in *The Nicene and Post-Nicene Fathers*, 2nd Series, Philip Schaff, ed., vol. 1: Eusebius, *Church History* (Grand Rapids: Wm. B. Eerdmans Pub. Co., 1976), 261. Clement's work to which Eusebius is referring is no longer extant.

THE FLOW OF JOHN'S GOSPEL

John's Gospel begins with a theological prologue in which the evangelist sets forth the incarnation of the pre-existent Word in human form (**1**:1-18). John describes the pre-existent relationship of the Word (1-5) to God by locating him with God and identifying him as God in the beginning (1-2). He also describes the pre-existent relationship of the Word to creation by affirming that everything that exists was created by the Word (3-5).

John the Evangelist sets the incarnation of the Word (6-18) in the historical context of the witness of John the Baptist to the Word as light (6-8) and then proceeds to describe the mixed effects upon humans of the coming of this light into the world (9-13). The evangelist states that the Word was manifested to us by becoming human flesh and tabernacling among us so that we might observe God's glorious grace and truth (14-18).

The main body of John's Gospel narrates selected historical events in the earthly ministry of Jesus that have been specifically chosen with the evangelistic purpose in mind of inspiring belief in him as the Son of God (1:19–20:31). Roughly the first half of the book is concerned with the public manifestation of Jesus to the Jewish people as the Messiah (1:19–12:50).

Before Jesus clashed with contrary preconceptions concerning what the Messiah should be, he enjoyed an initial period of openness to the possibility that he might be the one promised (1:19–4:54). The evangelist opens this period by structuring the manifestation of Jesus to the disciples around his first week of public ministry (1:19–2:12). Their introduction to Jesus' messiahship arose from the witness of John the Baptist, who was baptizing on the other side of the Jordan River (1:19-51).

On the first day of that week, John bore witness concerning himself to a delegation of religious leaders from Jerusalem (19-28). He clearly denied the popular speculations that he was the Messiah (19-23) and asserted to the contrary that he was greatly inferior to the Messiah (24-28). On the next day, John witnessed that Jesus was the Messiah (29-34). When he saw Jesus approaching, John identified him to the people standing around as 'the Lamb of God who takes away the sin of the world' (29-31). He vouched for this messianic identification on the grounds that the Holy Spirit had descended upon Jesus as a dove in accordance with the sign he had been given (32-34). On the third day, John introduced two of his own disciples to Jesus, and they followed him to the place where he was staying (35-39). After presumably spending the night with Jesus, Andrew, one of the two disciples, introduced his brother, Simon Peter, to Jesus (40-42). On the fifth day, Philip and Nathanael became followers of Jesus (43-51). First, Philip responded to Jesus' call (43-46), and then Nathanael responded to Philip's invitation to come and see the Messiah (47-51).

On the third day from Philip and Nathanael's response to Jesus, which by an inclusive reckoning would be one week from the first recorded witness of John the Baptist to the Messiah, Jesus manifested his glory to his disciples in the first of seven signs, the changing of water into wine at a wedding in Cana of Galilee (2:1-11). After the wedding, Jesus and his disciples stopped over at

The Seven Signs in John
John structures his Gospel around seven signs that witness to his conclusion that Jesus is the Son of God.
1. The changing of water to wine (2:1-11)
2. The healing of a royal official's son (4:43-54)
3. The healing of a lame man (5:2-9a)
4. The feeding of the five thousand (6:1-15)
5. Jesus' walking on the water (6:16-21)
6. The healing of a man born blind (9:1-41)
7. The raising of Lazarus (11:1-44)

Capernaum for a few days before they travelled to Jerusalem (12).

During the time from this visit to Jerusalem, which is the first of four recorded pilgrimages, until his return visit, Jesus had a short-lived opportunity to make a first impression on the wider public, who were not yet aware of his claims to messiahship (2:13–4:54). He began by manifesting himself in Jerusalem (2:13–3:21) upon his arrival for the Passover (13).

His first action, which gained him no favour with the religious leaders, was to cleanse the temple (14-22) by forcibly expelling

---

Jesus' 'Hour'

In his Gospel, John repeatedly refers to Jesus' 'hour' as a means of underscoring his conviction that Jesus' death unfolded in accordance with the divine timetable. At the outset of his public ministry, Jesus initially declined Mary's request to intervene at the wedding at Cana because his hour had not yet come (2:4). Later, as the opposition was becoming increasingly hardened, John reports two separate occasions on which the Jewish religious leaders wanted to seize Jesus but were unable to because his hour had not yet come (7:30; 8:20).

A major turning point from the public manifestation of Jesus to the preparation for his death comes in John 12:23. It follows shortly after John's final sign, the raising of Lazarus, and Jesus' triumphal entry into Jerusalem. When Jesus was told that some Greeks who had come to Jerusalem for the feast wanted to see him, he announced, 'The hour has come for the Son of Man to be glorified.' John notes, however, that this hour of glory would be an hour of suffering from which Jesus wished that he could be spared; nevertheless, he exclaimed, 'for this purpose I came to this hour' (12:27).

John introduces Jesus' demonstration of love for the disciples at their last Passover together with the comment that Jesus knew 'that his hour had come to depart from this world to the Father' (13:1). Before the last chain of events leading to Jesus' death is unleashed, Jesus offers one final, great intercessory prayer that opens with the request, 'Father, the hour has come; glorify your Son, in order that the Son may glorify you' (17:1).

---

the merchants who were selling animals and exchanging money (14-17). To their demand to know the authority behind this intrusion upon their business, Jesus gave the sign of the restoration of the temple of his body in three days (18-22). Although many people believed in Jesus, he did not trust them because he knew the shallowness of their enthusiastic response (23-25).

John records at length Jesus' conversation with a Pharisaic ruler of the Jews named Nicodemus (3:1-21). Nicodemus sought out Jesus privately because the signs that Jesus was performing proved to be a convincing confirmation that God had authorized his teaching (1-2). Nicodemus was caught by surprise, however, at Jesus' reply that he needed to be born again in order to see the kingdom of God (3-8). Although Nicodemus was one of the most eminent religious teachers in the nation, it quickly became evident that he needed greater spiritual understanding even to comprehend what Jesus was talking about (9-13). Jesus went on to assert that God had provided eternal life through his Son to everyone who believes in him (14-16) and that those who believe will escape divine judgment (17-21).

After making this initial appearance in Jerusalem, Jesus continued to manifest himself in the Judean countryside alongside the ministry of John the Baptist (3:22–4:3). The setting for the Judean ministry of Jesus (22-24) finds him, or more precisely, his disciples, baptizing (22) somewhere in the same general region as John (23-24). The occurrence of these two ministries in close conjunction with each other provoked some discussion suggesting that Jesus and John were conducting rival baptisms (25-30). John's disciples were jealous of Jesus' evident success (25-26), but John humbly deferred to Jesus, acknowledging his own inferiority to the one whose coming he had announced (27-30). The narrative pauses for a moment as John's comments provide an opportunity to reflect on how one will respond to the message of the one whom the Father sent from heaven (31-36). When the narrative resumes, Jesus has learned that some people were unjustly pitting him in competition against John, and he is trying to ease the tension by departing for Galilee (4:1-3).

The next phase in the manifestation of Jesus as the Messiah unfolds in Samaria, through which he passed on his journey northward, as well as in Galilee itself (4:4-54). The first half of this tour focuses on Jesus' evangelizing of a Samaritan woman (4-42). Jesus' encounter with her took place as she came to draw water from the well which Jacob had dug at Sychar (4-6). Jesus struck up a conversation with her (7-26), in which he was able to turn his immediate need for physical water into a spiritual discussion about his ability to provide her with living water that would quench her thirst eternally (7-15). Jesus then proceeded to apply this figurative lesson to the woman personally (16-26). By his prophetic insight, Jesus revealed that she was guilty of a life of adultery (16-18). She attempted to avoid scrutiny by diverting the discussion to religious issues concerning the proper way and place to worship God (19-24), but Jesus announced to her that he was the very Messiah whom she hoped would answer all her religious questions (25-26). At this point, the discussion shifts to the disciples (27-38), who arrived with some food while the woman hurried away to call the men of the city (27-30). The disciples were so preoccupied with satisfying their immediate physical appetites that Jesus had to redirect their attention to the eternal importance of reaping a spiritual harvest while it is ripe (31-38). Many of the Samaritans from that city returned with the woman to see Jesus for themselves, and believed in him (39-42).

The second half of Jesus' tour through Samaria and Galilee is taken up with the healing of a royal official's son (43-54). John sets the stage for the healing by noting the mood of expectation with which Jesus was received upon his return to Cana of Galilee (43-46a). The royal official, who had left his dying son in Capernaum to seek out Jesus, believed Jesus' word that his son would live, and returned home to find that he had recovered (46b-53). John counts this healing as Jesus' second sign, although he is clearly aware of other signs which he chose not to include in his Gospel (54).

Following this brief period of initial openness to Jesus, comes a period extending from his second visit to Jerusalem until just before his third visit which is marked by unsettled controversy over his claims to deity (5:1–6:71). The first of two major controversies during this time-frame arose in response to Jesus' healing of a lame man in Jerusalem during an unnamed feast (5:1-47). John marks the beginning of the section by noting Jesus' journey to Jerusalem for the feast (1). As the third sign in his Gospel, John records the incident of Jesus' miraculous healing of the lame man, who had been lying by the pool of Bethesda for thirty-eight years (2-9a). When the Jews saw the man carrying the mat on which he had been lying, they immediately voiced their disapproval (9b-18) because it was the Sabbath, and in their minds carrying one's mat and healing were both violations of the Mosaic prohibition against working on the Sabbath (9b-16). Jesus made the Jews even more angry by claiming that both he and his Father were working until the present, thus implicitly making himself equal with God (17-18).

The contention between Jesus and the Jews occasioned by the healing gives way to an extended discourse (19-47) in which Jesus asserted clear claims to deity (19-29). He claimed to perform the Father's work, including raising the dead (19-23); furthermore, he claimed that the Father had given him authority to judge all of the dead (24-29). Jesus also reaffirmed his solidarity of will with the Father (30). To support his claims, Jesus appealed to valid witnesses (31-47). He cited the human witness of John the Baptist (31-35), but his primary appeal was to a greater witness, namely the Father himself (36-40). Both the works of Jesus, which were given by the Father (36), and the words of Scripture, which were spoken by the Father (37-40), bore witness to him. Jesus then turned from defending himself to expose the Jews' unbelief (41-47). He revealed

---

'After These Things'

The phrase 'after these things' is one of several structural clues that John uses in his Gospel. Although it is not as basic to his literary structure as the seven signs attesting to Jesus' deity or the mention of the annual Jewish feasts, John often uses this literary device to signal a transition to a new section.

For example, it marks the transition from Jesus' initial manifestation to the disciples to Jesus' manifestation to a wider public (2:12); and again it marks the transition from the first phase of Jesus' public manifestation at Jerusalem to a second phase in Judea, where John was baptizing (3:22). As the initial openness to Jesus gives way to increasing controversy, we find the phrase bridging Jesus' healing of a royal official's son and the healing of a lame man on the Sabbath (5:1). Following the controversy arising from this healing, John uses the phrase to introduce the further controversy surrounding Jesus' feeding of the five thousand and the hard teaching that accompanies it (6:1). 'After these things' also introduces the period of determination to kill Jesus that follows the feeding of the five thousand (7:1). After Jesus' resurrection from the dead and John's statement of the purpose of this Gospel, the phrase is used once more to introduce the epilogue, in which Jesus makes a special appearance to the disciples in Galilee (21:1)

---

that the Jews had rejected his glory because they sought glory from men instead (41-44); and he further showed that they disbelieved his words because they disbelieved Moses' words, for Moses wrote about him (45-47).

The second major controversy of this period follows Jesus' provision of bread in Galilee before the Passover (6:1-71). After healing the lame man, Jesus went away to the other side of the Sea of Galilee, where he performed his fourth sign, the feeding of the five thousand (1-15). John briefly notes the setting for this miraculous sign (1-4) before recounting how Jesus multiplied five loaves and two fish to feed over five thousand people (5-13). They responded overwhelmingly to this miraculous sign (14-15). They recognized the identity of Jesus as the prophet who was predicted to come into the world (14) and would have forcibly made him king if he had not withdrawn by himself to a mountain (15). Late that night, Jesus performed his fifth sign: in order to rejoin the disciples, who had departed by boat for Capernaum and were struggling against a heavy storm, he came to them walking on the water (16-21).

The next day Jesus gave an extended discourse on the bread of life (22-71) to many of the people who were present at the feeding of the five thousand (22-40) and came searching for him at Capernaum (22-25). When they found him, he revealed that their true motive for seeking him was not that they genuinely believed the signs he had performed but that they selfishly desired more of the bread he had multiplied (26-29). They requested a sign from him so that they might believe, suggesting that he top Moses' sign of feeding their fathers in the wilderness with manna from heaven (30-35), but Jesus reprimanded them for their unbelief (36-40).

The discussion carried over to the synagogue, where the leaders of the Jews became Jesus' most vocal opponents (41-59). They began by disputing Jesus' claim to be the bread that came down from heaven (41-51). In response to their grumbling (41-42), Jesus asserted that they needed the Father's spiritual illumination to accept what he was saying (43-46), and he reaffirmed that he was, indeed, the provision for the world's eternal sustenance (47-51). The dispute continued concerning the seeming absurdity of eating the flesh of Jesus, upon which he solemnly insisted (52-58). As a historical postscript, John notes the setting where this dispute took place (59).

As a result of the controversy, the larger group of Jesus' disciples was divided (60-71). Many superficial disciples stumbled over Jesus' hard sayings (60-65), but Peter, speaking for the twelve, affirmed that they would remain loyal to Jesus because he possessed life-giving words and they had no one else to whom they could turn (66-71).

From this point on, the Jews became increasingly hardened in their resolve to kill Jesus (7:1–11:54). John develops their hardening around three occasions on which they clashed with him, the first of which was Jesus' third visit to Jerusalem for the Feast of Tabernacles (7:1–8:59). John includes Jesus' journey from Galilee to Jerusalem for the feast to introduce this occasion for the Jews' hardening (7:1-13). Because of threats from the Jews against his life, Jesus had protracted his stay in Galilee at first (1) and avoided going up to Jerusalem contrary to his brothers' advice (2-9). A little later, however, he arrived in Jerusalem secretly amid widespread controversy about him (10-13).

He began teaching in the temple (14-52) upon making his public appearance in the middle of the feast (14-36). As might be expected, the Jewish leaders reacted negatively to Jesus' teaching (14-24). Jesus indicated that they were unable to accept his teaching because they were selfishly seeking their own interests rather than God's (14-18), and he attributed their desire to kill him to their distorted sense of legalism, which condemned him for healing on the Sabbath (19-24). Some of the inhabitants of Jerusalem began to speculate about why the Jewish authorities did not take immediate action to silence Jesus (25-29). The common people even entertained what they considered to be an unlikely possibility, that their rulers might actually know that Jesus was the Messiah (25-27). To their doubtful musings, Jesus boldly asserted in the presence of all that he came from God (28-29). His bold declarations incited the attempts of the Jewish leaders to arrest him (30-36). Those who were present spontaneously attempted to seize Jesus, but they were unable to lay a hand on him because his appointed hour had not yet come

(30). Later the chief priests and Pharisees made a formal attempt to have him arrested by the temple guards (31-36).

On the last day of the feast, Jesus made a climactic appeal to the crowd (37-52). He promised that from those who believed on him the Spirit would flow like rivers of living water (37-39). The crowd's response was mixed: some identified him as the Messiah; others denied that he could be (40-44).

The temple guards, who had been sent earlier by the religious leaders, found themselves unable to arrest Jesus because they were spellbound by his words (45-52).

The following section on Jesus' forgiveness of the woman caught in adultery is not found in the oldest manuscripts and was probably not originally a part of John's Gospel, but most modern versions have included it within square brackets because it represents an ancient tradition that became attached to the canonical text at this point (7:53–**8**:11).

Originally, John's narrative continued uninterrupted with Jesus' debates in the temple after the feast (8:12-59). First we find Jesus debating with the Pharisees (12-30). The immediate issue was his claim to be the light of the world (12-20). After introducing Jesus' claim (12), John records the Pharisees' contention with Jesus over the validity of his testimony concerning himself (13-19); then the evangelist adds his own comment on the openness with which Jesus spoke (20). Following this brief pause, the debate resumes over

---

'I Am' Sayings in John

Seven times in John's Gospel, Jesus uses an 'I am' saying to describe who he is. These sayings usually present profound theological truths through concrete metaphors.

1. I am the bread of life (6:35; cf. 6:41, 48, 51)
2. I am the light of the world (8:12; 9:5)
3. I am the door of the sheep (10:7)
4. I am the good shepherd (10:1, 14)
5. I am the resurrection and the life (11:25)
6. I am the way, and the truth, and the life (14:6)
7. I am the true vine (15:1, 5)

Jesus' claim to go where the Pharisees could not follow (21-30). The interchange falls into two parts revealing a stark contrast between the unbridgeable gulf separating Jesus from the Pharisees (21-24) and the inseparable relationship between Jesus and the Father (25-29). In conclusion, John appends a note that many who heard the debate came to believe in Jesus (30).

A second debate follows between Jesus and these 'believing' Jews, who, as quickly becomes evident, were very shallow (31-59). They rejected Jesus' teaching that the Son was able to liberate them through their knowing the truth about him because they denied that they had ever been enslaved (31-36). Notwithstanding their claim to be free because they were physical descendants of Abraham, Jesus demonstrated that they were in spiritual bondage because they were, in fact, the devil's children (37-47). In response to their disparaging comments about the purity of his lineage, Jesus asserted that he pre-existed with his Father before Abraham's day (48-58). For this claim, the Jews attempted to stone him, but he escaped from them (58).

A series of events associated with Jesus' attendance at the Feast of Dedication later that year turned into a second occasion for the Jews to become hardened in their resolve to kill Jesus (9:1–10:42). The build-up begins with Jesus' activities outside the temple some time prior to the feast (9:1–10:21). The initial source of conflict was Jesus' healing of a man born blind, which is now the sixth sign in John's Gospel (9:1-41). John briefly records the actual restoration of the man's sight (1-7) before discussing its more lengthy aftermath. The people who saw the man, especially those who had known him previously, were amazed at the miracle (8-12), but the Pharisees vehemently opposed Jesus (13-34). First, they questioned the man because they thought it incredible that anyone sent from God could perform such a miracle on the Sabbath (13-17). Next, they questioned the man's parents because they disbelieved that he had been blind (18-23). Then, in exasperation, they questioned the man again because they were convinced that Jesus was a sinner who would not be heard by God (24-34). John was quick to see the spiritual outcome of the miracle, which he paints in two contrasting pictures (35-41). Upon talking further with Jesus, the man who had been blind believed in him (35-38), but, as Jesus pointed out, the Pharisees, who claimed to see, remained blind to their sin (39-41).

Following the healing of the blind man, John records Jesus' discourse on the Good Shepherd, which apparently also took place before the feast and outside the temple (**10**:1-21). Jesus began the discourse by uttering an enigmatic saying about a shepherd and his sheep (1-6). He then went on to explain the saying for the sake of his listeners, who did not understand (7-18). He identified himself as the door of the sheepfold (7-10) and the Good Shepherd (11-18), whom he characterized as one who lays down his life for the sheep (11-13), who knows his sheep intimately (14-18) and is loved by the Father (17-18). This saying caused a division among the Jews between those who wrote Jesus off as an insane demoniac and those who were open to seeing something divine about him (19-21).

During the Feast of Dedication, Jesus gave a discourse in Solomon's portico of the temple in response to the demands of the Jews that he clearly state whether or not he was the Messiah (22-39). After pointing out that they had not believed his earlier statements, Jesus unequivocally claimed unity with the Father (22-30); and they responded by attempting to stone him for blasphemy (31-39). Consequently, Jesus withdrew beyond the Jordan (40-42).

Before his last Passover, Jesus arrived at Bethany, a village just outside Jerusalem, to perform one final sign, which became a further occasion for the hardening of the Jews' resolve to kill him (**11**:1-54). Jesus' seventh and climactic sign, not counting his own resurrection, was the raising of Lazarus from the dead (1-44). The narrative begins with Jesus discussing Lazarus' illness with his disciples, beyond the Jordan (1-16). When he received news that his friend Lazarus was ill (1-5), Jesus purposely delayed for two days before leaving to visit him amid the protests of the disciples, who were fearful of returning to Judea (6-10). Jesus informed them that Lazarus had already died, but he was going to awaken him (11-16). While he was still on the road to Bethany, Jesus was met by Lazarus' two sisters (17-37). First, he was met by Martha (17-27), who came running out to greet him (17-19). Although she expressed regret that he had not come sooner, he comforted her with the promise that her brother would rise again (21-27). Mary also came out to met Jesus (28-37) after Martha hurriedly returned home to call her (28-31). Upon seeing the mourning of Mary and the Jews who accompanied her, Jesus was deeply grieved to the point of tears (32-37).

He went to the tomb, commanded that the stone be removed, and called Lazarus to come out – which the dead man did, still wrapped in his grave clothes (38-44). This amazing sign produced two very different responses (45-54). Many of the Jews who witnessed it believed in Jesus (45-46), but the Sanhedrin resolved upon the recommendation of Caiaphas, the high priest, that Jesus would have to be put to death before his popularity upset their national security (47-53). With his death warrant sealed, Jesus withdrew to a city called Ephraim, where he could more easily escape from public view (54).

In John's Gospel, the rejection of the sign of Lazarus is a hinge upon which the door of opportunity rapidly begins to swing closed, leaving only a very brief period during which one final chance remains to accept Jesus as the Messiah before his death (11:55–12:50). Although his fate has now been irreversibly set as far as the religious leaders are concerned, events, particularly with respect to other people, are still building up to the climactic end of Jesus' public ministry (11:55–12:36a). John fills the air with tension by revealing that the Jewish authorities were lying in wait to seize Jesus if he should venture to come up for the Passover (11:55-57).

Well aware of their intentions, Jesus, nonetheless, returned to Bethany before the feast to visit Lazarus and his sisters (**12**:1-11). While they were eating, Mary anointed Jesus with expensive perfume in symbolic preparation for his burial (1-8). Because many people were believing in Jesus on account of Lazarus, the chief priests plotted to kill him as well (9-11).

The fourth visit of Jesus to Jerusalem began triumphantly on the next day with enthusiastic crowds of pilgrims cheering and hailing him as the King of Israel as he rode into the city upon a donkey (12-19). In God's timing, Jesus' appointed hour had now come (20-36a). This hour is described, first, as an hour of glorification (20-26). In response to the request of some Greeks to see him (20-22), Jesus replied that the hour had come for the Son of Man to be glorified (23-26). But, paradoxical as it might seem, this hour was also an hour for the Son of Man to suffer (27-36a). In response to Jesus' prayer that the Father's name be glorified, the Father spoke in a voice from heaven offering the reassurance that he would be glorified in Jesus' death (27-33). The crowd, however, was perplexed about the mention of the Son of Man being put to death because Jesus seemed to identify the Son of Man with the Messiah, whom they thought was eternal (34-36a).

The announcement that the appointed hour had come is followed by a brief transition from the public ministry of Jesus to his private preparation of the disciples for his death and the new challenges that his departure would bring (36b-50). This transition is developed in two parts: first, the evangelist makes some parenthetical comments based on Isaiah to explain the unbelief of the Jews (36b-43); then Jesus gives a final public appeal calling for belief in him (44-50).

Jesus' manifestation as Messiah having been rejected by the most part of the Jews, especially the religious leaders, John now moves on to consider the redemptive work of the Saviour in the second half of his Gospel (13:1–20:29). He begins by noting in some detail Jesus' private preparations of the disciples for the departure of their master (13:1–17:26). Jesus began to prepare his disciples during the Passover meal by means of two symbolic actions (13:1-30). The first action was his washing of the disciples' feet (1-20), a humble service which he willingly stooped to perform (1-11). After cleansing the group (1-5), he included Peter, who protested until Jesus made acceptance of the rite a condition of belonging to him (6-11). When he had finished, Jesus drew out the implications of his example for the disciples (12-20). He expected the same attitude of humble servanthood to be demonstrated by them (12-17), with the exception of the betrayer, of course (18-20). Jesus's second symbolic action, although the disciples did not understand it, was to identify the betrayer by dipping a piece of bread and handing it to him (21-30).

After Judas got up and left the gathering, Jesus gave a lengthy farewell discourse (13:31–16:33), which began in the house (13:31–

14:31) and was continued later. In light of the impending events, Jesus introduced his discourse by announcing (31-35) that the Son of Man would be glorified very shortly (31-33) and that he was giving his disciples a new commandment, namely to love one another (34-35). In response to Peter's query about where he was going, Jesus asserted that Peter was not able to follow yet (36-38), but he encouraged all of the disciples by promising them a future home with his Father (**14**:1-4). In response to Thomas' protest that it was impossible for them to know the way since they didn't know where he was going, Jesus claimed to be the way himself (5-7). In response to Philip's request for Jesus to manifest the Father, Jesus claimed to reveal him perfectly (8-11). Jesus also gave further assurances to the disciples that they would be enabled to face the future after his departure (12-21). He promised them that they

---

The Annual Jewish Feasts in John's Gospel

Unlike the synoptic writers, who mention only the final Passover before Jesus' death, John builds his chronological framework upon the recurrence of Passover and other annual Jewish feasts. His mention of three, or possibly four, Passovers allows Jesus' ministry to span from two to three and one half years.

From the very outset, John the Baptist's identification of Jesus as the paschal lamb alerts the reader to the typological significance of this schema (1:29, 35). The first Passover in John's Gospel provides the occasion for the cleansing of the temple and Jesus' conversation with Nicodemus about the new birth (2:13–3:21). An unnamed feast, which could possibly be Passover, is mentioned in 5:1, but that identification is open to question.

John sets the feeding of the five thousand against the backdrop of a second, or third, Passover (6:4). He overlooks any details of the celebration of this Passover, however, and doesn't even mention if Jesus went up to Jerusalem for it because he is more interested triggering a chain of theological associations from this feast to eating the multiplied loaves, to eating the manna in the wilderness, and finally, to eating the flesh of Jesus and drinking his blood. Many people found the saying about feasting on Jesus hard to accept, but John takes pains to develop it in its earliest Paschal connection; whereas, the synoptic writers reserve it for Jesus' last Passover with his disciples.

From Passover, which took place in the spring, John skips over to the

would be able to do greater works than he had done (12-14), that the Father would give them another Helper (15-17), and that he, himself, would be manifested to them after a period of absence (18-21). In response to the surprise of Judas (not Iscariot) at the apparent exclusivity of Jesus' manifestation to them and not the world, Jesus explained that this manifestation was conditioned upon loving him (22-24). Jesus then concluded the first part of the discourse with two promises and a warning (25-31). He promised that the Holy Spirit would be sent to them as a revealer of truth about him (25-26) and that he would leave his peace with them in the world (27-29). Finally, he warned that the ruler of the world was coming quickly (30-31).

After leaving the room where they had eaten the Passover meal, Jesus continued his farewell address on the way to a garden on the

---

Feast of Tabernacles, a week-long harvest festival during which all Jews lived in temporary shelters to commemorate their wilderness wanderings and anticipate their eternal heavenly dwellings. John notes that at first Jesus considered it too dangerous to go up to Jerusalem for this great feast even though his brothers urged him (7:1-9), but later he went in secret and began teaching publicly in the temple (7:10, 14). On the last day of the feast, which climaxed with the priest's pouring out water on the altar from a golden pitcher in symbolic anticipation of the outpouring of the Spirit, Jesus, in conscious fulfillment of this symbolism, stood up and invited anyone who was thirsty to drink from him (7:37-39). In 8:12-59, we find Jesus still in the temple disputing with the Pharisees, probably on the Sabbath following the Feast of Tabernacles.

The next feast mentioned in John's Gospel is the Feast of Dedication, which is also known as the Festival of Lights, or Hanukkah (10:22). It was celebrated in late December to commemorate the restoration of the temple by Judas Maccabeus. Although the connection is debated, the mention of this feast probably governs the preceding time period rather than introducing a new section.

The raising of Lazarus, which took place shortly before Passover of the following year (11:55), becomes the event that irreversibly seals Jesus' fate in the minds of the religious leaders (11:47-53). John tells us more explicitly that Jesus revisited Lazarus' home in Bethany six days before Passover (12:1) and made his triumphal entry into Jerusalem on the following day (12:12).

---

other side of the Kidron ravine (**15**:1–16:33). The first of three major topics that he addressed was the disciples' relationships to others (15:1–16:4a). He exhorted the disciples to maintain an abiding relationship to the vine (15:1-11). Using the illustration of branches abiding in the vine as their means of bearing fruit (1-8), Jesus instructed them to abide in his love by keeping his commandments (9-11). He also commanded them to live in a loving relationship to one another (12-17).

He warned them, however, that they would experience hostile relations with the world (15:18–16:4a). Jesus pointed out that the psychology of the world's hostility to him implied (18-25) that the world would also hate his disciples (18-21) and that the worldly people of that day who hated him were guilty of sin because he had spoken to them and performed unprecedented works in their presence (22-25). Over against the world's hostile mood, Jesus promised that the coming Spirit of truth would bear witness concerning him (26-27). To prevent them from stumbling, Jesus warned his disciples in advance that the world would persecute them zealously (**16**:1-4a).

The second major topic which Jesus addressed was the coming of the Spirit in his place (4b-15). He assured the disciples that it was to their advantage that he go away so that the Spirit could come to them (4b-7). Jesus taught them that upon his arrival the Spirit would perform a dual function of convicting the world (8-11) and instructing them in the truth (12-15).

The third topic was Jesus' return in a little while (16-33). The initial disclosure of Jesus' new relation to the disciples (16-24) caused them perplexity because they did not understand how Jesus could be absent for a little while and then return to them again (16-18). Jesus promised, however, that their grief would be replaced by overwhelming joy (19-22) and that the Father would give them whatever they asked in his name (23-24). After having introduced the topic in somewhat vague language, Jesus proceeded to elaborate upon his new relation to the disciples (25-33). He promised that a time would come when he would no longer speak in enigmatic sayings but plainly declare the Father to them (25-28). Just when they thought that they grasped what he was saying, Jesus predicted that they would soon desert him (29-32), but he concluded by promising them triumphant peace in the midst of tribulation (33).

Following his discourse to the disciples, Jesus offered an intercessory prayer to the Father, in which he expressed his deepest concerns upon his imminent departure from the world (17:1-26). First, he requested his own glorification together with the Father (1-5). He then interceded for his disciples (6-19). After affirming their spiritual understanding of his identity and mission (6-8), he requested their spiritual well-being (9-19) in terms of their preservation in the Father (9-12), their protection from the evil one (13-16), and their sanctification in the truth (17-19). Finally, he interceded for all future believers (20-26) that they might be united with one another (20-23) and experience fellowship with the Godhead (24-26).

As soon as Jesus was finished praying, he moved directly from preparatory matters to the heart of his redemptive work of suffering as a substitute for the sins of the world (18:1–19:42). The first step in accomplishing salvation was willingly yielding to betrayal in the garden across the Kidron ravine (1-11), where he had retired with the disciples after the Passover meal (1). While they were there, Judas arrived accompanied by officers from the chief priests and Pharisees along with a detachment of Roman soldiers to arrest Jesus (2-9). Before Jesus could stop him, Peter drew a sword and cut off the ear of the high priest's slave, not understanding the necessity of Jesus' death in the Father's plan (10-11).

In order for Jesus to be condemned, he had to be tried before the authorities (18:12–19:16a), starting with the Jews (18:12-27). Jesus remained steadfast throughout his appearance before Annas (12-24), before whom he was arraigned first because Annas exercised great influence as the former high priest and father-in-law to the current high priest, Caiaphas (12-14). While Jesus was being tried, Peter, who had followed up to the high priest's courtyard, denied that he was one of Jesus' disciples to the slave-girl who let him through the gate (15-18). After questioning Jesus concerning his disciples and his teaching, Annas sent him on to Caiaphas (19-24). During Jesus' appearance before Caiaphas, Peter repeatedly denied his association with Jesus (25-27).

Jesus also had to appear before Pilate, the Roman governor, because the Jews did not have the right to inflict capital punishment (18:28–19:16a). Having led Jesus to the governor's official residence, the Jewish religious leaders demanded his condemnation (18:28-32). Pilate took Jesus inside and inquired about his kingship, but Jesus' spiritual kingdom did not seem to pose a political threat to Pilate (33-38a). Not finding any grounds for a charge against Jesus, Pilate repeatedly attempted to release him, but he failed each time (18:38b–19:7). He tried appealing to the custom of releasing a prisoner at the feast, but the Jewish leaders demanded that he release Barabbas instead (18:38b-40). He also failed in his attempt to appeal to the sympathy of the crowd (**19**:1-5) by ordering Jesus to be scourged (1-3) and then presenting to them the pathetic sight of his beaten body, dressed in a purple robe and wearing a crown of thorns in mockery of his unbelievable pretensions to kingship (4-5). When the religious leaders started calling out for Jesus' crucifixion, Pilate attempted to shift the responsibility for judging the case to them, but they would not accept it because their real charge of blasphemy demanded the death penalty, which they could not legally execute (6-7). Their hint of Jesus' divine origin made Pilate very nervous so he inquired further of Jesus, only to find himself placed on the defensive (8-11). Although Pilate made further efforts to release Jesus, he eventually capitulated to the Jewish leaders' political threats to blackmail him with treason for protecting a rival to Caesar (12-16a).

John reports the brutal realities that follow in straightforward, factual language, but he looks past the outward appearances of Jesus' death and burial to view their true spiritual significance in terms of the sacrifice of God's Passover Lamb to effect salvation for the world (16b-42).[1] Pilate's complicity with the Jewish leaders meant that Jesus was put to death at the hands of Romans (16b-37). The soldiers who attended to his crucifixion (16b-30) led Jesus out to Golgotha, where they positioned his cross between two others and affixed the inscription which Pilate had written, declaring Jesus to be 'The King of the Jews' (16b-22). While Jesus hung on the cross, the soldiers divided his garments among them (23-24).[2]

---

1. On the versification see the note in the outline.

Standing nearby was Jesus' mother, whom he entrusted into the care of the beloved disciple, John (25-27). After being given a drink to moisten his lips, Jesus said, 'It is finished,' and gave up his spirit (28-30). When the soldiers saw that he was already dead, they did not break his legs, as they had done to hasten the death of the men on the other two crosses, but one of the soldiers verified that he really was dead by thrusting a spear into his side (31-37). Jesus was buried in a new tomb belonging to Joseph of Arimathea, who had obtained permission from Pilate to remove the body (38-42).

But Jesus did not remain in the tomb; John reports several appearances of the resurrected Jesus in Jerusalem (**20**:1-29). The first of these appearances happened by the empty tomb on the first day of the week (1-18). Before anyone saw Jesus, it became evident that the tomb was empty (1-10). The discovery was initially made by Mary Magdalene (1-2) and confirmed by Peter and John, who found the linen wrappings lying there without the body inside (3-8). Later Jesus appeared to Mary Magdalene (11-18). At the time, she was peering through her tears into the tomb and discussing with two angels the disappearance of Jesus' body (11-13). When she turned around, she did not realise at first that the person standing behind her was Jesus; but when he spoke her name, she instantly recognized him and clung onto him, at once overjoyed and afraid to let him go (14-18).

Jesus also appeared to the disciples behind closed doors on the next two subsequent Sundays (19-29). On the first of these appearances, Jesus symbolically bestowed the Holy Spirit upon them in anticipation of their future ministry (19-23). On the second occasion, Thomas, who had been absent the first time, was with the others (24-29); he refused, however, to believe their report that they had seen Jesus (24-25) until Jesus appeared in their midst and Thomas's doubt was instantly transformed into worship (26-29). The fourth evangelist concludes the main body of his Gospel by stating that he recorded the signs contained in it for the apologetic purpose of persuading his readers that Jesus is the Messiah, the Son of God, so that they might have life through believing in his name (30-31).

---

2. On the versification see the note in the outline.

He rounds out his account, however, with a personal epilogue, which is primarily taken up with the parting words of the risen Lord (**21**:1-25). Jesus manifested himself again to the disciples at the Sea of Tiberias in a scene that allows us to step within the inner circle and feel the warmth and depth of his personal relationship to them (1-23). After a brief introduction (1), John describes their miraculous catch of fish (2-14). Peter had decided to go fishing and took most of the disciples along with him, but they caught nothing all night (2-3). At dawn, Jesus, who was standing on the shore, told them to cast their net on the other side of the boat, which they did, and caught more fish than they could haul in (4-8). When they reached the shore, Jesus already had a charcoal fire going and invited them to join him for breakfast (9-14). The conversation after breakfast (15-23) focused on the restoration of Peter (15-19). Jesus proved the depth of Peter's love by asking Peter three times if he loved him, and he commissioned Peter for service by commanding him three times to care for his sheep (15-17). Along with this call to service, Jesus forewarned Peter that he would suffer an unnatural death (18-19). This prediction made Peter curious about Jesus' purpose for John, but Jesus replied that the length of John's life was none of Peter's business (20-23).

The evangelist maintains the personal tone of the epilogue in his conclusion by identifying himself as the unnamed disciple throughout the Gospel, who by process of elimination must be John; he also appends a note that Jesus did far more than could ever be recorded (24-25).

OUTLINE OF JOHN'S GOSPEL

---

1. John is probably following through with the analogy to Genesis 1:1 which he had suggested in John 1:1 by drawing a parallel between the seven days of creation in Genesis and the first week of Jesus' ministry as the beginning of a new creation. If the disciples stayed overnight with Jesus, as John 1:39 implies, verses 40-42 become the fourth day and verse 43 the fifth. Using the Jewish inclusive method of reckoning time, which counts part of a day as one day, and counting the 'third day' in John 2:1 from 1:43, which is the last day mentioned, the miracle at the wedding in Cana falls on the seventh day relative to John 1:19-28, with no mention being made of the sixth day.

2. Some MSS read *the* Feast, i.e. Passover, but the textual support for this reading is weak, and the identification of the feast remains uncertain.

3. The centrality of Jerusalem to the narrative carries through to John 10:39. The first feast mentioned in this connection, the Feast of Tabernacles, took place in September/October.

4. John 10:22 draws a thematic connection with the preceding sections in 9:1–10:21. The Feast of Dedication, also known as the Festival of Lights, or Hanukkah, occurred in late December.

---

5 Some English versions (NASB, RSV) list verse 16b of the Greek text as verse 17.

6 Some English versions (NASB, RSV) list verse 24b of the Greek text as verse 25.

ACTS

OVERVIEW OF THE BOOK OF ACTS

Theme: the spread of the Gospel from Jerusalem to Rome

Key Verse: Acts 1:8, 'You shall receive power when the Holy Spirit comes upon you; and you shall be My witnesses both in Jerusalem, and in all Judea and Samaria, and even to the remotest part of the earth' (NASB).

Introduction: a recapitulation of Luke's former treatise	1:1-5
I. The birth of the church in Jerusalem	1:6–8:1a
A. The period of waiting	1:6-26
B. The day of Pentecost	2:1-47
C. The growth of the early church amidst opposition	3:1–8:1a
(SUMMARY: the word kept on spreading and numbers continually increased)	6:7
II. The expansion of the church into Samaria and beyond	8:1b–9:31
A. The scattering of the Jerusalem church by persecution	8:1b-3
B. The evangelistic ministry of Philip	8:4-40
C. The conversion of Saul on the road to Damascus	9:1-30
(SUMMARY: the church had peace and was strengthened)	9:31
III. The opening of the Gospel to the Gentiles	9:32–12:24
A. The ministry of Peter in western Palestine	9:32-43
B. First conversion of Gentiles in Cornelius' household	10:1–11:18
C. The birth of a Gentile church in Syrian Antioch	11:19-30
D. The persecution of the apostles by Herod	12:1-23
(SUMMARY: the word continued to grow and be multiplied)	12:24

HISTORICAL BACKGROUND

The Book of Acts is generally ascribed to Luke, the author of the third Gospel and travelling companion of Paul. Acts is the second volume in Luke's two-part history of early Christianity. It begins where the Gospel leaves off and traces the continued works of the risen Jesus through the apostles by the power of the Holy Spirit as Christianity rapidly spread from Jerusalem to Rome, the capital of the empire (cf. Acts 1:8). This work is our most valuable historical source for the background of the majority of Paul's epistles. Both Luke and Acts are addressed to Theophilus (Lk 1:1-4; Acts 1:1-3), who may have sponsored their publication, but they were intended to reach a wider Gentile audience as well.

Luke probably completed the Book of Acts at Rome during Paul's first imprisonment there. If the abrupt ending of the book indicates that it was written shortly after the last events that it narrates, we should date it around A.D. 61 or 62.

THE FLOW OF THE BOOK OF ACTS

The book of Acts moves beyond the actions and teachings of Jesus while he lived upon earth, which are recorded in the first volume of Luke's two-part history, to the continued actions of Jesus through the apostles after he had risen and ascended. Luke introduces this sequel to his Gospel by recapitulating his former treatise for the benefit of Theophilus, to whom both volumes are dedicated (**1:1-5**).

He begins by telling the story of the church's birth in Jerusalem (**1:6–8:1a**). The disciples had to go through a period of waiting for this event (1:6-26) following Christ's ascension into heaven (6-11). During the interim they gathered in the upper room for prayer

---

Luke's Abridgement of the Speeches in Acts

In order to make the speeches in Acts fit, Luke had to condense them. As a result, we often have the gist of what was said rather than a verbatim account. It is not surprizing that these speeches should come in abridged form since all historians work under similar constraints of space. In most cases a verbatim account is neither desirable nor humanly possible. Thucydides, the model Greek historian, freely acknowledges that, even though he took great pains to report the events of the Peloponnesian War with detailed accuracy, he made no attempt to reproduce the speeches verbatim because he could not remember, and his sources did not record, every word that was spoken:

As to the speeches that were made by different men,...it has been difficult to recall with strict accuracy the words actually spoken, both for me...and for those who brought me reports. Therefore the speeches are given in the language in which, as it seemed to me, the several speakers would express...the sentiments most befitting the occasion, though at the same time I have adhered as closely as possible to the general sense of what was actually said.

(Thucydides, *History of the Peloponnesian War*, 1.22.1, trans. Charles Forster Smith, Loeb Classical Library [Cambridge: Harvard University Press, 1980], 1:39.)

(12-14) and chose Matthias as a replacement for Judas (15-26).

On the day of Pentecost the church was born (**2**:1-47) by the coming of the Holy Spirit (1-13). While the first believers were gathered together, the Spirit came upon them with the sound of a rushing wind and the appearance of tongues of fire being distributed to each of them; as a result they were filled with the Spirit and enabled to speak in other languages (1-4). The visitors who had come for Pentecost from all over the world were bewildered as they heard the mighty acts of God being proclaimed in their own languages (5-13).

To explain what had happened, Peter preached a sermon (14-40) in which he linked these events to Joel's prophecy of the outpouring of the Spirit (14-21),[1] which he claimed was now being fulfilled because of Jesus' resurrection from the dead and ascension to the Father's right hand (22-36). About three thousand people responded to Peter's invitation to repent and be baptized so that they might receive the promised gift of the Holy Spirit (37-42). The resultant life of the early church was characterized by a sense of awe, generosity in sharing with the needy, a spirit of unity in its fellowship, exuberant praise to God, and continued daily growth (43-47).

The church's growth, however, took place amidst strong opposition (**3**:1–8:1a). Very early in the church's existence, the healing of a lame man provided an excellent opportunity for witness to both the common people and the hostile religious leaders (3:1–4:31). As Peter and John were going up to the temple to pray, they met a lame beggar whom they restored to health at once (3:1-10). Peter explained to the crowd that had gathered (11-26) that this sign was accomplished by the power of the risen Jesus, whom they had put to death (11-16), and that it pointed to their opportunity to repent in view of the Messiah's promised restoration of all things (17-26). As a result of their preaching, Peter and John were imprisoned by the Sanhedrin (**4**:1-12). Even before they had finished speaking, they were arrested by the captain of the temple guard, who was accompanied by some of the priests and Sadducees (1-4). The next day the high priest assembled with the Sanhedrin (5-12) to inquire by what power the apostles had healed the lame

---

1. Joel 2:28-32.

Summary Statements in Acts

Luke usually closes a major literary section in Acts with a summary statement that describes the condition of the growing church up to that point:

1. And the word of God kept on spreading; and the number of the disciples continued to increase greatly in Jerusalem, and a great many of the priests were becoming obedient to the faith (Acts 6:7).
2. So the church throughout all Judea and Galilee and Samaria enjoyed peace, being built up; and, going on in the fear of the Lord and in the comfort of the Holy Spirit, it continued to increase (Acts 9:31).
3. But the word of the Lord continued to grow and to be multiplied (Acts 12:24).
4. So the churches were being strengthened in the faith, and were increasing in number daily (Acts 16:5).
5. So the word of the Lord was growing mightily and prevailing (Acts 19:20).
6. And he [Paul] stayed two full years in his own rented quarters, and was welcoming all who came to him, preaching the kingdom of God, and teaching concerning the Lord Jesus Christ with all openness, unhindered (Acts 28:30-31; NASB).

---

man (5-7). Peter boldly affirmed that the power to heal him, or to save anyone, can be found only in the name of Jesus, whom they had crucified (8-12). The Sanhedrin did not know what to do so they released Peter and John with a warning not to speak in Jesus' name, but the apostles forthrightly refused to be silenced (13-22). After their release, they gathered with the other believers to pray that they might speak the word with boldness, which in fact they did (23-31).

The early believers gained great respect from the common people because they cared for their needy by holding their goods in community (4:32–5:11). Those who had some means adopted the practice of selling their land or houses and entrusting the proceeds to the apostles for distribution to the poor (32-35). Luke singles out Barnabas as a noble example of one such person who sold a tract of land and donated the money to the poor (36-37). Ananias and his wife, Sapphira, however, were severely punished for wilfully misrepresenting their gift as the full amount received from the sale of their property when in fact it was only a portion (5:1-11). When Ananias brought the money, Peter confronted him with his deceit and reminded him that he was under no obligation to give anything; then Ananias dropped dead at Peter's feet (5:1-6). Several hours later, Sapphira, who had not yet heard what had happened to her husband, affirmed the same lie and also died on the spot (7-11).

The great respect and popularity that the apostles had among the people only served to intensify the antagonism of the Sanhedrin (12-42). The apostles were increasing in popularity by performing many extraordinary miraculous signs (12-16); the Sadducean members of the Sanhedrin, filled with jealousy, responded by arresting them a second time (17-42). With the help of an angel, the apostles escaped their custody during the night and were back preaching in the temple early the next morning (17-26). When the apostles were returned to the Sanhedrin for questioning, they defied its injunction to stop preaching, claiming higher allegiance to God (27-32). They were released upon the counsel of a leading Pharisee named Gamaliel, who advised letting things run their course and leaving the outcome to God's sovereignty (33-42).

About that time, the Jerusalem church decided to select seven deacons to handle the administration of aid to the poor so that the Hellenistic widows would not be overlooked and the apostles would not be detracted from their primary task of praying and preaching (6:1-6). Luke summarizes the history of the church to this point by stating that the word kept on spreading and the number of disciples in Jerusalem continually increased (7).

He then narrates how the ongoing opposition from zealous Jews culminated in the martyrdom of Stephen, which became the point of transition into the church's expansion beyond the borders of Jerusalem (6:8–8:1a). The Jews had accused Stephen of speaking blasphemously against Moses and the temple (6:8–7:1). He responded with a historical defence of the related doctrines of God's universal redemptive working with the entire human race, regardless of ethnic or geographic boundaries, and God's transcendence of any physical habitation, such as the temple (7:2-53). Stephen pointed out that God's call to Abraham came when the patriarch was in Mesopotamia, far away from the promised land, which he never actually possessed himself (2-8). Stephen also reminded his accusers that although Joseph was sold into slavery by his brothers, God's presence was with him in Egypt, where the nation of Israel was formed (9-16). Furthermore, God's appointment of Moses, whom Stephen's opponents regarded as sacrosanct, occurred outside of the promised land and was repeatedly questioned by the ancient Israelites (17-43). Moses, as Stephen recounts, was providentially brought up in a pagan environment in the Egyptian palace (17-22). The first time Moses attempted to deliver his fellow Israelites, he was misunderstood, rejected, and forced to flee the country (23-29). Forty years later, God encountered Moses at a remote place in the wilderness near Mount Sinai, which became sacred by virtue of God's presence, and there God commissioned him to deliver the Israelites from their bondage (30-35). Although Moses was specially chosen by God and led the Israelites out of Egypt by many miraculous signs, they wanted to turn back and continued to reject him, preferring to be led by idols (36-43). Stephen also argued that God was content with a temporary dwelling place until Solomon built the temple; and, even then, it was not capable of containing God because he fills the heavens and earth (44-50). Having made his case for God's universality and transcendence, Stephen applied the underlying thread of Israel's constant rejection of the prophets throughout history to his opponents' present resisting of the Holy Spirit (51-53). The enraged Jews rushed upon Stephen and stoned him to death while a young man named Saul looked on approvingly (7:54–8:1a).

The persecution that broke out following Stephen's death forced the church to expand into Samaria and beyond (8:1b–9:31). The whole Jerusalem church, except for the apostles and perhaps some Hebrew Christians, scattered throughout Judea and Samaria to escape this persecution, which was led by Saul (8:1b-3). One of those forced to flee was Philip, who preached the Gospel in the places where he went (4-40) starting at Samaria (4-13). His preaching was confirmed by many powerful signs (4-8), and many Samaritans believed and were baptized, including a well-known sorcerer named Simon (9-13). When the apostles in Jerusalem heard of the conversion of the Samaritans, they sent Peter and John to give their official endorsement to this new movement (14-25). As the apostles laid their hands upon them, the Samaritans received the Holy Spirit (14-17). When Simon saw what happened, he attempted to purchase this authority to confer the Spirit through the imposition of hands, but he was sharply rebuked (18-24). As the apostles travelled back to Jerusalem, they extended the Gospel to other Samaritans in villages along the way (25). From Samaria, an angel directed Philip to a desert road leading to Gaza, where he met an influential Ethiopian eunuch who was ready to hear the Gospel and was baptized as soon as they came to water (26-40).

The church continued to expand beyond Samaria and acquired its most powerful agent for an even greater expansion to the Gentiles with the conversion of Saul as he was travelling to Damascus to arrest more believers (9:1-30). On the road, he encountered the risen Lord in a blinding light and an audible voice asking, 'Saul, Saul, why are you persecuting me?' (1-9). After three days, the Lord sent Ananias to Saul to restore his sight and tell him what he was to do (10-19a). He got up and began proclaiming Jesus (19b-30). First he entered the synagogues of Damascus (19b-25), where he confounded the Jews by demonstrating that Jesus is the divine Messiah (19b-22) until their plot to kill him forced him to escape over the city wall by night in a basket (23-25). Saul then returned to Jerusalem, where he gained the confidence of the frightened disciples through the help of Barnabas and argued boldly with the Hellenistic Jews until they also attempted to kill him and he had to flee to Tarsus (26-30). In a second summary statement, Luke draws attention to the significant transition that Saul's conversion marks into a new period in the history of the early church, during which it initially enjoyed peace and was strengthened (31).

As well as temporary relief from persecution, the historical period inaugurated by Saul's conversion also witnessed the beginning of the Gospel's extension beyond all ethnic boundaries to include full-fledged Gentiles, although Saul was not the first to break the cultural barrier (9:32–12:24). The stage for the opening up of the Gospel to the Gentiles is set in Peter's ministry in western Palestine (9:32-43). Peter travelled to Lydda, where he healed Aeneas, who had been bedridden for eight years (32-35). From there, he was called to Joppa by a group of disciples who were grieving the loss of their friend Dorcas, whom they loved greatly for her acts of charity, but Peter raised her back to life (9:36-43).

Peter's stay in Joppa becomes the background for the conversion of the first Gentiles, who were from the household of Cornelius (**10**:1–11:18). Cornelius, a devout Roman centurion who was known for his philanthropy to the Jews, had a vision in which an angel told him to dispatch some messengers to Joppa to call Peter (10:1-8). Meanwhile, the Lord was preparing Peter by a vision in which a large sheet filled with unclean animals was let down from heaven to him (9-16). While Peter was still thinking about what the vision meant, the messengers arrived at the door of the house where he was staying (17-23a). The next day he returned with them to find all of Cornelius' relatives and close friends assembled together waiting to hear his message from God (23b-33). Peter preached the Gospel to them, making clear that God is impartial and extends his forgiveness to anyone who believes (34-43). While Peter was still speaking, the Holy Spirit fell upon his listeners, who began speaking in other languages just as the Jews had done at Pentecost, thus making it impossible for anyone to refuse them the right to water baptism (44-48). When Peter returned to Jerusalem, the Jewish believers took issue with him for eating with uncircumcised Gentiles, but when he explained his vision and the way that the Holy Spirit fell upon Cornelius' household, they acknowledged that God had extended salvation to the Gentiles (**11**:1-18).

Luke now turns from Palestine to pick up another thread of the early church's history in Antioch of Syria, which gave birth to a large Gentile church (19-30). Luke's history of the beginnings of the church in Antioch revolves around two of its leaders: Barnabas and Saul (19-26). The church got off to a good start when some

Hellenistic Jews who were scattered by the persecution following Stephen's martyrdom[2] began speaking to the Greeks at Antioch, and it grew considerably larger under the encouragement of Barnabas, who was sent from Jerusalem to assist this new venture (19-24). Barnabas, in turn, sought out Saul, who helped bring the church to Christian maturity by his teaching ministry (25-26). One way that the church demonstrated its maturity was in reaching out beyond itself to the famine stricken believers in Judea by sending a gift at the hands of Barnabas and Saul (27-30).

Luke lets his narrative line follow Barnabas and Saul to Jerusalem so that he can report King Herod's persecution of the apostles (**12**:1-23) before he returns to mention other important developments in Antioch. Herod had James, the brother of John, executed with a sword, and he imprisoned Peter as well (1-5). But Peter was miraculously released (6-19). During the night while Peter was sleeping between two guards, an angel entered his cell, threw off his chains, and led him past the sentries and through the iron gate into the city (6-10). After the angel left, Peter realized that he was not dreaming, so he walked to the house of Mary, John Mark's mother, and knocked at the gate, but those who had gathered inside to pray for his release would not believe that it was Peter until his persistent knocking finally persuaded them to look (11-19). When Herod awoke the next morning, he was greatly disconcerted at Peter's disappearance and ordered the guards to be executed (18-19).

To this incident, Luke appends a brief record of the untimely death of Herod, who was suddenly struck dead with an intestinal disorder and eaten by worms because he arrogated to himself the glory due to God (20-23). In contrast with Herod's demise and as a fitting summary to the opening of the Gospel to the Gentiles, Luke states that the word continued to grow and be multiplied (24).

Now that the Jerusalem church officially endorsed the conversion of Gentiles, the foundation was laid for the Gospel's next phase of expansion throughout Asia Minor and into Europe (12:25–28:31). This outward movement of the Gospel to the whole

---

2. Cf. Acts 8:4.

The Death of Herod Agrippa

Agrippa came to...Caesarea... Here he celebrated spectacles in honour of Caesar.... Clad in a garment woven completely of silver...he entered into the theatre at daybreak. There the silver, illumined by...the first rays of the sun, was wondrously radiant and by its glitter inspired fear and awe in those who gazed intently upon it. Straightway his flatterers raised their voices...addressing him as a god.... The king did not rebuke them nor did he reject their flattery as impious. But shortly thereafter he looked up and saw an owl perched on a rope over his head. At once, recognizing this as a harbinger of woes..., he felt a stab of pain in his heart. He was also gripped in his stomach by an ache...that was intense.... Leaping up he said to his friends: 'I, a god in your eyes, am now bidden to lay down my life, for fate brings immediate refutation of the lying words lately addressed to me....' They hastened, therefore, to convey him to the palace.... Exhausted after five straight days by the pain...he departed this life....

(Josephus, *Antiquities* 19.8.2 [343-350], trans. Louis H. Feldman, Loeb Classical Library [Cambridge: Harvard University Press, 1969], 9:377-381).

---

world begins in earnest with the first missionary journey of Paul, on which he was accompanied by Barnabas into Asia Minor (12:25–14:28). To begin at the starting point of the journey, Luke returns his readers to the church in Syrian Antioch (12:25–13:3), which he had momentarily left behind[3] to record important events in Jerusalem. He neatly accomplishes this move by following back Barnabas and Saul, who returned with John Mark after they had delivered the offering for famine relief (12:25). Under the Holy Spirit's direction, the church at Antioch commissioned Barnabas and Saul to do the missionary work for which they had been called (**13**:1-3).

On the first leg of their journey, they passed through the island of Cyprus, where the proconsul, Sergius Paulus, came to faith after Saul, who was also known as Paul, brought a curse of temporary blindness upon a magician who was trying to dissuade the proconsul

---

3 Cf. Acts 11:19-30.

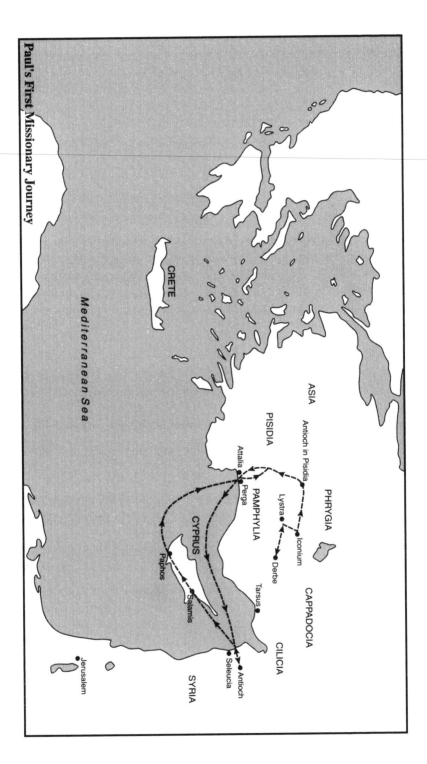

Paul's First Missionary Journey

Mediterranean Sea

CRETE

ASIA

PISIDIA

PHRYGIA

Antioch in Pisidia

Attalia
Perga
PAMPHYLIA

Lystra

Iconium

Derbe

CYPRUS

Paphos

Salamis

Tarsus

CAPPADOCIA

CILICIA

Antioch
Seleucia

SYRIA

Jerusalem

A Light to the Gentiles

Many years before Christ's birth, Isaiah predicted that the Servant of YHWH would carry the Gospel to the Gentiles:

It is too small a thing that you should be My Servant
To raise up the tribes of Jacob, and to restore the preserved ones of Israel;
I will also make You a light of the nations
So that My salvation may reach to the end of the earth (Isa 49:6, NASB).

Isaiah's prophecy is picked up at several places in the New Testament. When Simeon held the baby Jesus in his arms, he declared that this child would be 'a light of revelation to the Gentiles' (Luke 2:32). Paul was commissioned on the Damascus road to bear Christ's name 'before the Gentiles' (Acts 9:15). When Paul and Barnabas turned from the unbelieving Jews in Pisidian Antioch to preach to the Gentiles, they grounded their action on this prophecy (Acts 13:47). Paul again alluded to Christ's fulfillment of this prophecy through him when he had to defend his ministry, both before the angry mob at the temple and before King Agrippa (Acts 22:21; 26:17-18).

from believing (4-12). Their next major stop was Antioch in the province of Pisidia; here Paul and Barnabas faced a strategic turning point in spreading the Gospel to Gentiles (13-52). They arrived in Pisidian Antioch after having sailed north to the province of Pamphylia and trekking overland, although John Mark dropped out along the way (13-15). Luke records the essence of the sermon that Paul preached in the synagogue on the Sabbath following their arrival (16-41). He began by reviewing Israel's redemptive history from the exodus to the baptism of John (16-25); then he applied Jesus' atoning death and resurrection to his listeners' need of forgiveness (26-41). Many of the people, especially the God-fearers and proselytes, were interested in what Paul had to say and begged him to speak to them again (42-43). When a large crowd assembled on the next Sabbath, the Jews became so disruptive that Paul and Barnabas decided to give up on them and turn to the Gentiles, much to the delight of the Gentiles and the indignation of the Jews, who drove them out of their district (44-52).

From Antioch, Paul and Barnabas toured through Iconium, Lystra and Derbe (**14**:1-20). Some people at Iconium believed, but the Jews stirred up trouble and the missionaries had to flee for their lives (1-7). At Lystra the crowds attempted to worship Barnabas and Paul, whom they mistakenly identified as the gods Zeus and Hermes because Paul had healed a man who was lame from birth (8-18). But the mood quickly changed. Irate Jews who had pursued Paul from Antioch and Iconium won over the crowd and stoned Paul until they thought he was dead, but he got up and escaped to Derbe the next day (19-20). After making many disciples in Derbe, Paul and Barnabas returned to their home church in Syrian Antioch, retracing their steps through the cities where they had so recently been persecuted (21-28).

Following Paul's first missionary journey, the first church council was convened in Jerusalem (**15**:1-35). It was called at the request of the church in Syrian Antioch to resolve the heated question of whether the Mosaic law should be imposed upon Gentile converts (1-5). After much debate, Peter stood up and argued that God's bestowal of the Holy Spirit upon Cornelius' household on the basis of faith without making any distinction of race, proved that salvation was by grace for both Jew and Gentile; therefore, they should not place a legalistic burden, which they themselves had been unable to bear, upon the Gentiles (6-11). Paul and Barnabas added to Peter's speech by relating some of the signs and wonders God had performed through them among the Gentiles (12). James summarized the discussion and made a recommendation that they not trouble the Gentiles but write them a letter setting out four minimal expectations: that they abstain from things contaminated by idols, from fornication, from meat that had been strangled, and from blood (13-21). The church agreed to draft James' recommendation into a letter, which Luke records for us, and send it to the church at Antioch with Paul and Barnabas, and two men chosen from their own congregation, Judas and Silas (22-29). The believers at Antioch rejoiced when they read the letter, and Paul and Barnabas spent some time there teaching and preaching (30-35).

From Antioch, Paul set out with Silas, and was later joined by

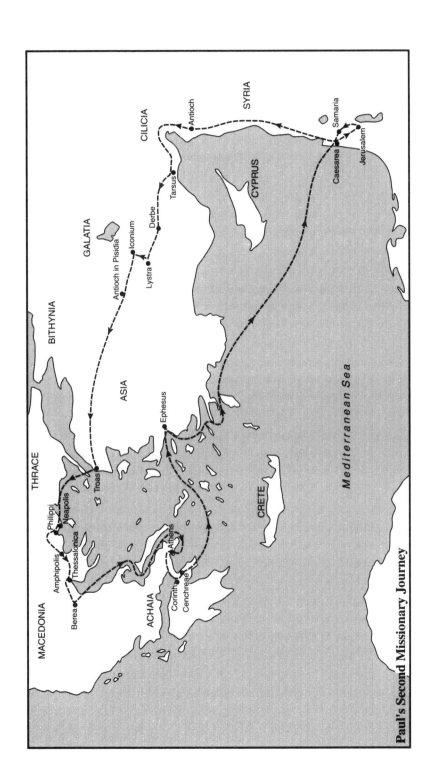

Paul's Second Missionary Journey

Timothy, on his second missionary journey, which took them as far as Macedonia and Achaia (15:36–18:22). The most significant ministry on this missionary journey did not occur until after they had travelled across Asia Minor, but some important developments which they had not planned took place along the way (15:36–16:10). Originally, Paul and Barnabas had planned to revisit the cities where they had preached on their first journey, but they had such a sharp disagreement over whether or not they should take along John Mark that they split and went their separate ways (15:36-41). As Paul and Silas were passing through Derbe and Lystra delivering the decrees of the Jerusalem church council, they met a highly-regarded young disciple from Lystra named Timothy, whom they decided to take along with them (**16**:1-4). Luke summarizes the time from the beginning of the first missionary journey to the delivering of the council's decrees, which are associated here with the first journey in a logical rather than a geographical sense, as a period during which 'the churches were being strengthened in the faith and increasing in numbers daily' (5).

Paul and his companions hurriedly passed through the Phrygian region of Galatia and refrained from travelling northeast into Bithynia from Mysia because the Holy Spirit was strategically impelling them westward into Europe through the port city of Troas, where Paul saw a vision of a man calling him to come over to Macedonia and help them (6-10). Beginning with the Macedonian vision, Luke makes a subtle shift in pronouns from the third to the first person plural, from which the reader is to infer that Luke accompanied Paul for the duration of the 'we' section (10-17) until he returns to the third person at Philippi.

The evangelism of Macedonia (16:11–17:15) began at the important Roman colony of Philippi (16:11-40). Paul and his companions arrived there by sailing to the island of Samothrace and then on to Neapolis, the seaport of Philippi (11-12). On the Sabbath, they found a place of prayer by the river, where Lydia, a God-fearing business-woman who sold purple fabrics, was converted along with her household (13-15). Luke also shows the grace of God at work at the opposite end of the social spectrum in the conversion of a demon-possessed slave-girl who was earning

---

'We' Sections in Acts

At several places in the Book of Acts, the narrative switches from the third person plural 'they' to the first person plural 'we'. The simplest explanation for this change of person is that Luke accompanied Paul during the 'we' sections and relied upon the reports of other people for the rest of Acts. The first 'we' section covers 16:10-17, which begins with Paul's response to the vision of the man from Macedonian asking for help and ends with the encounter with the demon-possessed slave-girl at Philippi. The second 'we' section picks up somewhere in Macedonia as Paul is *en route* to Jerusalem to deliver the offering for the poor and it ends when Paul arrives in Jerusalem (20:5–21:18). The final 'we' section covers Paul's journey to Rome (27:1–28:16).

From the association of the first two 'we' sections with Macedonia in general and Philippi in particular, some scholars have suggested that Luke might be the man from Macedonia in Paul's vision. Philippi could have been Luke's hometown, which would explain Luke's dropping out at this point and reconnecting with Paul there again later. While Paul was in prison at Caesarea, Luke could have remained in Palestine gathering material for his Gospel from written sources and eyewitnesses who were still living.

---

a sizeable profit for her masters by fortune-telling until Paul exorcised her evil spirit (16-18). Her masters, who saw their source of income lost, dragged Paul and Silas before the chief magistrates and had them thrown into prison (19-24). At midnight, a great earthquake broke the prison doors open, releasing the prisoners; the jailer, who was undoubtedly impressed by a combination of providential circumstances and the character of Paul and Silas, readily accepted their offer of salvation in Jesus Christ, making him and his household the third trophy of God's saving grace at Philippi (25-34). The chief magistrates, upon realizing the next day that Paul and Silas were Roman citizens, publicly apologized for their injustice in punishing them without a trial and sent them away as quickly as possible (35-40).

After travelling through Amphipolis and Apollonia, they came to Thessalonica (**17**:1-9), where Paul reasoned with the Jews in the synagogue for three Sabbaths. A few of them were persuaded, but a very large number of God-fearing Greeks along with some prominent women accepted the Gospel (1-4). The Jews, who were jealous of the following Paul and Silas had gained, incited the riff-raff from the marketplace to riot, but failing to find the missionaries at home, they dragged Jason, their host, before the city authorities (5-9).

As a result of the unrest, Paul and Silas were forced to move on to Berea (10-15). The members of the Berean synagogue, whom Luke commends for their noble-mindedness, eagerly investigated the Scriptures to see if what they were being taught was true; and consequently, many of them came to believe (10-12). The Jews from Thessalonica, however, came down to Berea and agitated the crowds so that the believers sent Paul away for his own safety, while Silas and Timothy remained behind (13-15).

Thus the evangelistic thrust of the second missionary journey

---

Pagan Quotations in Paul's Sermon at the Areopagus

Paul's sermon at the Areopagus contains two references to pagan poets. The first one is from the Ctretan poet Epimenides, whom Paul also quotes in Titus 1:12:

They fashioned a tomb for thee, O holy and high one—
The Cretans, always liars, evil beasts, idle bellies! (Tit 1:12)
But thou art not dead; thou livest and abidest for ever;
For in thee we live and move and have our being (Acts 17:28).

The second quotation is from the *Natural Phenomena* of Aratus, a Cilician poet:

Let us begin with Zeus:
Never, O men, let us leave him unmentioned.
Full of Zeus are all the ways and all the meeting-places of men;
The sea and the harbours are full of him.
It us with Zeus that every one of us in every way has to do,
For we are also his offspring (Acts 17:28) (As cited by F. F. Bruce, *Paul: Apostle of the Heart Set Free* [Grand Rapids: Wm. B. Eerdmans Pub. Co., 1983], 242.)

**The Decree of Claudius Expelling
the Jews from Rome (A.D. 49)**

'Since the Jews constantly made disturbances at the instigation of Chrestus, [Claudius] expelled them from Rome.'

Chrestus is probably a Latin misspelling for Christos, the Greek name for Christ. The disturbances mentioned were probably disagreements between orthodox Jews and Jews who had converted to Christianity. This decree forced Aquila and Priscilla to leave Rome (Acts 18:2), but by the time that Paul wrote his Epistle to the Romans they had returned (Rom 16:3-5). Claudius' decree may also form the background for the former persecution that the readers of Hebrews had endured (Heb 10:32-35).

(Suetonius, *Twelve Caesars, Claudius*, 25.4, trans. J. C. Rolfe, Loeb Classical Library [Cambridge: Harvard University Press, 1979], 2:53).

---

was carried over into the province of Achaia (17:16–18:17) beginning at Athens, the ancient seat of Greek philosophy and culture (17:16-34). While Paul was waiting at Athens for his friends to join him, he became provoked at seeing the city full of idols so he began reasoning in the synagogue with the Jews and in the market-place with some Epicurean and Stoic philosophers, who asked him to address an assembly at the Areopagus (16-21). Using an idol he had seen to a unknown god as a point of contact, Paul began to explain that the God who had made heaven and earth was offering them an opportunity to repent before judging the world through a man whom he had raised from the dead (22-31). At the talk of the resurrection, some of them began to sneer, but others were interested in hearing more, and a few believed (32-34).

From Athens, Paul continued south to Corinth (**18**:1-17). Upon arriving there, he worked at tent-making during the week along with Aquila and Priscilla, a Jewish couple who had been expelled from Rome by Claudius' decree; and on the Sabbaths he reasoned in the synagogue (1-4). When Silas and Timothy rejoined him, Paul devoted himself completely to teaching, first in the synagogue

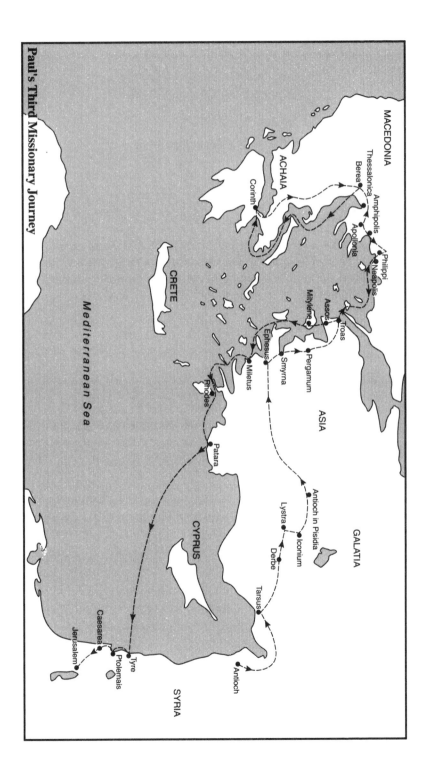

Paul's Third Missionary Journey

MACEDONIA

ACHAIA

Thessalonica
Berea
Amphipolis
Apollonia
Philippi
Neapolis

Corinth

CRETE

Mediterranean Sea

Mitylene
Assos
Troas

Ephesus
Miletus
Smyrna
Pergamum

Rhodes

ASIA

Patara

Antioch in Pisidia
Lystra
Iconium
Derbe

GALATIA

CYPRUS

Tarsus

Caesarea
Jerusalem
Ptolemais
Tyre

Antioch

SYRIA

until the Jews rejected his message, and then in the house of a God-fearer next door to the synagogue, where he taught for a year and a half (5-11). The embittered Jews arraigned Paul before Gallio, the proconsul of Achaia, but he was not interested in becoming involved in religious debates and threw the case out of court (12-17).

After remaining in Corinth for some time longer, Paul returned to the church in Syrian Antioch, from which his journey had originated (18-22). On the way, he made a brief stopover at Ephesus, promising to return later (18-21). After landing on the coast of Palestine at Caesarea, he went to visit the church at Jerusalem and then continued on to Antioch (22).

On his third missionary journey, Paul fulfilled his promise to the Ephesians by spending most of his time with them, but he also made a hurried visit of the churches in Macedonia and Greece before returning to Palestine (18:23–21:16). Before Luke becomes involved in the actual details of Paul's ministry at Ephesus, he briefly describes its setting (18:23-28). In just one verse, he passes over Paul's trip through the Galatian region and Phrygia (23); but then he takes some time to describe the teaching ministry of Apollos at Ephesus prior to Paul's arrival there because Apollos' limited knowledge about Jesus, which at first only extended up to John's baptism, was probably responsible for the strange theological phenomena that Paul encountered at Ephesus among some of John's disciples (24-28).

Paul's lengthy and productive stay in Ephesus began shortly after Apollos had departed for Corinth (**19**:1-41). After Paul related the fulfilment of the prophecies of John the Baptist to some of his disciples who had not even heard about the Holy Spirit, they received the Spirit and spoke in tongues (1-7).

Paul's ministry at Ephesus, which lasted for almost three years, had a great impact upon many people who came in contact with the Gospel (8-19). As a result of his teaching, first in the synagogue and then in the school of Tyrannus, the word of the Lord spread throughout all of Asia Minor (8-10); and as a result of his miraculous works, many sick people were healed and many who practised sorcery burned their magic books (11-19). In another summary statement, Luke reports that the word was growing mightily and prevailing (20). Having gained a sense of completion to his work at Ephesus, Paul began planning for a future journey to Rome, but first he determined to bring his third journey to a close by travelling through Macedonia and Achaia before going to Jerusalem (21-22).

By summarizing the effects of the Ephesian ministry and disclosing the apostle's travel plans before mentioning the riot that broke out under the instigation of the Ephesian silversmiths (23-41), Luke leaves the impression that rather than the riot being the reason for Paul's leaving, the great inroads that the Gospel was making was the reason for the riot. Upon observing the declining fortunes of the idol manufacturing business at Ephesus, a silversmith named Demetrius stirred up other craftsmen in related trades to riot against Paul (23-27). The mob dragged two of Paul's travelling companions, Gaius and Aristarchus, into the theatre and chanted for about two hours, 'Great is Artemis of the Ephesians,' while the disciples and some of his friends from among the leaders of the province desperately urged Paul not to venture into the theatre (28-34). Finally, the town clerk managed to subdue the mob by reassuring them that Artemis, the city's patron goddess, was in no great danger and at the same time scolding them for their unruly behavior, advising them instead to take their case to the provincial court (35-41).

Paul's return trip to Jerusalem (**20**:1–21:16) took a long loop through Macedonia and Greece, probably because Paul and the representatives of the various churches that Luke mentions were collecting an offering for the poor in Jerusalem (20:1-6). Luke picks up his 'we' section again at Philippi (20:5–21:18), implying that he rejoined the apostle at the same city where he left him earlier.[4] When Luke and Paul caught up with their other travelling companions at Troas, Paul preached such a long message that a drowsy young man named Eutychus fell out of the third floor window where he was sitting and had to be restored back to life (20:7-12). Because Paul was in a hurry to reach Jerusalem in time for Pentecost, he decided to embark upon a ship that sailed past

---

4. Acts 16:17.

Ephesus to Miletus and bid farewell to the Ephesian elders from there (13-38). Luke records a detailed itinerary of the ship along the coast to Miletus (13-16). When the ship had docked at Miletus, Paul called for the elders to come to him overland and, upon their arrival, delivered an emotional farewell address (17-35). He began by recounting how he had faithfully and humbly taught the Ephesians all that was profitable for them, even though the Jews had plotted against him (17-21). He informed the elders that he felt constrained to go to Jerusalem although he expected to be imprisoned there (22-24), and he warned them to be on their guard because false teachers would come in among them, seeking to destroy the flock (25-31). Finally, he committed them to God's grace (32-35). After a tearful farewell, they accompanied him to the ship (36-38).

After sailing down the coast of Asia Minor, they boarded another ship bound for Tyre, where Paul received another prophetic warning not to set foot in Jerusalem (**21**:1-6). When the ship had discharged its cargo, they continued down the coast to Ptolemais and Caesarea (7-14). While they were staying at the home of Philip the evangelist (7-9), a prophet named Agabus predicted that Paul would be bound at Jerusalem and delivered over to the Gentiles, but Paul, who was not concerned for his own safety, could not be dissuaded (10-14). Having accepted Paul's determination as the Lord's will, the group continued the last miles overland to Jerusalem (15-16).

Their arrival in Jerusalem set in motion a chain of events that providentially led Paul to Rome by an indirect route that he had not planned (21:17–28:31). Before he reached Rome, he was arrested in Jerusalem, as the Spirit had repeatedly warned (21:17–23:11). Without judging the inherent rightness or wrongness of Paul's action, Luke implies in retrospect that the ultimate human cause for the lengthy delay and circuitous route by which the apostle eventually came to Rome may be traced back to his meeting with the elders of the Jerusalem church (21:17-26). Luke also implies that he left Paul after their meeting with the elders at Jerusalem, because at this point the 'we' section stops.[5] Paul reported to them many of the wonderful things God had done through his ministry

---

5. Acts 21:18.

to the Gentiles (17-19). Although they were delighted by his report, the elders were deeply concerned about the perception among myriads of zealous Jews that he was teaching Jews in Gentile lands to abandon circumcision and the Mosaic Law, so they suggested that he pacify them by personally joining in the purification rites for four men who had taken a vow (20-25). Paul did as they had instructed and went up to the temple to give notice of the days of purification (26).

On a subsequent visit to the temple, a riot broke out (27-36). Some Jews from Asia Minor mistakenly supposed that Paul had brought Trophimus, one of his Gentile friends from Ephesus, into the temple, so they seized Paul in outrage and dragged him outside the sacred precincts (27-30). When news of the uproar reached the Roman commander, he immediately rushed down with his soldiers and rescued Paul before the Jews beat him to death (31-36). Not being able to determine the reason for the uproar, he granted Paul's plea for a hearing before the crowd (37-40).

Standing on the stairs, Paul made his defence to the crowd in the Hebrew language (**22**:1-21). He recounted how he had been so zealous for Judaism that he persecuted followers of Christ to death (1-5) until one day as he was travelling to Damascus to persecute more Christians, the risen Jesus encountered him in a blinding light and an audible voice (6-11). Later he received a visit from a devout Jew named Ananias, who restored his sight and made known God's purposes to him (12-16). Paul went on to explain that when he returned to Jerusalem, the Lord warned him in a vision that his testimony would not be accepted there and commanded him to leave the city and go far away to the Gentiles (17-21). As soon as Paul mentioned the Gentiles, the crowd became violent again and kept calling out for his death until the commander had to remove him and carry out his own interrogation (22-29).

Wanting to get to the bottom of the disturbance, the commander ordered Paul to appear before the Sanhedrin (22:30–**23**:10). The hearing got off to a poor start with a head-on confrontation between Paul and the high priest (22:30–23:5), but Paul succeeded in splitting the opposing parties of the Sadducees and Pharisees over the issue of the resurrection (23:6-9). Such a heated dispute broke out between them that the commander had to remove Paul again (10). That night the Lord appeared to Paul and reassured him that he would witness for him at Rome (11).

Before he got to Rome, however, Paul had to undergo an extended imprisonment at Caesarea (23:12–26:32) as the result of a plot by the Jews against his life (23:12-15). Paul's nephew, who had learned of their plot to ambush Paul on his way to appear before the Sanhedrin, disclosed this information to the commander (16-22), and he immediately transferred Paul to Caesarea (23-35). That night he dispatched a large convoy of soldiers and horses to accompany Paul (23-24) along with a letter of introduction to Felix, the governor (25-30). When the convoy, minus the foot soldiers, who were no longer needed, arrived in Caesarea, the governor promised to hear the case after Paul's accusers also arrived (31-35).

Five days later the high priest came with a lawyer named Tertullus, and Paul went on trial before Felix (**24**:1-27). Tertullus accused Paul of stirring up dissention throughout the world and trying to desecrate the temple (**24**:1-9). Paul, who spoke in his own defence, admitted that he believed in the resurrection, but denied that any of the charges against him were true (10-21). Felix decided to postpone the trial until the commander arrived and permitted Paul considerable freedom while he remained in custody (22-23). In fact, Felix, who was hoping to receive a bribe, prolonged Paul's detention for two years until he left office (24-27).

When the new governor, Festus, assumed office, Paul's case came up for a retrial (25:1–26:32). The Sanhedrin wanted Paul to be tried in Jerusalem (25:1-5); but when Festus asked him if he was willing to stand on trial at Jerusalem, Paul exercised his right of appeal to Caesar's tribunal (6-12). When King Agrippa came to pay his respects to the new governor, Festus consulted with him about Paul's case (13-22). Agrippa wanted to hear Paul himself, and Festus did not know what to write to Caesar so he arranged a hearing for the next day (25:23–26:32). Festus opened the hearing by briefing Agrippa on the details of the case thus far (23-27). Paul then made his defence to Agrippa (**26**:1-23). He argued that formerly he lived according to the strictest sect of Judaism and did everything possible to persecute the followers of Jesus (1-11), but

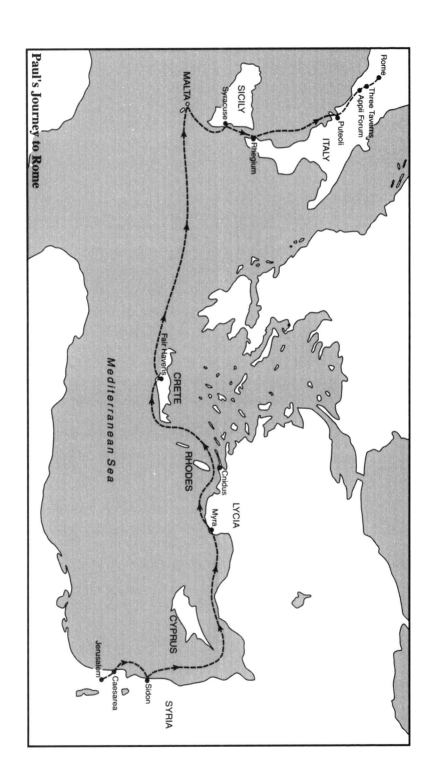

Paul's Journey to Rome

while he was on his way to Damascus, he saw a brilliant light and heard a voice commissioning him to preach to the Gentiles (12-18). Because he had been faithful to this divine calling in proclaiming the gospel on the grounds of Jesus' resurrection, the Jews sought to kill him (19-23). Paul then turned from defending himself to witness personally to Agrippa, who was not ready to be persuaded so quickly (24-29). Drawing those around him aside, Agrippa admitted that Paul was innocent and advised that he could have been set free if he had not appealed to Caesar (30-32).

Agrippa's ruling that Paul's appeal must be heard by Caesar now at last launched the apostle on his long-awaited voyage to Rome (**27**:1–28:31). From the commencement of a third 'we' section at this point (27:1–28:16), we may assume that Luke travelled with him to Rome. The voyage, however, was imperilled by a violent storm at sea (1-44). Although the winds were contrary from almost the outset, they managed to sail under the shelter of land most of the way; but they experienced great difficulty in rounding the south coast of Crete, which offered less protection, so they put in at Fair Havens (**27**:1-8). As it was already late in the shipping season, Paul warned of impending danger if they continued, but because the port was not suitable for wintering, the centurion sided with the advice of the pilot and ship-owner to continue up the coast to Phoenix (9-12). When a moderate south wind came up, they seized the opportunity and weighed anchor, but the breeze suddenly changed to a violent northeast gale that drove them helplessly out to sea for days, without sight of sun or stars to give them bearings (13-20). Paul encouraged the crew, who were despairing of life and had not eaten for days, by announcing that an angel had appeared to him in the night assuring him that he had to stand before Caesar and that God had granted him the lives of all his fellow passengers (21-26). On the fourteenth night, the sailors determined that they were approaching land and feared that the ship would run aground on rocks in the dark (27-32). As day was dawning, those on board finally heeded Paul's encouragement to take some food so that they would have sufficient strength to reach the shore alive (33-38). In the morning light, they observed a beach where they decided to run the ship aground, but it struck a sandbar and was broken up by the pounding of the waves, forcing everyone to reach land by swimming or clinging to pieces of the wreckage (39-44).

Only after they had all landed safely, did they learn that the island where they would have to stay the winter was called Malta (**28**:1-10). The natives, who were exceptionally hospitable and built a fire to dry them out, concluded that Paul was a god when he did not die from the bite of a viper that had crawled out of the firewood (1-6). In gratitude for Paul's healing of the leading man's father and others who were sick, the islanders provided their guests with necessary supplies to set out again (7-10).

Three months later, the travellers resumed their voyage to Rome on an Alexandrian ship that had wintered at the island (11-16). Luke lists their itinerary for the trip, which briefly stopped over on Sicily, and proceeded up the west coast of Italy to the main port of Puteoli, and then followed the Appian Way through the Forum of Appius and Three Taverns, where they were met by some believers from Rome (11-15). When they entered the city, Paul was allowed to stay by himself, with a soldier guarding him (16). At this point the 'we' section ends, but Luke probably remained in the area long enough to learn the information with which his history concludes.

While in Rome, Paul had opportunity to proclaim the Gospel (17-29). Initially, the Jews, who had heard negative reports about the Christian sect but knew nothing about Paul personally, were open to hear his views (17-22). On the date they had scheduled, Paul spent all day reasoning with them from the Scriptures concerning Jesus, but the majority rejected, so he announced that the gospel was turning to the Gentiles (23-29). Luke concludes his history at the heart of the Roman empire with a triumphant summary that leaves Paul openly preaching the Gospel to all who visited him at his own rented quarters over the next two years without any hinderance (30-31).

OUTLINE OF THE BOOK OF ACTS

Correlations of the Pauline Epistles with the Book of Acts

Epistle	Reference in Acts	Missionary Journey	Place of Worship	Clue	Date
Missionary Epistles					**Written before the close of Acts**
Galatians	13:14–14:23	1st	Syrian Antioch	S. Galatia before council	AD 49
	16:1-6	2nd	Macedonia?	(N. Galatia after council)	(AD 57)
	18, 23	3rd			
1 Thess.	17:1-15	2nd	Corinth	1 Thess 3:5-6 with Acts 18:5	AD 51
2 Thess.	17:1-15		Corinth		AD 51
1 Corinthians	18:1-18	2nd	Ephesus	(1 Cor 16:8, 9)	AD 55 or 54
2 Corinthians	18:1-18 20:2-3	2nd 3rd	Macedonia	(2 Cor 7:5-6, 13; 8:1	AD 56 or 55
Romans	28:16-31 (later than the epistle)	Rome	Corinth	(Rom 15:25-27; 16:1)	AD 57 or 56
Prison Epistles					**Probably written at the end of Acts**
Colossians	19:10; cf. Col 2:1	(2nd)	Rome	Col 4:3, 18; 4:7-8 with Eph 6:21-22	AD 60 to 61
Philemon	(see Col)	(2nd)	Rome	Phile 1, 10-12, 13, 22-24 with Col 4:8-9	AD 60 to 61
Ephesians	18:19-21	2nd	Rome	Eph 3:1; 4:1; 6:20	AD 60 to 61
	18:24–20:1	3rd			
	20:15–21:1	3rd			
Philippians	16:12-40	(2nd)	Rome	Phil 1:7, 12-14, 17, 19; 2:17; 4:22	AD 60 to 61
Pastoral Epistles					**Written after the close of Acts**
1 Timothy	(see Ephesians for earlier background)		Macedonia	1 Timothy 1:3; 3:14; went to Macedonia from Ephesus	AD 63-66
Titus	(27:7-13, 21; brief stopover)	Voyage to Rome	Macedonia?	Titus 3:12 headed for Nicopolis	AD 63-66
2 Timothy	(see Ephesians for background)		Rome	(2 Timothy 4:6, 16, 21)	AD 65-67

The Pauline Epistles

The Typical Literary Structure of Paul's Epistles

Introduction

     A.   A to B, greetings
               E.g., Paul, an apostle (or bond-servant) of Christ Jesus, to X (at Y), grace to you and peace from God our Father and our Lord Jesus Christ.
     B.   Thanksgiving for the spiritual status of his readers
     C.   Prayer for the spiritual health of his readers
     D.   Reference to his personal circumstances (sometimes scattered throughout the epistle)

Body of the letter
     A.   Doctrinal exposition
     B.   Practical application

Conclusion
     A.   Concluding exhortations
     B.   Travel Plans
     C.   Final greetings
           1.   To the readers
           2.   From his associates
     D.   Benediction

The Missionary
Epistles

A Biographical Sketch of the Apostle Paul

Paul, formerly known as Saul, was born in Tarsus, the capital of Cilicia (Acts 21:39; 22:3). Both of his parents were Jews (Phil 3:5; Rom 11:1), and at least his father must have had the privilege of Roman citizenship because Paul was born a citizen (Acts 22:28).

Tarsus was a Greek university city, which may account for Paul's fluency in the Greek language, but at some point early in his life, he moved to Jerusalem, where he was educated under Gamaliel, the leading Rabbi of the day (Acts 22:3; cf. 5:34). Paul was very zealous for the Mosaic Law and adhered strictly to the rigorous legalistic standards of the Pharisees (Phil 3:4-6; Gal 1:14). Although Paul became conversant with Greek thought, his philosophical outlook, even in his later life, remained true to its Hebrew origins.

We know little of Paul's family, other than that he had a sister and a nephew who lived in, or near, Jerusalem (Acts 23:16). At the time of his missionary travels, Paul was single (1 Cor 9:5), but since marriage was the normal expectation of Jewish Rabbis there is a good possibility that he had been widowed earlier, or perhaps, his wife may have left him when he became a Christian (cf. Phil 3:8; 1 Cor 7:15).

Even before his conversion, Paul was an intensely zealous man who acted upon his convictions, and a gifted leader who was rapidly advancing up the hierarchical ladder of the Jewish religious establishment (Gal 1:13). He was on his way to Damascus with letters from the high priest endorsing him to persecute the Christians when he encountered the risen Jesus through a blinding light (Acts 9:1-9). This dramatic experience completely transformed him from being a persecutor of the church to become its greatest apostle (1 Cor 15:8, 9; 1 Tim 1:12-13), and he looked back on it as his claim to apostleship (1 Cor 9:1).

Paul was a natural genius who possessed a rare combination of diverse gifts and abilities. His brilliant mind held a firm grasp of his own first century world, and he could insightfully analyze its problems and possibilities without ever losing the discernment necessary to separate the trivial from the important, or the cultural trappings from universal principles. But unlike most intellectuals, he also had the ability to transform abstract thought into practical action with the hard-nosed determination and rigorous physical discipline of a military strategist; yet all the while he maintained a genuine, warm-hearted, prayerful and personal concern for the people to whom he ministered.

Galatians

OVERVIEW OF GALATIANS

Theme: A Defense of Christian Liberty

Key verse: Galatians 5:1, 'It was for freedom that Christ set us free; therefore, keep standing firm and do not be subject again to a yoke of slavery' (NASB).

HISTORICAL BACKGROUND

Galatians is one of the undisputed Pauline epistles. Paul wrote this polemical defense of justification by faith in the heat of his battle with legalistic Judaizers who were attempting to impose the Mosaic Law on Gentile converts.

There are two major theories about the background of Galatians. The first view holds that the epistle was written to unknown churches in North Galatia that were composed of ethnic Galatians. The second one contends that it was sent to churches in South Galatia such as Pisidian Antioch, Iconium, Lystra, and Derbe. In this case the recipients would have been part of the Roman province of Galatia but would not have been ethnic Galatians. At one time the North Galatian view was predominant, and it still has serious defenders, but scholarly opinion has shifted in favour of the South Galatian view.

According to the North Galatian view, Paul's first and second visits to Galatia correspond to Acts 16:6 and 18:23 respectively, and the apostle's visit to Jerusalem mentioned in Gal 2:10 corresponds to the Jerusalem church council of Acts 15. If this were the case, the epistle would necessarily have to have been written after the Jerusalem church council, and probably after Acts 18:23, which would place it around A.D. 57. On this view Macedonia, Ephesus, and Corinth could all be possible places of writing.

The South Galatian view equates Paul's first visit to Galatia with Acts 13:14—14:24 and the visit to Jerusalem in Gal 2:1-10 with Acts 11:27-30. The epistle, then, would have been written before the Jerusalem church council of Acts 15, making it the earliest of Paul's epistles at A.D. 49. The place of writing would be Syrian Antioch. The presence of known churches in Southern Galatia, as opposed to the lack of any evidence that Paul ever visited Northern Galatia, and the absence of any appeal to the Jerusalem church council, even though it settled the very issue that Galatians addresses, both argue strongly for the South Galatian view.

Paul's Style of Writing

In writing to the churches that he had visited, Paul adopted the common literary form of his day. His epistles are similar in form to other letters of that period, but they reflect his own personal style of writing. Undoubtedly, he gave some thought to what he wanted to say, but his epistles often bear more resemblance to spontaneous writing than to polished literature. He usually has a general structure in mind, but he is so full of ideas that thoughts tumble out one after another. Often he leaves one idea to pursue another and forgets to come back to the first. F. F. Bruce describes the apostle's style very well:

'Something of Paul's native impetuousness is apparent in his epistolary style. His letters were regularly dictated to an assistant. At times the torrent of his thought rushes forward so swiftly that it outstrips the flow of his words, and his words have to leap over a gap now and then to catch up on his thought. How the scribe managed to keep up with his words we can only surmise. Time and again Paul starts a sentence that never reaches a grammatical end, for before he is well launched on it a new thought strikes him and he turns aside to deal with that. When he comes back on to the main track, the original start of the sentence has been forgotten. All this means that Paul is not the smoothest of authors, or the easiest to follow, but it does give us an unmistakable impression of the man himself. He has something worth saying, and in saying it he communicates something of himself; there is nothing artificial or merely conventional about the way he says it' (F. F. Bruce, *Paul: Apostle of the Heart Set Free* [Grand Rapids: Wm. B. Eerdmans Pub. Co., 1983], pp. 456, 457).

THE FLOW OF GALATIANS

The introduction to Galatians (**1**:1-10) begins with a formal greeting (1-5), which, in typical epistolary style, identifies the writer, the Apostle Paul (1-2a), and the readers, the churches of Galatia (2b). It then follows with Paul's customary salutation: 'grace to you and peace' (3-5).

But without pausing to give thanks for his readers, Paul immediately starts in by expressing bewilderment at their spiritual condition (6-10). He cannot understand how the Galatians are so quickly deserting the Gospel (6-7), and he warns that anyone who preaches a gospel contrary to what they received will be condemned without partiality (8-10).

Against this background of defection, Paul makes his defence of the true Gospel, which is one of Christian liberty. In the first main section of the epistle, he presents personal arguments for the authority of his Gospel (1:11–2:21). First, he argues that his Gospel did not depend on human agency (11-24). The fact that he received his Gospel directly from God (11-17) is supported both by his personal claim that it came by revelation (11-12) and by the chronological impossibility of his having been influenced by others. There simply was not sufficient time between his conversion and his withdrawal into Arabia for him to have picked up someone else's theology (13-17). Not only did his Gospel originate independently of human influence, it also developed independently (18-24). Paul argues from his limited contact with the Jerusalem apostles (18-20) and his lack of familiarity with the Judean churches (21-24) that the development of his Gospel could not have depended upon either of those sources.

Second, Paul argues that although his Gospel was not derived from the Jerusalem apostles (especially in regards to its requirements for Gentile converts), it was endorsed by them (**2**:1-10); therefore, it had an even stronger claim to be authoritative. Their endorsement of Paul's Gospel was demonstrated both in their non-insistence upon circumcision for Titus, who was a Gentile (1-5), and their welcoming of Paul into fellowship with the stated purpose that he go to the Gentiles (6-10).

Third, Paul argues that the authority of his Gospel is implicitly witnessed by his integrity over against Peter's duplicity in withdrawing from fellowship with Gentiles (11-14). Paul relates an earlier incident in which Peter stopped eating with Gentiles for fear of the Jews (11-13); because Peter was not acting consistently with his own convictions, Paul rebuked him publicly (14).

Fourth, Paul argues that the truthfulness of his Gospel was exemplified in his own experience (15-21). Even though he was a good, moral Jew, Paul recognized that he needed to be justified by faith (15-16). Having been justified by faith, it would be logically inconsistent to return to keeping the law as a means of attaining righteousness; rather, he had been crucified with Christ and died to the law so that he might lead a new life based on faith (17-21).

In the second main section of the epistle, Paul presents doctrinal arguments for the enjoyment of Christian liberty (3:1–5:1). He begins by arguing from the experience of the Galatians (3:1-5). Since their entrance into the Christian life came through receiving the Spirit by faith, not by works (1-2), it would be logically inconsistent to try to continue in the flesh by works (3-5).

The same principle of faith is evident in the example of Abraham (6-9). According to Genesis 15:6, Abraham was justified on the basis of faith (6), and so Gentiles are blessed along with him on the same basis of faith (7-9).

Paul reaches the same conclusion regarding faith by arguing from the curse of the law (10-14). Everyone who is under the law is under a curse because the law requires total obedience (10). It is not possible to be justified by law because it, being based on works, is incompatible with faith, the principle by which Scripture declares that we are justified (11-12). But Christ redeemed us from the curse of the law so that now blessings might come to the Gentiles by faith (13-14).

We also know that justification cannot come by the law because the promise preceded it chronologically (15-18). If human covenants that have been ratified cannot be changed or set aside unilaterally (15), then the law, which came later than the promise to Abraham's seed, cannot nullify the promise, as would necessarily be the case if the promised inheritance were realized on the basis of law (16-18).

The objection that given Paul's reckoning the law would have no purpose is invalid (19-25). The law served a limited purpose (19-22). It was added as a temporary measure to check sin until the promised seed arrived (19-20), but it was never intended to replace the promise as a means of imparting eternal life (21-22). Furthermore, the law had a preparatory function in holding us in confinement under sin so that it might direct us to faith in Christ as our only way out (23-25).

Building upon the claim of Galatians 3:16 that the promises to Abraham's seed are fulfilled in Christ, Paul argues that all believers are in mystical union with Christ; therefore, they are Abraham's spiritual descendants and heirs of the promises (26-29).

Paul also argues for the enjoyment of Christian liberty from the advantages of sonship (4:1-11). Using an analogy from Greco-Roman culture, in which a slave could be adopted to the full rights of sonship, Paul points to the advantages of being adopted (1-7). In that culture even a naturally born son had to wait until he reached the age of majority, which was predetermined by his father, before he could enjoy all the privileges of sonship and inherit his father's property (1-2). Paul draws out his analogy across the course of history in relation to humanity as a corporate whole: at the point when history had reached its fullness, Christ came to redeem us from slavery so that we might be adopted as God's sons (3-5). Having been adopted, believers now enjoy the benefits of sonship: we have the Spirit; we can call God Father; and we are his heirs (6-7). By contrast, Paul shows the folly of returning to those things by which we had previously been enslaved (8-11).

Next he argues from the contrasting motives of himself and his opponents, who were vying for the religious allegiance of the Galatians (12-20). The Galatians once whole-heartedly accepted the sincerity of Paul in ministering to them (12-16); by contrast, his opponents were deceitfully trying to use the Galatians for their personal advantage (17-18). He uses the metaphor of being in labour with a child to express the renewed earnestness of his parental concern and the intensity of his pain at their spiritual regression (19-20).

Paul highlights the Galatians' choice between legalistic bondage and Christian liberty by drawing some analogies out of the Old Testament incident of Sarah and Hagar (4:21–5:1). He begins by recounting the Old Testament narrative about Abraham's two sons:

one was born of a bondwoman by the flesh; the other was born of a freewoman according to promise (21-23). He then gives an allegorical interpretation (4:24–5:1). The bondwoman, Hagar, corresponds to the covenant given at Mount Sinai and to the present Jerusalem; her children are slaves (24-25). The freewoman, Sarah, corresponds to the heavenly Jerusalem, and her children are free (26-28). As it was then, so it is now: the one born by the flesh persecutes the one born by the Spirit in fulfilment of the promise (29). Since Scripture commanded Abraham to cast out the bondwoman, so, believers, who are children of the freewoman, must keep standing in the freedom that Christ has established and not subject themselves again to slavery (4:30–5:1).

At this point Paul shifts from his theological consideration of Christian liberty to its practical application to life in the Spirit (5:2–6:10). He begins negatively by noting the consequences of legalism (2-12), which may be further broken down into logical implications (2-6) and practical results (7-9). Accepting circumcision as a legal requirement for salvation logically implies that one rejects the benefits of Christ's sacrifice and accepts the obligation to keep the whole law (2-3). It also implies that one is severed from Christ, for justification by legalistic works is mutually incompatible with justification by faith in Christ (4-6). Practically, legalism had already seriously hindered the Galatians' spiritual progress (7-9), and it would also result in the judgment of those who were perpetrating the problem (10-12). Paul balances this negative tone, however, with a positive emphasis on the proper use of freedom in serving one another, rather than perverting freedom into a licence to sin (13-15).

He then sets forth two contrasting ways of life: life in the flesh and life in the Spirit (16-26). Continuously walking in the Spirit would enable the Galatians to live a spiritual life and not carry out the opposing lusts of the flesh (16-18). Paul identifies a fleshly life by a representative list of vices (19-21), and he also identifies a spiritual life by a contrasting description of the fruit of the Spirit (22-24). He concludes the contrast with an exhortation to adopt the attitude of the Spirit rather than that of the flesh (25-26).

Finally, he exhorts the Galatians to work out their spirituality practically in relation to people around them (6:1-10). They should lighten the burdens that others are carrying by bearing them for them (1-5). Special attention should be given to picking up those who have fallen and restoring them in a spirit of gentleness (1-2). At the same time that they were helping others, each one was to pull his own weight with an attitude of humility (3-5).

They should shoulder their responsibility for doing good, which Paul delineates with respect to three principles (6-10). He lays down a principle of material remuneration for those who teach the word (6). In this context, he spells out the principle of sowing and reaping and exhorts the Galatians to sow to the Spirit rather than the flesh (7-8). More generally, he summarizes their responsibilities under a principle of social obligation in doing good to everyone, starting with believers (9-10).

Paul now draws his epistle to a close (11-18). He pens a personal note assuring the Galatians that the letter is authentic (11). He re-emphasizes the contrast he had drawn earlier between the selfish motives of the legalists and his own selfless ones (12-16).[1] The Jewish legalists wanted to impose circumcision on the Galatians so that they might avoid persecution and boost their own egos (12-13), but Paul had no vested interest in the issue. For him externals were unimportant; the only important thing was the cross of Christ, which produces a new creation by our dying to the world (14-16). After one last warning to the troublemakers (17), Paul closes with a short and simple benediction reminding his readers of God's benevolence in doing more for us than we deserve (18).

---

1. Galatians 4:12-20

OUTLINE OF GALATIANS

1 Thessalonians

OVERVIEW OF 1 THESSALONIANS

Theme: The Lord's return as a motivation to progress in faith

Key verses: 1 Thessalonians 3:12-13: 'may the Lord cause you to increase and abound in love for one another, and for all men ... so that He may establish your hearts unblamable in holiness before our God and Father at the coming of our Lord Jesus with all His saints' (NASB).

HISTORICAL BACKGROUND

Scholars generally accept that 1 Thessalonians was written by Paul along with Silvanus and Timothy, whose names are also attached to the greeting (1 Thess 1:1). In the first century, Thessalonica was the leading commercial center of Macedonia due to its excellent harbour and its strategic location on the Egnatian Way. The church that Paul founded there was composed primarily of Gentile converts, and it was still in its infancy when persecution from jealous Jews forced Paul to leave town. His great anxiety for his young converts was relieved, however, when Timothy caught up to him at Corinth with the good news that they were standing firm. In response, Paul sent back this letter. From an inscription referring to Gallio, the proconsul who dismissed the charges brought against Paul at Corinth (Acts 18:12-17), we are able to date 1 Thessalonians fairly precisely at A.D. 50 or 51, which makes it one of Paul's earliest epistles, second only to Galatians.

The Book of Acts provides significant information about the background of 1 Thessalonians at several points. It records the birth of the church at Thessalonica on Paul's second missionary journey (Acts 17:1-9) and the departure of Paul and Silas because of persecution from local Jews (Acts 17:10-15; 1 Thess 2:14-16). It also records the lonely stay of Paul in Athens by himself while he was worrying about the steadfastness of the church at Thessalonica (Acts 17:16-34; 1 Thess 2:17-18; 3:1-5) and Paul's reunion with Silas and Timothy at Corinth with good news about the Thessalonians (1 Thess 3:6-10; Acts 18:5). A later visit to the Macedonian churches, including Thessalonica, on Paul's third missionary journey is mentioned in Acts 20:1-5.

THE FLOW OF 1 THESSALONIANS

The First Epistle to the Thessalonians begins with a standard introduction (**1**:1), in which Paul and his associates, Silvanus and Timothy (1a), address their readers at Thessalonica (1b) with the typically Pauline greeting, 'Grace to you and peace' (1c).

The first half of the epistle is taken up with the apostle's grateful rejoicing over the progress of the Thessalonians in faith (1:2–3:13). Paul is so filled with thanksgiving for their exemplary conversion that he dwells on this theme for a while (1:2-10). After employing an introductory formula reassuring the Thessalonians that he is always praying for all of them (2), he lists three specific reasons why he thanks God for them (3-5). First of all, he is thankful for their godly character, which was displayed in actions stemming from the traditional triad of Christian graces (3). Their faith motivated them to work (3a); their love prompted them to labour (3b); and their hope inspired them to endure (3c). He is thankful, secondly, that they were chosen by God (4) and, thirdly, that the power of the Gospel was evidenced among them (5).

Paul continues in an attitude of thanksgiving by listing some of the practical results of their conversion that made him particularly thankful (6-10). The way that they imitated the apostles in joyfully handling tribulation became a positive example to other believers (6-7). They proclaimed the Gospel so well that their faith became known throughout the world (8). They turned from idols to serve the true and living God (9), and they were waiting for Christ's return from heaven (10).

Upon reflecting on his stay with the Thessalonians, Paul quickly adds to his thanksgiving for their exemplary conversion his personal thankfulness for the positive relations that he enjoyed with them (2:1–3:13). He begins by reminding them of the blamelessness of his ministry among them (2:1-12). From the outset he had boldly proclaimed the Gospel to them in the face of strong opposition (1-2), and he asserts that his motives for exhorting them are still pure before God (3-4). He came to them with the gentle attitude of a mother tenderly caring for her children (5-7), and he served them sacrificially, giving his whole life to them (8-9). They were well aware of how devoutly and sincerely he had ministered to them (10-12).

He is very thankful that they had responded positively to his ministry (13-16). They had accepted the divine authority of the Gospel (13) and suffered for it at the hands of their fellow countrymen (14-16). But Paul became anxious to know how they were doing when he was forced to leave them for a short while, because he felt that the personal success of his ministry was bound up with them (17-20). Shortly before Paul wrote this epistle, Timothy arrived with an encouraging report about them (**3**:1-10). Paul had sent Timothy back to Thessalonica because he was particularly anxious that these young converts might have given up their faith under the pressure of persecution (1-5), so he was greatly relieved and happy when Timothy returned with the news that they were standing steadfast in their faith (6-10). Paul continued to pray for them that they might increase in love and be established without blame at the coming of the Lord Jesus (11-13).

References to Christ's Return in 1 Thessalonians

Thoughts of Christ's return permeate Paul's first epistle to the Thessalonians. Each of its chapters closes with a reference to this doctrine. Although the literary structure of the epistle transcends modern chapter divisions, these references to Christ's return often coincide with the end of a structural unit.

Paul closes his thanksgiving for the Thessalonians' conversion by rejoicing that they turned from serving idols to wait for Christ's return from heaven (1:10). In a further section of thanksgiving for the positive relations that he enjoyed with the Thessalonians while he was among them, Paul confesses that being separated from them made him anxious about their spiritual condition because he shared in their rewards at Christ's coming (2:19). He concludes this section with a prayer that they will, indeed, be found unblamably holy when Jesus returns (3:13). At the heart of the epistle, lies Paul's attempt to correct the Thessalonians' mistaken belief that those who had already died would miss Christ's return (4:13-18). In his conclusion, the apostle offers a benedictory prayer, similar to his earlier prayer, that his readers would be preserved complete and blameless at the coming of the Lord Jesus Christ (5:23).

Now that Paul has brought his relationship with the Thessalonians up to date, he concentrates the second half of his epistle on practical instructions that would help them to realize continued progress in their Christian walk (**4**:1–5:22). He opens with a series of ethical exhortations (4:1-12), which he introduces by encouraging them to progress in their Christian walk by following the commandments which he previously passed down to them under Christ's authority (4:1-2). Specifically, they are to maintain sexual purity (3-8), to excel in their love for one another (9-10), and to be industrious in their work (11-12).

Paul also encourages their continued progress by clarifying a couple of eschatological misunderstandings which were threatening to impede them (4:13–5:11). First, he clarifies their misunderstanding of the status of deceased Christians (4:13-18). Believers may rightly hope that those who have died in the Lord will be raised just as Jesus was (13-14). When Christ returns, the believers who have died will be raised first, and then those who are still alive at his coming will be caught up with them to meet the Lord in the air (15-17). The Thessalonians were instructed to use this doctrine to console one another (18).

Although they should not have needed further instruction, Paul clarifies what seems to have been a misunderstanding concerning the timing of the day of the Lord (**5**:1-11). That day will come suddenly and unexpectedly, like a thief in the night (1-3); but since the Thessalonians belong to the day, and not the night, they do not need to be caught unawares, provided they keep themselves armed and awake (4-8). They may be encouraged because that day will result in salvation for them, and not wrath (9-11).

Paul draws his instruction to a close by grouping the exhortations that he has not found time to elaborate upon together into a general list (12-22). Although the associations between these brief exhortations are fairly loose, they may be conveniently divided into two sub-groupings, the first of which concerns community life (12-15). The Thessalonians are to respect their leaders in the Lord (12-13) and to help the members of their church who are faltering (14-15). The second sub-group concerns the personal sanctification of the Thessalonians (16-22). In relation to their inner selves, they are to maintain a joyful attitude of prayer and thanksgiving continually (16-18); and in relation to the body, they are not to quench the Spirit or despise prophecies but, after having tested everything, to hold on to what is good and shun whatever is evil (19-22).

In conclusion (23-28), Paul offers a benedictory prayer assuring the Thessalonians that God will be faithful in carrying out their sanctification to its final completion at the return of Christ (23-24); he also requests them to pray for him and his co-workers (25). He conveys his parting salutation to the Thessalonians (26) and charges that his letter be read in the presence of all of them (27). Finally, he closes with a benediction that repeats the theme of grace with which he introduced the letter (28).

OUTLINE OF 1 THESSALONIANS

2 Thessalonians

OVERVIEW OF 2 THESSALONIANS

Theme: Steadfastness in the light of the Lord's return

Key verses: 2 Thessalonians 2:14-15, 'And it was for this He called you through our gospel, that you may gain the glory of our Lord Jesus Christ. So then, brethren, stand firm and hold fast to the traditions which you were taught, whether by word of mouth or by letter from us' (NASB).

HISTORICAL BACKGROUND

Although some questions have been raised about this epistle's relationship to 1 Thessalonians, 2 Thessalonians is generally accepted as having been written by Paul along with Silvanus and Timothy, whose names are also attached to the greeting (2 Thess 1:1-2; cf. 3:17). Both epistles were sent to the same group of young, Gentile converts in Thessalonica, the capital of Macedonia.

Only a few months after he had written 1 Thessalonians, further news about the condition of the church at Thessalonica reached Paul at Corinth (see Acts 17:1–18:18a and the notes on 1 Thessalonians). Paul had taught that the return of Christ was imminent (i.e., that he could return at any moment), but apparently some of the Thessalonians were so convinced that he would return immediately that they had stopped working and had become a burden on others (1 Thess 1:11-12; 2 Thess 2:1-3; 3:6-12). Paul wrote 2 Thessalonians to follow up his first epistle and to correct their misunderstanding both theologically and practically. The proximity of this letter to 1 Thessalonians would place it in A.D. 51.

THE FLOW OF 2 THESSALONIANS

The introduction to the Second Epistle to the Thessalonians is almost identical to that of First Thessalonians: Paul and his associates, Silvanus and Timothy, address the church at Thessalonica with the greeting, 'Grace to you and peace ...' (**1**:1-2).

The epistle begins with an introductory thanksgiving for the initial growth of the Thessalonians, which extends to such a length that it becomes a main point in its own right (3-12). Paul praises God for their progress in the midst of persecution (3-4), and he encourages them in light of God's judgment upon their persecutors (5-10). He also prays that they will realize God's purpose that the Lord Jesus be glorified by them and they in him (11-12).

Paul's primary theological concern in writing to the Thessalonians was to correct a troubling misapprehension concerning the timing of Christ's return (**2**:1-12). Paul warns them not to be shaken by anyone claiming that the day of the Lord had already arrived (1-2), and he corrects this mistaken doctrine by delineating two important events that must precede the day of the Lord (3-12). First, the apostasy which had been predicted will occur (3a), and, second, the man of lawlessness will be revealed (3b-12). This man who will be characterized by lawlessness is vividly described in terms of his extremely insolent and arrogant attitude towards God and religion (3b-4), but the Thessalonians should not have been surprised because Paul had previously instructed them about him (5). They should have been aware of the personal force who was restraining him until the time for him to be revealed (6-7). When he is revealed (8-12), the Lord's coming will suddenly and decisively seal the doom of this lawless man (8), who will be empowered by Satan to perform false signs and wonders (9) and will deceive those who do not love the truth (10-12).

After dealing with this doctrinal misapprehension, Paul returns to his note of thanksgiving for the Thessalonians, this time emphasizing the spiritual progress that he anticipates from them (2:13–3:5). He is thankful that God has chosen them from the beginning for salvation and called them to share in Christ's glory (13-14). Accordingly, he exhorts them to remain steadfast in the doctrine that he had taught them (15) and prays that they will be encouraged by God's love for them to make continued progress in their faith (16-17). In turn, he asks them to intercede for the deliverance of him and his co-workers from their religious opponents so that the Gospel might spread rapidly without hindrance (3:1-2). Paul affirms that God will be faithful in watching over the Thessalonians (3), and he expresses his confidence that they will continue to practice the things he had commanded them (4-5).

Paul thought it necessary, however, to give the Thessalonians some practical directives concerning one issue that seems to have been a problem for some of them, namely their lack of diligence in their labour (6-15). He commands them to shun disorderly brethren (6) and to follow his example of working hard so that he would not become a burden to anyone (7-10). In particular, he commands the slothful among them to earn their own living (11-12), and he exhorts the church as a whole not to become weary of well-doing (13). If anyone does not obey his instruction given in this letter, he commands the church to discipline such a person (14-15).

Paul concludes the epistle in three short lines (16-18). First, he pronounces a benediction of peace upon his readers (16), and then he signs his name to assure them of the epistle's authenticity (17). Finally, he leaves them with a benediction of grace (18).

OUTLINE OF 2 THESSALONIANS

1 Corinthians

OVERVIEW OF 1 CORINTHIANS

Theme: Paul's problem church

Key verse: 1 Cor 1:10, 'I appeal to you, brothers, in the name of our Lord Jesus Christ, that all of you agree with one another so that there may be no divisions among you and that you may be perfectly united in mind and thought' (NIV).

HISTORICAL BACKGROUND

First Corinthians is an undisputed Pauline epistle. Corinth, the city to which Paul wrote, was the political and commercial capital of Achaia. Its strategic location at the crossroads of Greece contributed to its reputation for wealth and immorality. Corinth was situated on the narrow isthmus joining Peloponesus to the South with the northern mainland; it was also the connecting point for East-West shipping traffic across the Aegean and Ionian seas through ports on either side at Cenchrea and Lechaeum. The cosmopolitan flavour of the city found expression in the diversity of the church at Corinth, which was composed primarily of Gentile converts from paganism who were still influenced by the morality and philosophical views of their pagan neighbours.

Acts records the founding of the church at Corinth by Paul on his second missionary journey (Acts 18:1-17) and the later ministry of Apollos there (Acts 18:24–19:1). Paul wrote this epistle to the Corinthians from Ephesus (1 Cor 16:8-9) in the spring of A.D. 55, or perhaps 54, in response to verbal (1 Cor 1:11) and written reports (1 Cor 7:1) about various problems in the church (see also notes on 2 Corinthians).

THE FLOW OF 1 CORINTHIANS

The introduction to 1 Corinthians (**1**:1-9) begins with a salutation in which its writer, the apostle Paul, together with Sosthenes, his brother in Christ, send the church at Corinth their wish for grace and peace (1-3). The introduction also includes Paul's thanksgiving for the Corinthians' reception of God's grace, through which they received every spiritual gift and the assurance that Christ would continue to establish them until his return (4-9).

In the first main part of the epistle, Paul responds to verbal reports that had been brought to him concerning spiritual problems within the Corinthian church (1:10–6:20). First of all, he responds to reports, specifically said to be from members of Chloe's household, that there were factions within the church (1:10–4:21). Before he attempts to analyze this problem in detail and to offer his resolution, Paul gives an introductory statement of what had gone wrong (1:10-17). Some of the Corinthians apparently were claiming to follow him, others were claiming to follow Apollos or Cephas, and still others Christ (10-12), but Paul remarks that such factions are inconsistent with the unity of Christ and his own subservient role as a minister of the Gospel (13-17).

Paul then begins to look more closely at the underlying cause of these personality-centered factions (1:18–2:16). He identifies the problem with the seeming incompatibility of the Gospel with human wisdom (1:18–2:5). To the world, the message of the cross is foolishness (1:18-25), and God primarily called those who were of no significance in the world's eyes to believe in this message so that he might effectively remove any basis for human pride (26-31). Paul, himself, admits that his presentation of the Gospel to the Corinthians, which concentrated on Christ crucified, was undertaken in a state of personal weakness and accompanied by feelings of fear and rhetorical inadequacy; consequently, the only adequate foundation for their faith was God's power in the cross, and not his own ability (**2**:1-5).

Paul starts to resolve the problem by pointing out the genuine wisdom of the Gospel to those with spiritual discernment (6-16).

Although God's wisdom, which Paul was proclaiming, remains hidden from the rulers of this age (6-9), it has been revealed by the Holy Spirit (10-13) and can be apprehended by those who are spiritual, while those who are natural reject it (14-16).

Keeping in mind the natural inclination to follow the world in placing one's confidence in human leaders rather than something so seemingly foolish as the cross of Christ, Paul defines the proper role of Christian leaders (**3**:1-23). He chides the Corinthians for their immaturity in idolizing men (1-9). To be specific, they were childishly setting up their leaders as heroes and forming divisive allegiances according to their personal preferences (5-4), but Paul points out that their leaders, whether himself or Apollos, were merely fellow-servants through whom God worked for their benefit (1-9). Using the imagery of the construction of a temple, Paul goes on to warn leaders in any capacity that they are responsible for how they build upon the foundation, which is Christ, because the quality of their work will be tested by fire (10-17). He also corrects the inverted positions of wisdom and folly in the confused thinking of some Corinthians by lowering leaders from their elevated status as objects of boasting by rival factions in the church to a subservient role as the common possession of all believers (18-23).

Without detracting from what he has already said about the servanthood of leaders, Paul found it necessary to defend his own apostleship against some of the Corinthians who apparently were not just preferring some other leader over him but calling his apostolic authority into question (**4**:1-21). He gives little weight to their criticism because, although he was a servant for their sake, his master to whom he will have to render a final account is the Lord, who will judge him more thoroughly and accurately than even he could himself (1-5). Nevertheless, it should have been evident to them that he bore the marks of a true apostle: poverty, humiliation, and suffering, which ironically stood in sharp contrast with their own wealth, honor, and ease (6-13). Paul closes the defense of his apostolic authority by appealing to the Corinthians on the basis of his historical position as their spiritual father (14-21). After reminding the Corinthians of his historically undeniable claim to be their spiritual father (14-15), Paul exhorts them to imitate him (16-17), and he threatens to discipline those of them who are arrogant if they do not respond to his fatherly love (18-21).

The second report to which Paul responds, for which no source is stated, concerns the involvement of a church member in incest (5:1-13). Paul rebukes the church for its failure to take disciplinary action and calls for the excommunication of the offending brother (1-8), who is to be removed by the united action of the church (1-5) so that it might recover its moral purity (6-8). With respect to this case, Paul found it necessary to correct the Corinthians' misunderstanding of a comment he had made in an earlier letter to the effect that they were not to associate with immoral people, by which he had meant immoral people who claimed to be part of their fellowship rather than those who were outside of the church (9-13).

The third problem reported to Paul concerns cases of litigation between Christians (6:1-11). He tells them that they should be ashamed of their taking other Christians to court in front of unbelievers (1-6). It would be better for the innocent party to accept injustice, but as it was, Christians were defrauding other Christians (7-8). Paul places these issues of wrongdoing and justice in an eschatological perspective by warning that those who practice immorality will not inherit the kingdom of God (9-11).

The fourth problem concerns reports that some Corinthians were visiting prostitutes (12-20). Apparently some of them were arguing that it was legitimate for them to indulge their sexual appetites because what they did with their bodies had nothing to do with their spirits, but Paul counters that their bodies were created for the Lord, not for immorality (12-14). He carries his point further by arguing that since they are united with Christ in body and spirit, it is unthinkable that they should also be united with a prostitute (15-17). Furthermore, God has a claim upon a Christian's body because he has purchased it at a great price to be a temple for the Holy Spirit (18-20).

In the second main part of the epistle, Paul predominantly replies to a letter in which representatives of the church had posed a series of questions for him concerning practical issues that were troubling them (7:1–16:4). Unfortunately, their letter has been lost so we are left to reconstruct the wording of their questions from the answers, which are usually introduced by the formula, 'now concerning ....' Paul's first answer deals with the general topic of marriage and several smaller related issues (7:1-40). He instructs those who are married not to abstain from sexual relations, except by mutual consent so that they might devote themselves to prayer for a limited period of time; otherwise, they might be tempted by their lack of self-control (1-7). He instructs those who are not bound by marital obligations not to worry about their circumstances (8-16). In this category, he includes the unmarried and widows, whom he personally advises to remain single provided they can control their passions (8-9), and also spouses who have been deserted, whom he releases from a false sense of obligation to try to hang on to the partner who has left, although he instructs believers not to leave an unbelieving spouse who is willing to live with them (10-16). Paul extends the general principle that he has already implicitly applied to marriage to all social stratifications: whether circumcised or uncircumcised, slave or free, believers are to remain as they were when Christ called them without worrying about their status, although slaves should gain their freedom if they have the opportunity (17-24). Paul now explicitly applies this general principle to virgins, but by way of personal advice rather than dominical command (25-40). He advises that when marriage is viewed from several different perspectives, there are decided advantages to remaining single (25-35). In view of the crisis that the church was experiencing at that time, it would be pragmatically advantageous for them to remain single because they would be spared from some of the troubles that would come to married people (25-28). In view of the coming eschaton, the fleeting enjoyment of marriage, which cannot be perfectly realized in this life, would be equalized by the rapidly approaching enjoyment of greater eternal rewards (29-31); and in view of the greater potential that single people have for devoting themselves completely to the service of the Lord without distractions, singleness is spiritually advantageous (32-35). But Paul quickly balances his advice by stating that it is permissible for virgins to marry without any fear that they are sinning by so doing (36-38). Finally, he states that death releases a widow from the bonds of marriage, leaving her the freedom either to remarry or not, although in his opinion she will be happier if she does not remarry (39-40).

The second question of the Corinthians which Paul addresses concerns eating food sacrificed to idols (**8:1–11:1**). He begins by laying down some guiding principles for them in questionable matters such as this (**8:1-13**). The essential problem, as he analyzes it, lay in an arrogation of knowledge over love for those who did not share the same understanding (1-6). First, he states the general principle that knowledge leads to arrogance (1-3); then he identifies the knowledge that idols have no real existence, as the specific point that was causing the Corinthians to become arrogant (4-6). The solution is found in showing consideration for the conscience of a weaker brother who might be caused to stumble by seeing believers partake of food sacrificed to idols (7-13).

Paul encourages the stronger Corinthians to show consideration in the exercise of their liberty by setting before them his own example of placing voluntary restraints upon his liberty as an apostle (**9:1-27**). He asserts that his claim to be an apostle is legitimate (1-2); and along with his apostolic office, he may expect certain rights, such as the right to financial remuneration (3-12a). These rights are supported by the common practice of other ministers of the Gospel and ordinary workers, who enjoy the fruits of their labor (3-7), as well as by the Mosaic Law, which by way of analogy even legislates payment for working oxen (8-12a). But Paul voluntarily waived his apostolic rights so that he might not cause any hindrance to the Gospel (12b-18). Furthermore, he asserts that, although he is free, he has become a slave by accommodating himself to the social customs of all ethnic groups so that he might save as many people as possible (19-23). Beyond all of that, he exercises personal self-control in all things, in the same way that an athlete in training would, so that he might win the prize (24-27).

Paul goes on to warn the Corinthians of the spiritual danger of implicitly sanctioning idolatry by their participation in idolatrous feasts (**10:1-22**). He sounds this warning by way of a historical lesson from Israel's associations with idolatry in the Old Testament

(1-13). He reminds them that the majority of the Israelites fell from their privileged spiritual position, and their bodies were strewn across the wilderness in judgment (1-5). Paul warns the Corinthians that they are facing a similar danger of falling into idolatry and being judged because of over-confidence in their ability to associate with idolatry without being affected (6-13). He argues that their participating in idolatrous feasts is totally incompatible with their eating the Lord's Supper (14-22). By eating the Lord's Supper they share with fellow believers in the common body of Christ (14-18), and by participating in idolatrous feasts they fellowship with idolaters in the table of demons; their fellowship in one circle excludes their fellowship in the other (19-22).

Having clearly proscribed participation in idolatrous feasts in the name of Christian liberty, Paul now makes the necessary qualifications to permit the Corinthians true freedom from scrupulous questioning in their social contacts with the world (10:23–11:1). He lays down the fundamental principle of edifying the other person as a gauge for determining the limits of one's liberty (10:23-24). Within these limits, he permits the Corinthians the freedom to eat meat of unknown origin (25-30), whether it is bought in the market (25-26) or offered to them by an unbelieving host (27-30). He concludes the issue of religious liberty by circumscribing it with the obligation to do all things for God's glory, which means that they will avoid placing unnecessary hindrances to the Gospel in the paths of others (10:31–**11**:1).

The next subject that Paul addresses, propriety in public worship (11:2-34), lacks the formula 'now concerning ...' so we cannot be sure if the Corinthians asked about it or if he introduced it at this point, either in reply to a verbal report or out of his own concerns, because it fits topically with his prohibition of participation in idolatrous worship and his discussion of the use of gifts in the church, about which they did ask. Under this general heading, two issues are addressed, the first of which is the demeanour of women in public worship (2-16). Paul argues that women should have their heads covered while praying or prophesying because not to do so would be shameful within an assumed hierarchy in which God is the head of Christ, Christ the head of man, and man the head of woman (2-6). He also argues for the same point from the created order (7-12). Because man was created directly as the image and glory of God, whereas woman was created from man and for man as his glory, women should give appropriate outward recognition to man's priority in creation (7-10). Without altering this conclusion, Paul adds the qualification that man and woman are interdependent in Christ (11-12). Finally, he argues from the nature of things, which was attested by the dominant instincts of the Corinthians themselves and the unanimous practice of the other churches (13-16).

The second issue calling for propriety with respect to the public worship of the Corinthians was their celebration of the Lord's Supper (17-34). In this regard, Paul can find nothing good to say because the Lord's Supper, which had become associated with a fellowship meal, was being so badly abused by the exclusivism of the rich, who were gorging themselves on their own food and getting drunk while the poor went away hungry and humiliated, that it would have been better if they had not come together at all (17-22). Paul brings the true meaning of the Lord's Supper back into focus by reminding the Corinthians of its institution by Jesus (23-26). From Jesus' institution of the Lord's Supper, Paul moves to application concerning the proper attitude with which the Corinthians should observe it (27-34). They are to examine themselves individually to ensure that the manner in which they observe the Lord's supper is not deserving of God's judgment (27-32), and they are to show consideration for one another in the way that they eat (33-34).

Ancient Jewish Blessings for the Bread and the Cup

On the night that he was betrayed, Jesus took bread and gave thanks. He probably used the words of an ancient blessing that Jewish people still recite today before meals: 'Blessed are you, O LORD our God, King of the Universe, who brings forth bread from the earth.' In the same way he took the cup, and he probably offered the corresponding blessing for it: 'Blessed are you, O LORD our God, King of the universe, who created the fruit of the vine.'

Early Christian Worship

'And on the day called Sunday, all who live in cities or in the country gather together to one place, and the memoirs of the apostles or the writings of the prophets are read...; then...the president verbally instructs, and exhorts to the imitation of these good things. Then we all rise together and pray, and, as we before said, when our prayer is ended, bread and wine and water are brought, and the president in like manner offers prayers and thanksgivings...; and there is a distribution to each,...and to those who are absent a portion is sent by the deacons. And they who are well to do, and willing, give what each thinks fit; and what is collected is deposited with the president, who succors the orphans and widows and those who...are in want.... But Sunday is the day on which we all hold our common assembly, because it is the first day on which...God made the world; and Jesus Christ our Savior on the same day rose from the dead' (Justin Martyr, *First Apology*, 67, in *The Ante-Nicene Fathers*, Alexander Roberts et al., eds. vol 1: *The Apostolic Fathers*, trans. A. Cleveland Coxe [Grand Rapids: Wm. B. Eerdmans Pub. Co., 1975], 1:186.)

The next issue that Paul addresses, concerning which the Corinthians inquired in their letter, is the exercise of spiritual gifts in the church (**12**:1–14:40). To correct their abuse of the gifts, which was fostering spiritual pride by elevating those who possessed the more spectacular gifts to a superspiritual status, Paul lays out a global picture of the diversity of gifts within the unity of the body (12:1-31a). First, he gives the Corinthians a simple test that they can use to determine the origin of gifts in general: no one speaking by the Spirit can curse Jesus, and no one can confess Jesus as Lord except by the Holy Spirit (1-3). Paul then states that the whole diverse range of gifts found among believers comes from one common source: the Holy Spirit, who, working in conjunction with the other members of the Godhead, distributes to each individual as he chooses (4-11). Using a human body, which is composed of many different members, as an analogy for the church with its diversity of gifts, Paul draws out three important lessons about the inner workings of Christ's body, the church (12-31a).

New Testament Lists of Spiritual Gifts				
1 Cor 12:8-11	1 Cor 14:28-31	Rom 12:6-8	Eph 4:11-13[1]	1 Pet 4:10-11
	apostles		apostles	speaking
prophecy	prophets	prophecy	prophets	
word of wisdom				
			evangelists	
word of knowledge	teachers	teachers	pastors and teachers	
faith				
effecting of miracles	miracles			
gifts of healing	gifts of healings			
	helps adminis- trations	service leading giving showing mercy		serving
distinguishing of spirits				
tongues	tongues			
interpretation of tongues	interpretation of tongues			

1. Technically the list in Ephesians does not refer to spiritual gifts *per se*, but rather to key offices in which leaders, who possessed corresponding gifts, were given to the church.

First, Christ's body is a unity, even though it is composed of many different members, because all those who are a part of it were incorporated into it by baptism in one common Spirit (12-13). Second, each of the members within the unity of this body are interdependent upon the others in such a way that each one needs all of the others and in turn is needed by all of them for the body to function properly; consequently, there is no room for an egocentric spirit of self-sufficiency or for self-effacing feelings of insignificance, but only for mutual care and respect (14-26). Third, the diversity of gifts that exists within the church makes it evident that everyone cannot have the same gift (27-31a).

Sandwiched in the middle of his discussion of spiritual gifts, Paul strategically places an elevated appeal to the supremacy of love over all of the gifts as a corrective to the Corinthians' selfish coveting of the more showy ones (12:31b–13:13). Love is fundamentally necessary in the Christian life, for without it nothing else has any value (12:31b–**13**:3). Paul extols love for its many virtuous qualities, which all show consideration for the interests of the other person (13:4-7). He demonstrates that love is more excellent than gifts by contrasting the transitoriness of prophecy, tongues and knowledge, which were all destined to cease because of their incompleteness, over against the abiding permanence of love, which is even greater than faith and hope and will last for eternity (8-13).

When Paul returns to speak more directly about the gifts themselves, he tries to convince the Corinthians of the superiority of prophecy over speaking in tongues (**14**:1-25). Prophecy, he argues, is more valuable than tongues because it edifies the listeners; tongues, on the other hand, only edify the speaker, unless they are accompanied by an interpretation (1-5). Tongues, conversely, are not profitable in the church because they are unintelligible to the listeners (6-19). In support of this theological conclusion, Paul uses several examples of musical instruments and foreign languages to teach the lesson that indistinguishable sounds are not profitable in ordinary life (6-12). He then applies this lesson to the tongues-speakers at Corinth with respect to the preferability of their uttering intelligible speech (13-19). He obligates them to seek the gift of interpretation so that their listeners may be edified (13-17), and he sets before them his own example of preferring to speak understandably, although he was perfectly able to speak in tongues (18-19). Prophecy, as he goes on to argue, is superior to tongues because although tongues are a sign to unbelievers, they are not convincing to unbelievers; whereas, although prophecy is intended for believers, it is effective in convicting unbelievers (20-25).

Paul brings the discussion of spiritual gifts to a close by laying down some regulations for their use within the public assemblies of the church (26-40). He restricted the improper use of gifts that was apparently taking place among the Corinthians by requiring that everything be done in an orderly manner for the purpose of edification and by limiting them to, at the most, three interpreted utterances in tongues and two or three prophecies, the content of which was to be subject to the judgment of the group (26-33a). He also prohibited women from speaking in church (33b-36). Suspecting that some of the self-confident Corinthians would challenge his spiritual judgment, Paul reminds them that these regulations carry apostolic authority (37-38). Before leaving the subject, Paul briefly summarizes the thrust of his teaching by permitting them to prophesy and speak in tongues provided that they do so in accordance with his instructions in a decent and orderly manner (39-40).

The next issue that Paul deals with is the resurrection (15:1-58), although here the introductory formula is lacking as was the case with matters of public worship, so we cannot be certain that the Corinthians brought it up in their letter. He begins by reaffirming the historical certainty of Christ's resurrection (1-11) on the grounds that Christ appeared to many witnesses and last of all to himself (1-8), even though he did not deserve to be included among the apostolic witnesses (9-11).

The Corinthians probably accepted the historicity of Christ's resurrection; the more difficult point for them, of which Paul needed to convince them, seems to have been the eschatological reality of their own resurrection (12-58). Paul begins to argue his case by hypothetically assuming the denial of a general resurrection of the dead and then exploring its logical implications, which prove to be so contradictory to what the Corinthians accept as established facts that the assumed premise must be false (12-19). 'If there is no resurrection of the dead, then not even Christ has been raised,' although the Corinthians accepted that he had been raised (12-13). If Christ has not been raised, then the Gospel, which is founded upon his resurrection, is false, although the Corinthians believed that it was true (14-15). If the Gospel is not true, then life is futile,

---

Appearances of the Risen Christ

In or near Jerusalem
    On resurrection Sunday
        To Mary Magdalene (Mark 16:9; John 20:11-18)
        To the other women (Matt 28:8-10)
        To Peter (Luke 24:34; 1 Cor 15:5)
        To two disciples on the Emmaus Road (Mark 16:12-13; Luke 24:13-35)
        To the disciples, minus Thomas (Luke 24:36-43; John 20:19-25)
    On the following Sunday to the eleven, including Thomas (Mark 16:14; John 20:26-29)

At an undisclosed place and time
    To five hundred people at once (1 Cor 15:6)
    To James (1 Cor 15:7)

In Galilee
    To a group of disciples by the Sea of Tiberias including Peter, Thomas, Nathanael, James and John, and two others (John 21:1-24)
    To the eleven disciples at a designated location (Matt 28:16-20)

At Bethany, outside of Jerusalem, as Jesus ascended before the apostles' eyes forty days later (Mark 16:19-20; Luke 24:50-53; Acts 1:4-12)

After the ascension
    To Paul on the Damascus road (Acts 9:1-6; 22:1-10; 26:12-18; 1 Cor 15:8)

---

although the Corinthians apparently still believed that it had meaning (16-19).

Next, Paul reverses the direction of the argument: assuming that Christ has been raised and that other theologically accepted premises are also true, he infers that the believer's resurrection is certain (20-28). Since Christ has been raised and we are in Christ as the second Adam, we will also be raised (20-22). Since Christ has been raised and all things, including death, will be put in subjection under his feet, the dead must be raised (23-28).

The final move in Paul's argument for the resurrection of the dead is to point out practices in the lives of his opponents and himself that are inconsistent with its denial (29-34). In an *ad hominem* fashion, he reveals the inconsistency of his opponents' own practice of being baptized for the dead with the assumption that the dead are not raised (29). To their inconsistency, he adds his own apparent folly of endangering his life for the Gospel rather than living for the pleasure of the moment, as some of them were apparently doing (30-34).

Having successfully argued that the dead are raised, Paul now moves on to clarify the implications of the resurrection with respect to the transformation of our earthly bodies into glorified heavenly ones (35-58). He claims that the nature of the glorified body should be evident, in its essence at least (35-49), because other bodies within the realm of nature contain intimations about it by way of analogy (35-41). The body of a plant, for instance, unfolds from a dead seed in a way that greatly transcends the seed but maintains continuity with it (35-38). Furthermore, many different kinds of bodies exist within nature, and their glory varies from one to the other (39-41). To these natural observations, Paul adds some basic theological knowledge and then draws two inferences regarding the glorified body (42-49). Our natural body, which is sown as a perishable seed, will be raised as a far greater spiritual body that will be imperishable (42-44); and the earthly image of Adam, which we have borne, will be superseded by the heavenly image of Christ (45-49).

Closely tied to Paul's inferences about the nature of the believer's glorified body is a related point about the necessity of our glorification (50-57). We must be glorified in order to inherit the kingdom because perishable flesh and blood are incapable of sustaining our eternal existence (50-53). Only when we are glorified will death finally be conquered, as Christ most certainly will ensure (54-57). Paul brings his discussion of the resurrection to a close by cashing in on the practical implications that this triumphant assurance has for the persistent manner in which believers ought to serve the Lord in this life (58).

The question to which Paul responds last concerns the collection for the saints that he intended to take up upon his arrival at Corinth (**16**:1-4). He probably reserved this question for the end because it nicely ties into his other concluding comments (5-24), including the travel plans of himself and other fellow ministers to the Corinthians (5-12). Paul did not want to leave Ephesus at the moment because a great opportunity for ministry stood before him in a setting of strong opposition, but he promised to pay the Corinthians a lengthy visit after passing through Macedonia on the way (5-9). Timothy was planning to come to them shortly in Paul's place and with Paul's orders that he be treated with all due respect (10-11). Apollos, whom Paul had also encouraged to visit the Corinthians, was not available at the moment but promised to come when he was free (12).

Among his concluding comments, Paul includes some pertinent exhortations for the Corinthians (13-18). He commands that their conduct be marked by steadfastness in the faith and motivated by love (13-14) and that they submit to their leaders who had laboured diligently for them, such as Stephanas, who, along with Fortunatus and Achaicus, had recently come to Paul from them (15-18).

Finally, he includes greetings (19-24), both from the churches of Asia, with special mention of Aquila and Priscilla (19-20), and from himself (21-24). He signs the greeting with his own hand (21) and pronounces a malediction on anyone who does not love the Lord (22), before closing with a benediction of the Lord's grace and his own love upon all of them in Christ Jesus (23).

OUTLINE OF 1 CORINTHIANS

Paul's Relations with the Corinthians

1. Paul's first visit to Corinth on the second missionary journey (Acts 18:1-17)

2. Apollos' ministry at Corinth while Paul was at Ephesus at the outset of his third missionary journey (Acts 18:24–19:1; 1 Cor 1:12; 3:6)

3. Paul's *'previous letter'* (Corinthians A; 1 Cor 5:9; probably from Ephesus), lost

4. Verbal report from Chloe's household (1 Cor 1:11)

5. Official letter from the church at Corinth (1 Cor 7:1; 16:17-18)

6. *1 Corinthians* (Corinthians B, written from Ephesus; 1 Cor 16:8-9)

7. Paul's dispatch of Timothy to Corinth (1 Cor 4:17; 16:10-11; Acts 19:22)

8. Paul's 'painful visit' (second visit; 2 Cor 2:1; cf. 2 Cor 12:14; 13:1-2)

9. Paul's *'sorrowful letter'* (Corinthians C; probably from Asia; 2 Cor 2:3-4; 7:8), lost

10. Paul's dispatch of Titus with the sorrowful letter (2 Cor 2:12-13; 7:5-7)

11. Paul's narrow escape from death in Asia (2 Cor 1:8)

12. Paul's reception of Titus' good news (2 Cor 2:13; 7:5-15)

13. *2 Corinthians* (Corinthians D, written from Macedonia)

14. Titus' return to Corinth to prepare the collection (2 Cor 8:6, 16-24; 9:3-5; 12:18)

15. Paul's *third visit* to Corinth on the return leg of the third missionary journey with the collection for the poor at Jerusalem (2 Cor 12:14; 13:1-2; Acts 20:2-3)

2 Corinthians

OVERVIEW OF 2 CORINTHIANS

Theme: Paul's ongoing, difficult relationship with the Corinthians

Key verses: 2 Corinthians 7:8-9 'For though I caused you sorrow by my letter, ... I now rejoice ... that you were made sorrowful to the point of repentance ...' (NASB).

---

1. Verses 12b and 13 in the Greek text are verses 13 and 14 in some English versions (KJV, NASB, NIV, RSV).

HISTORICAL BACKGROUND

Paul's authorship of 2 Corinthians is undisputed. The epistle is intelligible as a single unit, although some sections (e.g., 6:14–7:1; 10:1–13:10) have been thought to be interpolations from other letters. On the geographic and socioeconomic background of Corinth, see the notes on 1 Corinthians.

To understand the two canonical epistles to the Corinthians, we need to place them into the historical framework of Paul's dealings with the Corinthians. Paul's *first visit* to Corinth took place on the second missionary journey (Acts 18:1-17). While Paul laboured at Ephesus at the outset of his third missionary journey, Apollos ministered at Corinth (Acts 18:24–19:1; 1 Cor 1:12; 3:6). Paul probably wrote the Corinthians what is known as his "*previous letter*" from Ephesus (Corinthians A; 1 Cor 5:9), but it is lost to us. While he was still at Ephesus, Chloe's household brought him a verbal report about the state of affairs in the church (1 Cor 1:11), and the church dispatched an official letter asking his advice on certain issues (1 Cor 7:1; 16:17-18). Paul wrote *1 Corinthians* (Corinthians B, 1 Cor 16:8-9) to answer their sincere questions and to deal with some serious problems, such as divisions within the church (1 Cor 1:10-12) and a case of incest (1 Cor 5:1-5). Paul sent Timothy to Corinth to tend to these problems, but it is not clear if he accompanied this letter or went at another time (1 Cor 4:17; 16:10-11; Acts 19:22).

Paul planned to come himself later (2 Cor 1:15-16), but the worsening situation at Corinth compelled him to change his mind (2 Cor 1:17) and immediately pay a *second visit*, which is known as the 'painful visit'. The Corinthians had been resisting Paul's leadership for some time under the instigation of a group of Jewish pseudo-apostles who had infiltrated the church (2 Cor 11:13), but the opposition came to a head when an individual, who may have been the man guilty of incest, successfully defied the apostle's authority and forced Paul to leave in defeat (2 Cor 2:1; cf. 2 Cor 12:14, 21; 13:1-2). With the concerns of the church weighing heavily upon his heart as he travelled back through Asia (2 Cor 7:5), Paul wrote a '*sorrowful letter*' calling the church to repent (Corinthians C; 2 Cor 2:3-4; 7:8). He dispatched Titus to Corinth with this letter (2 Cor 2:12-13; 7:5-7), which is now lost to us. While he was in Asia, Paul narrowly escaped death from some very serious danger that he only speaks of vaguely (2 Cor 1:8-10). He had hoped to met Titus at Troas, but not finding him, he crossed over to Macedonia (2 Cor 2:12-13).

Everything was going wrong when Titus finally arrived with the good news that the Corinthians as a whole had repented (2 Cor 7:5-15). Their repentance relieved Paul of the unpleasant task of confronting them in person, and it encouraged him to write reaffirming his love for them. At the same time, he used the letter to deal with any remaining opposition (2 Cor 10:1–13:10) and to prepare for the collection for the poor at Jerusalem before he arrived with a delegation from Macedonia, who were accompanying their own offering (2 Cor 9:2-5; Acts 20:2-3). This letter is our *2 Corinthians* (Corinthians D), which would have been written from somewhere in Macedonia in the fall of A.D. 56 or perhaps 55 just before Paul returned from his third missionary journey. Paul sent Titus ahead with the letter (2 Cor 8:6, 16-24; 12:18), and he followed shortly afterwards, paying the Corinthians a *third visit* (2 Cor 12:14; 13:1-2;).

THE FLOW OF 2 CORINTHIANS

The introduction to 2 Corinthians (**1**:1-11) comes in two parts. First, there is a typical salutation of grace and peace from Paul and Timothy to the church at Corinth (1-2). A special note of thanksgiving follows (3-11), in which Paul thanks God for comforting him in his affliction (3-7) and for delivering him from a perilous situation in Asia from which he barely escaped with his life (8-11).

The first main part of the epistle is concerned with the restoration of Paul's relationship with the majority of the Corinthians, which had already taken place formally although some scars apparently still remained (1:12–7:16). Instead of immediately breaking into rejoicing over their change of heart, Paul finds it necessary to present his side of the story beginning with a defence of his own integrity (1:12–2:4). He affirms the sincerity of his character in all of his actions towards the Corinthians (1:12-14) and the stability of his purpose in planning to visit them earlier (1:15-22), but he explains that at the last minute he found it necessary to cancel his visit and send a letter instead in order to spare both them and himself from the grief that would have come by directly confronting the church with its lack of repentance (1:23–**2**:4). Now that the chief offender has repented, Paul instructs the church to forgive him and restore him to fellowship (5-11).

Paul also makes the Corinthians aware of some of the inner struggles of his ministry on their behalf (12-17). While he was at Troas, he became anxious at not finding Titus, who would have had news about the state of affairs at Corinth, and so he continued on to Macedonia (12-13); nevertheless, he was thankful that he could triumph in any situation through Christ (14-17). Since this interjected note of praise could sound like Paul was bragging about himself, he pauses to dispel any hint of self-commendation by pointing out that the lives of the Corinthians, to whom he had completely given himself in ministry, were the only letters of recommendation he needed (**3**:1-3). Paul places no confidence in himself, but only in the sufficiency of Christ working through him and in the greatness of the new covenant that God has entrusted to him (4-6).

He takes some time to extol the greatness of the Gospel that he preaches (3:7–4:15) by first of all contrasting the surpassing greatness of the new covenant with that of the old one (3:7-18). Although the condemning ministry of the old covenant written on tablets of stone came with such great glory that the people could not look at Moses' face directly, the life-giving ministry of the new covenant, which is written upon human hearts by the Holy Spirit, produces even greater glory (7-11). Under the old covenant, Moses had to veil his face, but the ministers of the new covenant can speak with greater boldness, and believers can all gaze upon the mirror image of God's glory into which they are being transformed (12-18). On a second level of contrast, Paul shows that the greatness of the gospel message far surpasses the weakness and humility of the messengers who proclaim it (4:1-15). The glory of the Gospel is like a brilliant light (1-6). Although the Gospel's glory is hidden from those who are spiritually blind (1-4), the same God who caused light to shine out of darkness at creation has shone in the hearts of believers so that they might see his glory in the face of Jesus Christ (5-6). By contrast, the messengers of the Gospel are very humble (7-15). They are like ordinary, breakable vessels of clay containing the priceless treasure of the Gospel (7-12); nevertheless, their firm conviction inspires them to proclaim the message boldly (13-15).

His reflection upon the greatness of the Gospel over against his inner struggles at trying to fulfil his ministry, leads Paul to explain the psychological drive behind his preaching (4:16–5:21). He found great personal encouragement to face hardships (4:16–5:10), first of all by looking at his circumstances in the light of eternity (4:16–5:5). The afflictions that he had endured were light and only lasted for but a moment when they were compared with the weighty eternal glory that they were producing (4:16-18), and he looked forward with anticipation to the day when the perishable earthly tent in which he lived would be exchanged for an eternal heavenly home (5:1-5). He also found encouragement to face hardships by walking by faith rather than by sight (6-10). But the driving force behind Paul cannot be explained by a psychology of passive endurance; rather, he was motivated by an overwhelming evangelistic zeal which resulted in hardships that he willingly endured in order to achieve his goal (5:11-21). His real motivation was, on one hand, the compelling love of Christ in dying for him so that he could no longer hold claim to his own life (11-15), and on the other hand, the reconciling grace of God (16-21), who took the initiative in reconciling the world to himself (16-19) and entrusted Paul as one of his agents of reconciliation (20-21).

In view of God's gracious redemption of them and his own sacrificial ministry for them, Paul appeals to the Corinthians to respond (**6**:1–7:4) by accepting God's saving grace (6:1-10), by returning his own freely given love (11-13), and by rejecting all worldly alliances with their unbelieving neighbours, especially in their associations with idolatry, so that they might be completely devoted to God (6:14–7:1). Once again he repeats his appeal for them to demonstrate their love by enlarging their hearts to make room for him inside, and he is confident that they will return his affection (2-4).

The reason for this confidence is that Paul had received the good news of Titus' report (5-16) and was greatly encouraged that the Corinthians had repented (5-13a). Earlier in the epistle, Paul mentioned his anxious search for Titus,[1] but by delaying the disclosure that he had actually found Titus and was able to rejoice because he brought good news (5-7), Paul allows the seriousness of the tension that had existed between himself and the Corinthians to be felt. Now he was relieved that the painful letter he had written to them had made them sorrowful to the point of repentance (8-13a). Along with his encouragement from meeting Titus, Paul adds an uplifting note of commendation for Titus' ministry to the Corinthians (13b-16).

The restoration of Paul's relationship with the majority of the Corinthians frees Paul to move on to the business of encouraging them to participate in his planned collection for the poor, which becomes the primary concern in the second main part of the epistle (**8**:1–9:15). He encourages the Corinthians to give generously (8:1-15) by challenging them with the example of the poor believers from the churches in Macedonia, who gladly gave even beyond

---

1. 1 Corinthians 2:12-13.

their ability (1-7). He also encourages them by reminding them of Jesus' example in willingly becoming poor so that they might become rich (8-9); and, finally, he appeals to the ideal of Christian equality by assuring them that the object is not to make others wealthy at their expense, but for their abundance to help those who are in need, with the understanding that they would also receive help if they should need it some day (10-15). In addition to giving generously, he encourages them to welcome Titus along with the other delegates who are coming to administer the collection (16-24) and to complete this project, which they had begun the previous year (**9**:1-15). Paul had boasted to the Macedonians about their readiness to contribute, and now he urges the Corinthians to follow through with their good intentions to avoid the embarrassment that would come if the Macedonians should find them still unprepared (1-5). For willingly participating in this ministry, Paul promises that they will be rewarded by God's supply of the means to give and by the recipients' thanksgiving to God for them (6-15).

In the last main part of the epistle, Paul turns to defend his apostleship to the remaining minority of Corinthians who still refused to acknowledge his authority over them (**10**:1–13:10). He begins to defend himself using a gentle approach (10:1-18) because, following the example of Christ, he does not want to be severe with them unless it is necessary (1-6). He reminds them, however, that he is able to be tough in person as well as in letter if need be (7-11). Unlike the false apostles, he was not arrogating authority to himself because, as the first to preach the Gospel to the Corinthians, his authority lay within the mandate that God had entrusted to him (12-18).

Although Paul knew very well that self-commendation does not make anyone approved, he engages in it tongue-in-cheek because he was rightly jealous for the loyalty of the impressionable Corinthians (**11**:1–12:13). Paul argues that since the Corinthians in their naive gullibility listened patiently to heretical teachers, they ought to bear with him a little, for he was in no way inferior to the greatest of these self-styled super-apostles (11:1-6). If he committed any sin, it was in robbing other churches so that he might serve the Corinthians without charge (7-11). In contrast with

---

Paul's Physical Appearance

For all his apostolic authority, Paul was not an imposing figure in person. The Corinthians sneered, 'His letters are weighty and strong, but his personal presence is unimpressive, and his speech contemptible' (2 Cor 10:1). We cannot be sure of what Paul looked like, but we have an interesting account from the second century that seems to bear the marks of an unembellished tradition:

And a man named Onesiphorous, who had heard that Paul had come to Iconium, went out with his children, Simmias and Zeno and his wife Lectra to meet Paul, that he might receive him to his house. For Titus had told him what Paul looked like. For (hitherto) he had not seen him in the flesh, but only in the spirit. And he went along the royal road that leads to Lystra, and stood there waiting for him, and looked at (all) who came, according to Titus' description. And he saw Paul coming, a man of small stature, with a bald head and crooked legs, in a good state of body, with eyebrows meeting and nose somewhat hooked, full of friendliness; for now he appeared like a man, and now he had the face of an angel (*The Acts of Paul*, trans. Wilhelm Schneemelcher and Rodolphe Kasser, in *New Testament Apocrypha*, ed. Edgar Hennecke; Wilhelm Schneemelcher; and R. McL. Wilson [Louisville, Kentucky: Westminster/John Knox Press, 1992], 2:239).

---

the pseudo-apostles, who deceitfully disguised themselves as apostles of Christ (12-15), Paul presents his credentials as a genuine apostle (16-33). Unlike the pseudo-apostles, Paul did not know how to exploit his converts (16-21a), but he was just as bold in claiming to be a servant of Christ because he had suffered far more than they had for the Gospel (21b-29). Although he had been driven to boasting, he refuses to put on the air of a self-reliant individual who brags about his own accomplishments; rather, he glories in his weakness, of which he relates the humiliating example of escaping persecution at Damascus by being lowered over the city wall in a basket (30-33). Because Paul must give evidence of his apostleship but hates bragging, he finds an indirect way of showing his credentials without calling attention to himself by using the third person to relate his own glorious experience of being caught up into heaven (**12**:1-5). The danger of becoming conceited from this extraordinary revelation was so great that God had to give Paul a thorn in the flesh to keep him humble and teach him that God's power is perfected in weakness (6-10). Paul had already boasted enough to make him foolish by his own standards, so he stopped using foolish arguments and remarked that the Corinthians should not have needed this defence of his apostleship because he had performed among them all the attesting miracles that could be expected of a genuine apostle (11-13).

Because he feared, however, that those at Corinth who were resisting his authority would not yield without a struggle, Paul continues to defend himself in a very personal way by placing the question of whether or not they will accept him in the uneasy context of how he and they will relate to one another when he arrives shortly to visit them for a third time (12:14–13:10). Using the image of parents sacrificing for their children, Paul lets the Corinthians know that he is willing to sacrifice himself completely for them because it is not their money that he wants but themselves (12:14-18). Even his defence of his apostleship was intended for their benefit in the hope that he could avoid the unpleasant confrontation that would be necessary if he should come and find that the recalcitrant Corinthians had not repented of their sin (19-21). As proof of his apostleship, Paul soberly threatens to exercise the authority God has given him to discipline any of them who are unrepentant (**13**:1-4). His real concern, however, is not to prove himself; the reason for writing to them is that he sincerely wants to build them up, if at all possible, rather than to tear them down by disciplining them severely (5-10).

With that wish, Paul comes to his conclusion (11-14). In it he offers some final miscellaneous exhortations (11) and general greetings (12)[1] before closing with a trinitarian benediction, which has commonly become known as 'the grace' (13).

---

1. Verses 12b and 13 in the Greek text are verses 13 and 14 in some English versions (KJV, NASB, NIV, RSV).

OUTLINE OF 2 CORINTHIANS

---

1. Verses 12b and 13 in the Greek text are verses 13 and 14 in some English versions (KJV, NASB, NIV, RSV).

The Collection for the Poor in Jerusalem

Paul's organization and delivery of a collection for the poor saints in Jerusalem draws the third missionary journey to a close. Paul hoped that this practical display of social concern and appreciation on the part of the Gentile believers of Asia Minor, Macedonia, and Achaia would become a means of unifying them with the Jewish Christians at Jerusalem, to whom they were spiritually indebted. This collection plays a strategic role in Paul's missionary program and provides a historical link between several of the Pauline epistles and the Book of Acts.

Taking an offering for the poor in Jerusalem was not a new enterprise for the Gentile church. On a previous occasion the Jerusalem church had been severely struck by famine, and the Gentile church at Antioch sent financial aid to them at the hands of Paul and Barnabas (Acts 11:27-30). When they met with leaders of the church at Jerusalem, they all eagerly affirmed the importance of remembering the poor (Gal 2:9-10).

Paul began planning the second collection more than a year prior to its completion. When he wrote to the Corinthians from Ephesus instructing them about how they should set aside funds for the collection and appoint delegates to ensure its safe delivery, he had already given similar instructions to the churches of Galatia (1 Cor 16:1-9). The participation of the Corinthians in the offering got side tracked temporarily, however, by a bitter dispute with the apostle over a matter of church discipline. Upon hearing of their repentance, Paul returned to Corinth by way of Macedonia, where the churches responded to the need generously and enthusiastically, even though they were experiencing great hardship themselves. With their sacrificial giving as an inspiring example, Paul sent Titus ahead of him to prepare the Corinthians for their contribution (2 Cor 8:1–9:15).

Paul spent about three months at Corinth, during which time he wrote his Epistle to the Romans (Acts 20:3). In it he expresses his intention to visit them after he has delivered the collection to Jerusalem (Rom 15:25-28). Shortly after writing Romans, he travelled to Jerusalem accompanied by delegates from the various churches that had contributed (Acts 20:4).

We know very little about the effect of the collection upon unifying the Jewish and Gentile Christians. The silence of Acts concerning the Gentiles' outpouring of love is stunning; the whole book contains only one direct reference to it in passing (Acts 24:17). Shortly after he arrive in Jerusalem, Paul was arrested and nearly lynched for supposedly bringing a Gentile into the temple (Acts 21:27-36). The best we can assume is that the Jewish Christians were genuinely appreciative, but the orthodox Jews who had rejected the Messiah also rejected this token of reconciliation.

ROMANS

OVERVIEW OF ROMANS

Theme: The revelation of God's righteousness in freely offering salvation to all people through faith

Key verse: Romans 1:17b, 'He who through faith is righteous shall live' (RSV).

Prologue: Paul's Gospel message	1:1-17
I. Doctrinal exposition of God's righteousness through faith	1:18–11:36
A. Righteousness by works excluded by the universal reality of sin	1:18–3:20
B. Justification by faith provided for universal accessibility to salvation	3:21–5:21
C. Justification by faith tied to the personal necessity of sanctification	6:1–8:39
D. Justification by faith reconciled with the national election of Israel	9:1–11:36
II. Practical application of God's righteousness to everyday life	12:1–15:13
Introduction: an appeal to sanctification on the basis of God's mercy	12:1-2
A. Sanctification in relation to other individuals	12:3-21
B. Sanctification in relation to civil government	13:1-7
C. Sanctification according to Christian standards	13:8-14
D. Sanctification in relation to the weaker brother	14:1–15:12
Benediction: a prayer for fulfillment through the Spirit's power	15:13
Epilogue: Paul's personal postscript	15:14–16:27

HISTORICAL BACKGROUND

No one seriously doubts that the Apostle Paul wrote Romans (cf. Rom 1:1), although he probably used Tertius as an amanuensis (Rom 16:22). Most people hold that the epistle is a unity, with the notable exception of Marcion, who deleted chapters 15 and 16 on unorthodox theological grounds. As a result of his omission, the closing benediction and doxology (Rom 16:20b, 25-27) became dislocated in some manuscripts.

The recipients were a mixture of Gentile and Jewish believers living at Rome. They had embraced Christianity long before Paul arrived and were probably meeting in several house churches throughout the city.

At the time of writing in A.D. 57 or 56, Paul was at Corinth and headed for Jerusalem with the collection for the poor (Rom 16:1, 23). He wrote this letter to prepare for a long-anticipated visit to Rome *en route* to Spain (Rom 1:11-13, 15; 15:22-24). Phoebe, a member of the church at Cenchrea, the eastern port of Corinth, probably delivered the letter (Rom 16:1, 2).

Historically, Romans fits into the Book of Acts near the end of the third missionary journey during the three-month stay in Greece just before Paul returned to Jerusalem with the offering for the poor (Acts 20:2-3; Rom 15:25-29). At that time he did not anticipate his intervening imprisonment at Jerusalem and Caesarea, or his survival of a storm at sea before he finally arrived in Rome as a prisoner under house arrest. For these details one must consult Acts 21:27–28:31. Theologically, Romans covers much of the same ground as Galatians concerning justification by faith apart from legalistic works, but the greater development of these themes in Romans implies that it was written later. The wonderfully liberating message of Romans has made it one of the most influential letters in all of history.

The Historical Impact of Romans

Paul's Epistle to the Romans may possibly be the most influential letter ever written. Apart from its immediate impact upon the first century, it has indirectly altered the direction of the church and secular history through its instrumentality in the conversion of several of Christianity's most outstanding leaders.

Augustine lived an immoral life before his conversion in AD 386; he wanted to change but could not find the power to do so. He recounts how the Epistle to the Romans confronted him one day while he was reflecting upon his spiritual condition:

> [28]But as this deep meditation dredged all my wretchedness up from the secret profundity of my being and heaped it all together before the eyes of my heart, a huge storm blew up within me and brought on a heavy rain of tears.
>
> [29]I went on...weeping in the intense bitterness of my broken heart. Suddenly I heard a voice from a house nearby—perhaps a voice of some boy or a girl, I do not know—singing over and over again, 'Pick it up and read, pick it up and read....' Stung into action, I returned to the place where...I had put down...the apostle's letters. I snatched it up, opened it and read in silence the passage on which my eyes first lighted: 'Not in dissipation and drunkenness, not in debauchery and lewdness, nor in arguing and jealousy; but put on the Lord Jesus Christ, and make no provision for the flesh or the gratification of your desires' [Rom 13:13-14]. I had no wish to read further, nor was there need. No sooner had I reached the end of the verse than the light of certainty flooded my heart and all dark shades of doubt vanished away (Augustine, *The Confessions*, 8.12 [28-29], trans. Maria Boulding, *The Works of Saint Augustine*, ed. John E. Rotelle, Part I Vol 1, The Confessions (Hyde Park, New City Press, 1977), 205-208).

Augustine instantly decided to break with the old life and turn to Christ. Eventually he became one of history's most noted thinkers. He set much of the course that theology would take for Roman

Catholics and Protestants alike, helped to define the relationship between the church and state, and provided an effective apology to the surrounding pagan society, which blamed the fall of the Roman Empire on the Christians.

Martin Luther's discovery of justification by faith came as he began to lecture on Romans at the University of Wittenberg in 1515. In the preface to his Latin writings, Luther recounts his conversion experience:

> I had indeed been captivated with an extraordinary ardor for understanding...the Epistle to the Romans...but a single word in Chapter 1 [:17],... 'the righteousness of God'...stood in my way. For I hated that word 'righteousness of God,' which,...I had been taught to understand philosophically regarding the formal or active righteousness...with which God is righteous and punishes the unrighteous sinner.
>
> Though I lived as a monk without reproach, I felt that I was a sinner before God with an extremely disturbed conscience, I could not believe that he was placated by my satisfaction. I did not love, yes, I hated the righteous God who punishes sinners, and secretly, if not blasphemously, certainly murmuring greatly, I was angry with God.... Nevertheless, I beat importunately upon Paul at that place, most ardently desiring to know what St. Paul wanted.
>
> At last, by the mercy of God, meditating day and night, I gave heed to the context of the words, namely, 'In it the righteousness of God is revealed, as it is written, "He who through faith is righteous shall live." ' There I began to understand that the righteousness of God is that by which the righteous lives by a gift of God, namely by faith. And this is the meaning: the righteousness of God is revealed by the gospel, namely, the passive righteousness with which merciful God justifies us by faith, as it is written, 'He who through faith is righteous shall live.' Here I felt that I was altogether born again and had entered paradise itself through open gates. There a totally other face of the entire Scripture showed itself to me....
>
> And I extolled my sweetest word with a love as great as the

hatred with which I had before hated the word 'righteousness of God.' Thus that place in Paul was for me truly the gate to paradise. (Martin Luther, 'Preface to Latin Writings,' in, *Luther's Works*, ed. Jaroslav Pelikan et al, vol. 34, *Career of the Reformer IV*, trans. and ed. Lewis W. Spitz [Philadelphia: Muhlenberg Press, 1960], 336-37).

This personal discovery from Romans soon led this insignificant monk to protest against the Roman Catholic Church's sale of indulgences. The Reformation that followed rapidly changed the religious landscape of Europe and left an indelible political, social, and economic impact on all of western society.

After returning from Georgia, John Wesley attended a meeting at Aldersgate St. in May 1738. There someone was reading from Luther's Preface to Romans. Wesley remarks that 'while [Paul] was describing the change which Christ works in the heart through faith, I felt my heart strangely warmed. I felt I did trust in Christ, Christ alone for my salvation, and an assurance was given me that he had taken away my sins, even mine, and saved me from the law of sin and death.'

That experience was the beginning of Methodism and sparked a revival that probably saved Britain from a revolution similar to the one that threw France into turmoil (John Wesley, *The Works of John Wesley*, ed. Richard P. Heitzenrater, Vol. 1, Journals and Diaries I, [Nashville: Abingdon Press, 1988], 249-50).

In addition to changing the world through these outstanding leaders, Romans has directly impacted countless ordinary individuals. Millions of its readers have come to a joyful understanding and acceptance of its liberating offer of a right standing before God through faith and freedom from the power of sin and death.

THE FLOW OF ROMANS

Paul opens his epistle to the Romans with a prologue introducing himself and the gospel message of justification by faith that he preaches (**1:1-17**). First, he gives an apostolic salutation (1-7) identifying himself as a bond-servant of Christ and an apostle who has been set apart for the Gospel (1), which he summarizes as the good news that the salvation promised by God in the Old Testament prophetic Scriptures has been fulfilled in Jesus Christ, David's natural descendant who has been powerfully attested by the resurrection to be the Son of God (2-4). Paul remarks that through Jesus Christ, he was graciously commissioned as an apostle to the Gentiles, including his readers at Rome whom he greets with his typical salutation of grace and peace (5-7).

In the second paragraph of the prologue, Paul introduces himself in a less formal and more personal way (8-15). He assures the Roman believers that he has been thanking God in his constant prayers for them (8-10) and that he persistently longed to meet them personally so that both he and they might be mutually encouraged by the other's faith (11-13). Because Paul saw it as his apostolic duty to evangelize all people, regardless of race or education, he was eager to preach the Gospel at Rome also (14-15).

His aspiration to preach at Rome naturally leads the apostle into a formal announcement of the central theme which he will develop in the main body of the epistle. The good news is that rather than condemning us, God declares both Jews and Gentiles to be righteous on the basis of faith (16-17).

In the first main part of the epistle, Paul gives a doctrinal exposition of God's righteousness which comes through faith (**1:18–11:36**). In order to establish that the only way to attain righteousness before God is by faith, Paul must first of all demonstrate that the alternative method of attaining righteousness by works is excluded by the universal reality that all people, Jews and Gentiles alike, have sinned and fall under God's condemnation (**1:18–3:20**). He begins by showing that the Gentiles cannot hope to attain righteousness by works because they all stand condemned as sinners before God (1:18-32). God's wrath justly rests upon them because they had received sufficient knowledge about God through nature to make them accountable for their rejection of him (18-23). From natural revelation, they knew that God was eternally powerful and divine (18-20), but they knowingly and willingly rejected this glorious and imperishable God, choosing instead to worship images of mortal men and animals (21-23). Because they sinned against what they knew, God allowed the Gentiles to degrade themselves by following their own sinful inclinations into various forms of moral depravity (24-32). Among these forms of depravity characteristic of the pagans, Paul mentions such sins as idolatry, which he closely links with sensuality (24-25), homosexuality (26-27), and other assorted vices, most of which are social sins against other persons (28-32).

Leaving his conclusion for later, Paul moves on to demonstrate that the Jews are also sinful and stand under God's condemnation (2:1-3:8). Most proud Jews would have readily accepted that the Gentiles were sinners, and even admitted that they themselves occasionally sinned, but they believed that God would overlook their sin because they had special status with him; consequently, Paul brings the Jews under condemnation by showing that God will judge them impartially (2:1-16). He begins to build his case by arguing that God must be impartial in judging them to be consistent with the standards by which they judge other people (1-4); and he asserts, moreover, that the principle by which God will judge Jews and Gentiles alike is one of works: God will punish the unrighteous and reward the righteous according to what they have done (5-11). To these strict affirmations of God's impartiality, Paul adds the qualifier, which does not help the Jews, that, in all fairness, God will judge all people on the basis of their knowledge of his law (12-16).

Paul makes the condemnation of the Jews even more certain by bringing against them specific charges which expose the inconsistency of their lives with their profession (17-29). First, he exposes the inconsistency of their actions with their own moral standards (17-24). Before he mentions their behavior, however,

Paul allows the Jews to build themselves up with lofty bragging about their knowledge of what is right and their ability to point out the shortcomings of others (17-20), so that the contrast will appear even more stark when he poses a series of rhetorical questions which, point by point, reveal that they as a whole were guilty of the very same sinful actions that they condemned (21-24). To follow through, Paul exposes the inconsistency of the Jews having the outward symbolism of circumcision but not practising inward conformity to the law, which he claims makes circumcision worthless; whereas, having the inward spiritual reality of circumcision without the outward physical sign will be counted as circumcision for Gentiles (25-29).

As a rhetorical device, Paul anticipates the objections that a typical Jewish opponent would raise to his arguments and then answers them himself, although he at times abbreviates the formal debate by leaving a premise or conclusion unexpressed with the expectation that his readers will fill it in from a general knowledge of the theological position of both parties (3:1-8). The first objection of Paul's imagined Jewish opponent is that if God is impartial and will judge the Jews in exactly the same way as the Gentiles, then the national privileges that God gave specially to them, such as the law and circumcision, have no value; but Paul replies that these things have great value – and he starts to enumerate some of the advantages of being Jewish, but he gets so caught up in his ideas that he does not make it past the first one (1-2).[1] To complete his thought from the context of the epistle, we must understand that although receiving the law and the sign of circumcision has great value, the benefit is not automatic exemption from judgment, as the Jews had supposed; rather, these privileges were intended to bring God's covenant people to repentance and obedient faith; without this response the privileges have no value in themselves.

Paul anticipates the second objection before it can be stated: even if the Jews are disobedient and unbelieving, God is duty bound by his own character to honour his covenant with them; therefore, all Jews will be saved. Paul replies by switching the argument around: God, indeed, is faithful to his covenant, but those Jews

---

1. He gives a further enumeration of Jewish advantages in 9:4-5.

Old Testament Quotations
Showing the Depravity of Mankind

In Romans 3:10-18, Paul strings together a series of Old Testament quotations from the Psalms and Isaiah to clinch his argument that all of mankind, Jews and Gentiles, are guilty before God. Notice how he refers to specific body parts to show that the whole person is depraved.

Romans 3:10-12
> Psalm 14:1: The fool has said in his heart, "There is no God." They are corrupt, they have committed abominable deeds; There is no one who does good. The Lord has looked down from heaven upon the sons of men, To see if there are any who understand, Who seek after God. They have all turned aside; together they have become corrupt; There is no one who does good, not even one (cf. Psalm 53:1-4)

Romans 3:13a
> Psalm 5:9: There is nothing reliable in what they say; Their inward part is destruction [itself]; Their throat is an open grave; They flatter with their tongue.

Romans 3:13b
> Psalm 140:3: They sharpen their tongues as a serpent; Poison of a viper is under their lips. Selah.

Romans 3:14
> Psalm 10:7: His mouth is full of curses and deceit and oppression; Under his tongue is mischief and wickedness.

Romans 3:15-17
> Isaiah 59:7: Their feet run to evil, And they hasten to shed innocent blood; Their thoughts are thoughts of iniquity; Devastation and destruction are in their highways. They do not know the way of peace, And there is no justice in their tracks; They have made their paths crooked; Whoever treads on them does not know peace.

Romans 3:18
> Psalm 36:1: Transgression speaks to the ungodly within his heart; There is no fear of God before his eyes. (NASB)

who do not believe do not receive the blessings of the covenant (which was made with the nation as a whole, and does not automatically provide for the salvation of every individual Jew); therefore, the condemnation of unbelieving Jews is not inconsistent with the faithfulness of God to his covenant with them (3-4).

The third objection is composed of two intertwining strands which, taken together, argue that if God justifies sinners on the basis of faith instead of works, as Paul claims, then God cannot judge unbelieving Jews because their sin brings about good consequences in demonstrating the righteousness of God and in bringing glory to him. When they are separated, the first strand of the argument reasons that if God justifies sinners on the basis of faith instead of works, the greater the sin, the greater God's grace, the greater the glory God receives;[2] therefore, one ought to sin more so that God will receive more glory; the second strand reasons that if the Jews had not sinned, God would not have received any glory in justifying them, as he does by justifying sinners on the basis of faith; therefore, he has no right to judge them since he profits from their sin. In both cases, the premises are true, but the conclusions are so absurd that they do not deserve an answer, although Paul suggests his response would be that God must be righteous in judging unbelieving Jews or else he would have no right to judge anyone at all, contrary to the Jews' accepted belief that the world must be judged for its sins (5-8).

Having satisfactorily answered these objections, Paul directs his demonstration of the sinfulness and consequent condemnation of all people towards its conclusion by moving beyond arguments that focus upon the Jews or Gentiles in particular, to ones that apply universally to the sinfulness of the entire world (9-20). On the basis of the evidence he has already presented, Paul states the charge that all people, whether Jews or Gentiles, equally fall under God's condemnation because of their sin (9). He then offers proof for this charge from a compilation of Old Testament scriptures (10-18), which he puts forward first of all to condemn everyone categorically (10-12), and then to describe the pervasiveness of

---

2. Paul will return to discuss the theology underlying this conclusion in greater detail in 5:20–6:2.

human depravity in terms of various corrupted parts of the body including the throat and tongue (13a-b), lips (13c), mouth (14), feet (15-17), and eyes (18). The biblical revelation to which Paul appeals may speak more directly to the Jews than the Gentiles, who have already been condemned by natural revelation, but the universal scope of these scriptures warrants Paul to conclude categorically that the law condemns everyone; therefore, no one will be justified before God on the basis of a legalistic performance of works (19-20).

Having shown that the universal reality of sin has precluded any possibility of attaining righteousness by works, Paul now goes on to show that God has made salvation universally accessible to all people through justification by faith (3:21–5:21). The heart of the Gospel is that God graciously provided a way for all who believe to be declared righteous (3:21-31) on the basis of Christ's saving work (21-26), which is seen as a redemptive event that enables God to act graciously in justifying us (21-24) and as a propitiatory sacrifice that permits God to act righteously in overlooking sin (25-26). Using a series of rhetorical questions, Paul draws out three ramifications of justification by faith being the means of attaining a righteous standing before God (27-31). First, because righteousness comes by faith rather than works, all boasting about one's own accomplishments is excluded (27-28). Second, since God, who is one, has only one method of justifying both Jews and Gentiles, namely faith, salvation is universally available to everyone (29-30). Third, justification by faith does not nullify the law; rather, it establishes it by acknowledging and fully meeting its requirements (31).

Now that Paul has set forth the essential features of the doctrine of justification by faith abstractly in theological terms, he proceeds to support the truthfulness of that doctrine with arguments drawn from the Old Testament (4:1-25). He begins by citing the precedent of Abraham, the first patriarch of the Jewish nation, who was reckoned righteous on the basis of his faith in God's promise rather than by works (1-5). Paul finds corroboration for Abraham's justification by faith in the experience of David, Israel's greatest king, who was forgiven apart from any works (6-8). He then returns to amplify Abraham's case and draw another argument for justification by faith from it: because Abraham was justified before he was circumcised,[2] circumcision must not have been the cause of his justification (9-12). Paul also argues that justification must be by faith in order to include all the world in God's promise to Abraham (13-17). This argument comes in two parts: first, if justification were by the law, it would nullify the promise to Abraham, which was by faith, but the promise to Abraham cannot be nullified; therefore, justification is not by the law (13-15). Second, if justification were by law, it could only include those who received the law (i.e. the Jews); but the promise specifically includes Gentiles, therefore justification must be by some principle other than law (16-17). As he concludes his confirmation of justification by faith from the Old Testament, Paul shifts from argumentation to application by holding up Abraham's faith in the promise of God as an example for us to follow (18-25). He highlights the strength of Abraham's faith in believing that God would keep his word even though all the natural circumstances seemed contrary (18-22), and he draws out the relevance of Abraham's example to those who also will be justified by believing in the same God, who raised Jesus from the dead (23-25).

Now that the case for justification by faith has been firmly established, Paul proceeds to enumerate some of the spiritual benefits of justification (5:1-11). Among these benefits, he includes the enjoyment of a newly found state of peace with God (1-2a), the ability to rejoice while patiently enduring tribulations confident that God, who has poured out his love into our hearts, will fulfill our expectations of sharing in his glory (2b-5), and, finally, freedom from God's wrath even though we were helpless and unworthy at the time that God reconciled us to himself (6-11). Paul takes a moment to elaborate upon this last benefit of justification by noting that while we were enemies with God, we were reconciled by Christ's death (6-8); therefore, we may expect to enjoy an ongoing relationship on the basis of Christ's life now that we are friends (9-11).

To extol the beneficial effects of Christ's act of righteousness

2. Genesis 15:6; 17:23-24.

in providing the means of justification for the entire human race, Paul contrasts it with the detrimental effects of Adam's sinful act, which resulted in the condemnation of the entire race (12-21). As a result of Adam's transgression, sin and death came to the whole world (12-14), but as a result of Christ's gracious gift, justification and life were made available to everyone (15-17). The actions of Adam and Christ both affect the entire race: through a single act of Adam's disobedience, the entire race became condemned as sinners, and through one act of Christ's obedience, life-giving justification was brought to everyone (18-19); the power of grace to bring life, however, greatly surpassed the power of sin to bring death (20-21).

Since the logic of being saved by grace rather than by works suggested to Paul's opponents that we may presumptuously continue sinning, Paul ties God's gracious provision of justification by faith to our personal need for sanctification (6:1–8:39). He gives two reasons why sanctification is absolutely necessary (6:1-23). The first of these is that justification never takes place in isolation from our union with Christ in his death and resurrection (1-11). It is unthinkable that we should continue to live in sin because baptism (1-4) symbolizes that we have died and been buried together with Christ in respect to sin (1-3) and have been raised to live a new life unto God (4). The fact that our old nature has been crucified with Christ and we have been raised with him to a new life (5-14) implies that we have been legally released from bondage to sin (5-7). We are to make our identification with Christ practical by giving sober consideration to our legal status as dead to sin and alive to God and then act accordingly (8-11). Because sin's legal power over us has been broken, it is possible for us to experience freedom from its domination by voluntarily placing our bodies at God's disposal as instruments of righteousness rather than at the disposal of sin as instruments of unrighteousness (12-14).

The second reason why sanctification is absolutely necessary is that having acknowledged God as our master, we are duty-bound to serve him completely (15-23). There are only two alternatives: either we are slaves who serve sin, which leads to death, or we are slaves who obey God, which leads to righteousness; being our own

> ### 'May it Never Be!'
>
> Paul uses the expression, 'May it never be!' ten times throughout Romans to underscore his abhorrence of an inference that he fears his opponents might falsely draw from his argument:
>
> **3:3** What then? If some did not believe, their unbelief will not nullify the faithfulness of God, will it? May it never be!
>
> **3:5** But if our unrighteousness demonstrates the righteousness of God, what shall we say? The God who inflicts wrath is not unrighteous, is He? (I am speaking in human terms.) May it never be!
>
> **3:31** Do we then nullify the Law through faith? May it never be! On the contrary, we establish the Law.
>
> **6:1** What shall we say then? Are we to continue in sin that grace might increase? May it never be!
>
> **6:15** What then? Shall we sin because we are not under law but under grace? May it never be!
>
> **7:7** What shall we say then? Is the Law sin? May it never be!
>
> **7:13** Therefore did that which is good become [a cause of] death for me? May it never be!
>
> **9:14** What shall we say then? There is no injustice with God, is there? May it never be!
>
> **11:1** I say then, God has not rejected His people, has He? May it never be!
>
> **11:11** I say then, they did not stumble so as to fall, did they? May it never be! (NASB)

master is not an option that is open to us (15-18). Having laid down the alternatives, Paul clarifies that slavery to righteousness, which, thankfully, the Roman Christians had wholeheartedly accepted, carries the advantages of sanctification plus the free gift of eternal life over slavery to sin, which only makes its captives ashamed and pays them death for wages (19-23).

Sanctification is not only a personal necessity that God requires of us but also a legal possibility that has come about by our new relationship to the law (7:1-6). To support the claim that our death annuls the law's power over us, Paul appeals to the analogy of the release of a married woman from her obligations to her marriage covenant by the death of her husband (1-3). He then applies this illustration to our release from our obligation to keep all of the law's requirements by our death in union with Christ (4-6).

In spite of this encouraging assurance that sanctification is legally possible, the depressing reality that human experience, in which the apostle himself shared, is often one of defeat, compelled Paul to suspend the forward thrust of his argument temporarily so that he might consider the Christian's struggle with sin, especially in the light of statements he had made earlier that might be misunderstood as disparaging the law (7-25). Speaking in the first person, he affirms that the law is intrinsically good, but rather than sanctifying him, it only condemns him by making him aware of his many violations (7-13). Paul does not blame his failure to attain his aspirations to sanctification on the law but rather on indwelling sin (14-25). He confesses to an internal tension between wishing to do what is right and doing what is wrong (14-19). This tension he attributes to the operation of two conflicting principles within him: his mind joyfully serves the law of God, but his flesh makes him a prisoner to the dictates of sin; rather than sinking into despair, however, as he could easily do, he bursts into a triumphant exclamation that victory can be found in Jesus Christ (20-25).

With this hopeful confidence in view, the positive tone returns to the argument as Paul begins to identify more precisely the source of our spiritual enablement for sanctification (**8**:1-11). He finds the foundation for that enablement in the implications of Christ's sacrifice (1-4). Building upon what he has said earlier about our legal release from the law,[3] Paul affirms that those who are in Christ are not subject to condemnation, even though we are not perfectly sanctified experientially, because the ruling power of the life-giving Holy Spirit has set us free from the authority of sin and death over us (1-2). By his sacrifice, Jesus Christ fulfilled all that the law required of us so that we might now be free to live according to the Spirit rather than the flesh (3-4).

Our legal freedom from the condemnation of the law and our fulfillment of its requirements in Christ, becomes the basis for the

---

3. Romans 7:6.

operation of the indwelling of the Holy Spirit to sanctify us experientially (5-11). The Holy Spirit works upon our minds in opposition to our sinful fleshly desires; by focusing our minds upon the Spirit rather than our flesh, we are enabled to live a holy life that pleases God (5-8). Furthermore, the Spirit who lives in us is the same one who raised Jesus from the dead, and he will also grant eternal life to our mortal bodies (9-11).

Paul sees sanctification as a process that is begun in this life, but he anticipates its glorious completion in the future (12-25). He assures those who by the Spirit are presently putting to death the deeds of the flesh that they will live because their following the Spirit is a sure sign that they are children of God and, therefore, also heirs who will be glorified together with Christ (12-17). Not only will God's children be glorified, but all of creation will share in that glory and be liberated from its involuntary subjection to futility and corruption (18-25). The goal to which all of creation looks with eager anticipation is the unveiling of our glory (18-21); in the meantime, while we along with the rest of creation groan under sufferings, we must patiently and confidently wait in hope (22-25).

We can be assured that we will reach the glorious completion of our sanctification because each member of the trinity is working on our behalf to ensure that we attain that goal (26-39). The Holy Spirit, who knows both us and the Father intimately, picks up where our feeble prayers leave off and intercedes for us himself with groanings that are too deep to be expressed in words (26-27). We who love the Father may be certain that he is working all things for our ultimate good because he planned from the beginning that those whom he foreknew should resemble his Son; furthermore, he acted in accordance with this plan by calling and justifying us, and, as far as he is concerned, our glorification is as certain as if it were already accomplished (28-30). So that the Father's wonderful plan for us might be realized, the Son provided everything necessary to carry it to completion (31-39). At great personal sacrifice to both the Father and himself, the Son died on our behalf so that we might freely receive all the good things intended for us (31-32). Because Jesus Christ himself is now interceding for us at the Father's right hand, we may be certain that no one can convict us of wrongdoing (33-34). The love of God for us as expressed in Jesus Christ is so powerful that nothing in heaven or earth, natural or demonic, present or future can separate us from it (35-39).

Having shown that since all people, Jews and Gentiles alike, are condemned sinners, and that the only way for anyone to be saved is by faith in Christ, with whom the believer is united in death and resurrection so as to be freed from sin and made alive to righteousness leading eventually to personal glorification and the restoration of the entire created order, Paul has now reached the logical conclusion of his exposition of justification by faith. But if justification only comes through faith, Paul's confident assurance that God is faithful in bringing our salvation to its glorious completion raises the question of how God can be faithful in fulfilling his promises of salvation to Israel when it as a nation has rejected this method of attaining righteousness (9:1–11:36). Paul's answer to this question, which demanded explanation in view of the large-scale apostolic movement of the gospel from the Jews to the Gentiles, unfolds within the grand sweep of redemptive history, one step at a time, beginning with a review of God's election of Israel in the past (9:1-29).

Paul's deep personal grief over the unbelief of most Jews draws the apostle back to enumerate some of the great national privileges that still belong to his people,[4] which lifts his spirit into a doxology (1-5).[5] After the 'amen', he returns to argue that the rejection of Israel is consistent with its election because the seed promised to Abraham was restricted to his spiritual descendants and did not necessarily include all of his physical descendants (6-13). In support of this restriction, Paul cites first God's promise that Abraham's seed would be reckoned through Isaac (6-9), and then God's choice of Jacob over Esau, although he is probably thinking of the two brothers here in terms of corporate solidarity as heads of two races rather than as individuals in themselves (10-13).

Paul also cites two examples to support his next point that God's freedom in acting mercifully is by no means incompatible with

---

4. In Romans 3:1-2 he had started to mention some advantages of being Jewish but only got as far as the first one.

5. Cf. Romans 1:25. Paul will break forth into a doxology again in 11:33-36 and introduce benedictions in 15:13 and 33 before he concludes with a final doxology in 16:25-27.

justice, contrary to what his opponents were arguing (14-18). In the case of Moses, God's freedom in showing, or withholding, mercy was clearly consistent with justice because God demonstrated more mercy than Moses had any right to expect (14-16). One might suppose that Paul would reinforce the same point in the case of Pharaoh – and, in fact, the very signs that resulted in the hardening of Pharaoh by his persistent rejection of them can be understood as God's mercy in giving him an unprecedented opportunity to acknowledge God and repent – but there is a lingering sense that God might not be completely just in Pharaoh's case because rather than demonstrating clearly why God is just, Paul simply asserts that he is (17-18).

The objection of Paul's interlocutor, which refuses to lie silent for long, resurfaces in the complaint that God should not find fault with anyone if he chooses to show mercy to some and harden others because no one can resist his will, to which Paul responds that God's sovereignty is, in fact, compatible with human responsibility (19-29). Before Paul presents his arguments against this objection, however, he puts the objector in his proper place by reminding him that no creature has a right to talk back to its Creator in an accusing tone of voice (19-21). Paul then offers at least a partial explanation, even though it does not fully address the problems of freedom and determinism, by showing from redemptive history that God's mercy exceeds our merits (22-29). We cannot find fault with God because he has been far more patient in putting up for a long time with vessels of wrath who did not deserve mercy (i.e. the Jews, who were part of the elect nation) and far more merciful towards vessels of mercy (i.e. the redeemed, who in Paul's day were primarily Gentiles who were not part of the elect nation) than anyone has a right to expect (22-24). Paul supports his contention by quoting first from the prophet Hosea to show that God was merciful in calling Gentiles to be his children although they were not his own, and then from Isaiah to show that God was merciful in leaving the Jews a remnant rather than destroying them completely (25-29).[6]

In view of Israel's election in the past, Paul now proceeds to

---

6. Hosea 2:23 (LXX, MT 2:25); 1:10 (LXX, MT 2:1); Isaiah 10:22-23; 1:9.

offer a theological explanation of Israel's present rejection of the Gospel (9:30–10:21). He identifies the legalistic approach of Israel to righteousness as the reason why the nation as a whole rejected Christ and failed to attain the righteousness required by the law (9:30–10:4). To be more specific, the Jews failed to attain righteousness because they went about it by works rather than by faith; ironically, they missed the goal of righteousness, even though they tried very hard, because they pursued the right object by the wrong method; whereas, the Gentiles, who were not looking for righteousness, stumbled across it by the great discovery of justification by faith (9:30-33). Although the Jews were very zealous for God, they failed to attain righteousness because, not knowing about God's righteousness that comes through believing in Christ, they directed all their energy into a misguided and futile attempt to establish their own legalistic righteousness **(10:1-4)**.

Having identified the reason why most Jews rejected the Gospel, Paul now proceeds to contrast their distorted method of legalistically seeking to earn their own righteousness, with God's intended method of imputing Christ's righteousness through faith (5-13). He points out that the requirements of God's method of righteousness are very simple: no one needs to attempt the impossible heroic feat of climbing up into heaven to bring God down to mankind or of descending into the nether world to free its captives, because God's presence with us and our release from death have already been achieved by Christ's incarnation and resurrection – all one needs to do is to believe and act accordingly (5-10). Not only are the requirements of the Gospel simple, but its application extends universally to everyone who calls upon the Lord, whether Jew or Gentile (11-13).

The simplicity and universal availability of the Gospel lead to Paul's accusation that the Jews are morally culpable for rejecting it (14-21). Before he presents the case against them, however, Paul acknowledges that a logical chain of preconditions needs to be fulfilled before someone can call upon Christ for salvation (14-15). First, one must believe in Christ (14a), which presupposes one's hearing the Gospel (14b); and hearing, in turn, is only possible if the Gospel is proclaimed (14c); and it can only be proclaimed if

God commissions messengers to proclaim it (15). The Jews can be held accountable for rejecting the Gospel (16-21) because they, as a whole, had heard the message which God's commissioned apostles had proclaimed throughout the world (16-18). Against the objection that although the Jews may have heard the words being proclaimed, they had not really understood their meaning, Paul counters that they should have been able to understand because both Moses and Isaiah prophesied that Gentiles, who were characterized by their theological dullness and lack of interest in spiritual things, would respond to the Gospel to the Jews' embarrassment (19-20). The Jews of Paul's day were without excuse because the only precondition to their being saved that remained unfulfilled was the one that depended upon them: rather than believing in Christ, they copied the Jews of Isaiah's day in obstinately refusing the grace that God patiently held out to them (21).

The patient mercy of God towards his chosen people in the past forms a bridge for Paul to move beyond their present rejection to the hope that they will be reconciled in the future through God's continued efforts (**11**:1-32). Paul uses two rhetorical questions to frame his grounds for this hope. In answer to the first question, 'Has God rejected his people?' Paul affirms emphatically that God has not rejected them because a righteous remnant still persists down to the present time (1-10). Working back from himself to the seven thousand righteous men in Elijah's day, Paul argues that God has always preserved a righteous remnant for himself, even during the worst of times in Israel's history; therefore, he must not have completely rejected his people (1-6). Given that God has not rejected his people, Paul explains the nation's rejection of the Gospel as a temporary hardening of the spiritually insensitive majority until the present (7-10).

Paul answers the second question, 'Did Israel stumble so as to fall irrecoverably?' by emphatically affirming that the Jews will be reinstated in God's redemptive program (11-32). Looking back upon the great blessing that their rejection was in bringing salvation to the Gentiles, he pauses for a moment to anticipate the exciting prospect that even greater blessings will flow from their reinstatement (11-16).

With the glorious prospect of the Jews' reinstatement before him, Paul goes back to show the legitimacy of this hope by drawing an analogy to the cultivation of an olive tree (17-24). In this analogy, the Jews, whom he likens to natural olive branches, were cut off because of their unbelief, and believing Gentiles were grafted in because of their faith (17-21). The fact that the Gentiles were grafted in even though they were not natural branches implies that the Jews, who are natural branches, will much more readily be grafted back in if they meet the same condition of faith (22-24).

Until this point, Paul's argument for Israel's national restoration has been somewhat theoretical, but now he turns to ground it in the certainty of God's promise (25-32). He affirms that in the eschaton all Israel will be saved, even as Scripture promises, notwithstanding their present hardness of heart (25-27); and he explains their disobedience as God's means of extending mercy to the Gentiles so that the Gentiles' reception of mercy might in turn become the means for God to restore mercy to his elect people in fulfillment of his irrevocable promise to the patriarchs (28-32). The humanly unfathomable wisdom of God in planning redemption across the course of history in such a way that he might show mercy to as many people as possible from all races, whether Jews or Gentiles, moves Paul to break forth in a spontaneous doxology (33-36).

Now that Paul has finished expounding God's gracious provision of righteousness to all people by faith along with the theological implications of this doctrine for Israel's national election and for the believer's personal sanctification, he turns in the second main part of the epistle to apply the theological foundation of justification by faith to everyday living in intensely practical ways (12:1–15:13). He introduces the new section by appealing to his readers on the basis of God's great mercy to them, which he has just expounded, to work out their sanctification experientially by presenting themselves to God as living sacrifices and by being transformed by the renewing of their minds (12:1-2).

The first sphere in which they are to work out their sanctification is in their relations to other individuals (3-21). In relation to those within the body of Christ, Paul directs the believers at Rome to work out their sanctification by exercising their spiritual gifts as

God intended (3-8). To this end, Paul exhorts them individually to discern with humility and honesty the role that God has assigned to each of them within the body (3-5) and to exercise their gifts according to their varying God-given endowments (6-8). In relation to society, whether inside or outside the church, Paul instructs them to work out their sanctification by always conducting themselves in a Christian manner (9-21). First, he lists a series of significant areas of conduct in which he exhorts them to serve others in ways that roughly correspond to several of the gifts he has mentioned (9-13); then partway through his discussion of the Christian's conduct in society, he subtly shifts his perspective from areas in which believers are to serve to different types of people with whom they must relate (14-21). Paul exhorts them to sympathetic relations with people in general, although he probably has primarily other believers in mind (14-16), and to peaceful relations particularly with non-Christians who oppose them (17-21).

The second sphere in which they are to work out their sanctification is in relation to civil government (**13**:1-7). Paul commands them to submit to civil authorities out of fear of punishment if they do evil (1-4) and to pay taxes so that they may keep a clean conscience, knowing that God has ordained the state for the necessary administration of society (5-7).

This rationale for Christians to co-operate with civil government leads Paul to a consideration of universal standards by which Christians are to work out their sanctification, while the particular relationships in which they need to be sanctified momentarily slips into the background (8-14). The fundamental principle by which all of one's conduct should be gauged is that of love for one's neighbour, which is the essence of the Old Testament law (8-10). The motivation by which all of one's conduct should be inspired is a sober consideration of the present age of darkness in light of the coming age, which has already dawned and is about to break forth into full day (11-14).

Keeping in mind the principle of loving one's neighbour and the motivation of living in light of the coming age, Paul addresses one's relation to a weaker brother as the final sphere in which the Roman Christians needed to work out their sanctification (**14**:1–

15:12). First, he lays down some guidelines for mutual toleration with respect to disputable matters, such as eating meat and observing holy days (14:1-12). They are to accept one who is weak in faith without passing judgment on that person's opinions (1-4). At the same time, they are to be firmly convinced in their own minds about their convictions on these issues before God (5-8), but they are to leave judgment to him (9-12). Second, Paul sets limitations upon personal liberties (13-23). Instead of placing stumbling blocks in the way of those whose faith is weak (13-18), the strong are to pursue peace and mutual edification (19-21); and all of them are to limit their actions by what is consistent with their own convictions (22-23). Finally, Paul exhorts the Roman Christians to imitate Christ's example in two particular aspects (**15:**1-12): as Christ denied himself for our sake, so those who are strong ought to make personal sacrifices for the good of their neighbors (1-6); and as Christ accepted us, so both the weak and the strong ought to accept one another to the end that God might be glorified through their united praise (7-12). Paul draws the second part of the epistle to a close with a benediction wishing his readers hope, joy and peace as a consequence of carrying out his practical exhortations through the Holy Spirit's power (13).

This climax would have been a fitting place for Paul to leave off writing, but he adds an epilogue so that he might mention some matters of a more personal nature which would have intruded upon his development of the epistle proper (15:14–16:27). In his concluding remarks (15:14-33), Paul defines the nature of his apostolic ministry (14-21) as being directed primarily to Gentiles (14-16) who had not been reached by the Gospel (17-21). He also discusses a projected itinerary for a future missionary journey (22-33). As he mentioned earlier in the prologue to the epistle, he had wanted to visit the believers at Rome for some time, but he had always been hindered from coming to them (22). Now at last, he hoped to visit them on his way to Spain (23-24) as soon as he fulfilled his obligation of delivering the collection for the poor in Jerusalem (25-29). He requests prayer that all will go well in Jerusalem and that he will be able to come to Rome in a rejoicing spirit (30-33).

Following these remarks about his ministry, Paul includes a long list of personal greetings (**16**:1-24). He commends Phoebe, who was probably the bearer of the letter, asking that she be received warmly (1-2); and he greets by name many of the believers at Rome with whom he was personally acquainted (3-16). Speaking in more general terms, he interjects a warning about those who would cause dissention in the church by their false teaching (17-20); he then conveys the greetings of his fellow-workers and several good friends who were with him at the time of writing (21-24). Finally, he concludes with a doxology of praise to God (16:25-27).

The Inscription of Erastus

A large limestone slab dating to the time of Paul has been found at Corinth, from where the apostle wrote his Epistle to the Romans. It bears the words, ERASTVS. PRO. AED. S. P. STRAVIT; 'Erastus in return for his aedileship laid [this pavement] at his own expense.' This Erastus is probably the city treasurer mentioned in Romans 16:23 (John McRay, *Archaeology and the New Testament* [Grand Rapids: Baker, 1991], 331).

OUTLINE OF ROMANS

The Prison Epistles

Colossians

OVERVIEW OF COLOSSIANS

Theme: The pre-eminence of Jesus Christ

Key verses: Colossians 1:17-18, 'And He is before all things, and in Him all things hold together. He is also head of the body, the church; and He is the beginning, the first-born from the dead; so that He Himself might come to have first place in everything' (NASB).

HISTORICAL BACKGROUND

Colossians is generally considered to be written by Paul, although a few scholars have questioned its authenticity because of similarities to Ephesians (see the notes on Ephesians). Colossae was situated in the Asian province of Phrygia about twelve miles upstream from its sister cities, Laodicea and Hierapolis, which sat on opposite sides of the Lycus River forming a neat triangle (Col 4:13). Colossae had once been a great cosmopolitan city, but Laodicea grew while it diminished to the extent that it became the least important of any city to receive a letter from Paul. The apostle did not found the church at Colossae himself, and most of its members had never met him personally (Col 2:1). Rather, it was founded by Epaphras, a native of Colossae who had probably been converted during Paul's extended stay at Ephesus on the third missionary journey and had then carried the Gospel back home (Col 1:7; 4:12; Acts 19:1–20:1, esp. 19:10).

Paul probably wrote this epistle in response to a request from Epaphras, who had come to him seeking advice on how to deal with a false teaching that was infecting the church (Col 4:12-13; Phile 23). The Colossian heresy was a syncretistic mixture of incipient gnostic dualism that made Christ a lesser emanation from God and legalistic Judaism that insisted upon the observance of certain religious rituals and holy days. Often standing the false teaching on its head, Paul countered that the Christ, who became flesh, is supreme over everything in heaven and on earth and that in him we have everything we need without adding legalism, which is spiritually impotent.

Tychicus carried this letter to the Colossians (Col 4:7-8; cf. Eph 6:21-22) along with a letter to Philemon, who was a Christian slave-owner in the Colossian church. At the same time he took a letter to the Ephesians, which was probably circulated at Colossae and the other churches of the Lycus Valley (Col 4:16). Most likely Paul was writing from house arrest in Rome in A.D. 60 or 61 (cf. Acts 28:16-31), but some scholars have argued that he wrote earlier from prison at Caesarea or Ephesus.

Correlations between Colossians and Ephesians

Colossians and Ephesians bear great similarities to each other. Although they come from different perspectives, both epistles deal with the pre-eminence of Christ in the church. Colossians is primarily concerned with Christ, the head of the body (Col 1:18), while Ephesians emphasizes the body over which Christ is the head (Eph 1:22-23). Ephesians is a relatively short book, with only 155 verses, but over 75 parallels can be found in Colossians. The freedom with which words and concepts are interchanged between the two letters suggests that both of them were written by the same mind at about the same time.

Col 1:9-11   *we* **have not ceased** *to pray* **for you** and to ask **that** *you may be* filled with the **knowledge** of His will in all *spiritual wisdom* and *understanding,*...**strengthened with power**, according to His glorious might....

Eph 1:16-17   *I*...*do not* **cease** *giving thanks* **for you**, while making mention of you *in my prayers*; **that**...*God* ...*may give* to you *a spirit of wisdom* and *revelation* in the **knowledge** of Him.

Eph 3:16   that He would grant you... to be **strengthened with power** through His Spirit in the inner man

Col 1:14   **in** *whom* **we have redemption, the forgiveness of sins**

Eph 1:7   **In** *Him* **we have redemption** through His blood, **the forgiveness of** *our trespasses*

Col 1:16   in Him all things were created...whether thrones or **dominions** or **rulers** or **authorities**

Eph 1:21   far above all **rule** and **authority** and power and **dominion**

Col 1:25-27   I was made a minister according to **the stewardship** *from God bestowed on me* **for** *your benefit,* that I might fully carry out the preaching of the word of God, that is, **the mystery which** *has been hidden* from the past ages and **generations**; but **has now been** *manifested* to His saints, to whom God willed to make known what is the riches of the glory of this mystery among the Gentiles, *which is Christ in you*, the hope of glory.

Eph 3:2-8   you have heard of **the stewardship** *of God's grace* which was given *to me* **for** *you*; And...you can understand my insight into **the mystery** of Christ, **which** in other **generations** *was not made known* to the sons of men, as it **has now been** *revealed*...to be specific, *that the Gentiles are fellow-heirs and* *fellow-members of the body*...through the gospel, of which I was made a minister according to the working of His power.

Col 3:2   If then *you have been* **raised up with Christ,** keep seeking the things above where Christ is, **seated** *at the right hand of God.*

Eph 2:6   *[God]* **raised us up with Him [Christ]** and **seated** us together with Him *in the heavenly places,* in Christ Jesus

Col 3:9-10 Do not lie to one another, since *you laid* **aside the old self** with its evil practices, **and** *have put* **on the new self** *who is being renewed* to a true knowledge according to the *image of the One who created him*

Eph 4:22-24 *lay* **aside the old self,** which is being corrupted in accordance with the lusts of deceit, and...*be renewed* in the spirit of your mind, **and** *put* **on the new self,** *which in the likeness of God has been* **created** in righteousness and holiness of the truth.

Col 3:15–4:1 And let the peace of Christ rule in your hearts, to which indeed you were called in one body; and be thankful. *Let the word of Christ richly dwell within you*; with all wisdom **teaching and admonishing one another with psalms and hymns and spiritual songs, singing** *with thankfulness in* **your hearts to God.** And whatever you do in word or deed, do **all in the name of** *the* **Lord Jesus, giving thanks** through Him to God the Father.
Wives, be subject to your husbands.... Husbands, love your wives....Children, *be obedient to* **your parents....Fathers, do not** *exasperate* **your children....Slaves,...** *obey* **your masters.... Masters,** *grant to your slaves justice....*

Eph 5:18–6:9 *be filled with the Spirit,* **speaking** to one another in psalms and hymns and spirituals songs, singing *and making melody with* your heart to *the Lord*; *always* giving thanks for all things **in the name of** *our* **Lord Jesus Christ** to God, even the Father; and **be subject to one another** in the fear of Christ.
Wives, *[be subject to]* **to you** *own* **husbands....**
Husbands, love your wives....Children, *obey* **your parents....**
Fathers, do not *provoke* **your children.... Slaves,** *be obedient to*...**your masters.... Masters,** *do the same things....*(NASB)

THE FLOW OF COLOSSIANS

Following standard epistolary form, the introduction to Colossians (**1**:1-14) opens with the Apostle Paul and Timothy sending their greetings of grace and peace to the saints at Colossae (1-2). It also includes Paul's expression of sincere thanksgiving for the initial progress of the Colossians in the Gospel (3-8) and a prayer for their continued growth in spiritual understanding (9-14).

A Pre-pauline Hymn?

Many scholars speculate that Paul adapted the high christological passage in Colossians 1:15-20 from an earlier hymn. It is equally possible, however, that Paul composed it himself. The subject matter naturally elevates the language above ordinary prose, but the passage still falls short of a strict poetic structure.

15 Who is the image of the invisible God,
       The first-born of all creation,
16 For by Him were created all things,
       In the heavens and on the earth,
       The visible and the invisible,
           Whether thrones or dominions or rulers or authorities,
           All things through Him and for Him were created;
17 And He is before all things,
       And all things in Him hold together.

18 And He is the head of the body, the church,
       Who is the source,
           The first-born from the dead,
           In order that He might in all things
               come to have the pre-eminence,
19 For in Him all the fullness was pleased to dwell,
20   And through Him to reconcile all things to Himself,
                   Having made peace through the blood of His cross,
                   Through Him, whether things upon the earth or
                       things in the heavens.

As with many of Paul's epistles, Colossians begins with a doctrinal section which sets forth the aspects of Christian theology most relevant to the particular needs of the readers (1:15–3:4). The doctrinal section in Colossians is generally concerned with presenting the supremacy of the Christian Gospel over against the inferior alternatives that were posing a threat to it at Colossae (1:15–2:5). The first line of evidence to which Paul turns to demonstrate the supremacy of the Gospel is the person and work of Christ (1:15-23). Using a hymnic form, he declares that Christ is pre-eminent over the entire universe, including the invisible heavenly powers, by right of creation (15-17); he is also head of the church, his body, by right of redemption (18-20). Furthermore, Paul declares that Christ has reconciled the Colossians to himself by his death so that they might live holy lives (21-23).

To his christological presentation of the supremacy of the Gospel, Paul adds some personal notes about his ministry and sufferings for the sake of this Gospel (1:24–2:5). He comments first concerning his ministry to the church in general (1:24-29) by suffering for Christ (24), by being a steward of God's recently disclosed mystery, namely that Christ indwells Gentiles (25-27), and by admonishing all believers so that he might present them to God complete in Christ (28-29). Following these general comments, he notes his concern for the Colossians in particular (2:1-5). Although he had not met most of them personally, he was deeply concerned that they realize the full spiritual wealth that was theirs in Christ (1-3), especially in view of the threat to their well-being posed by the misleading theology of some persuasive false teachers (4). Even though he was physically absent from them, Paul assures the Colossians that he was one with them in spirit and was rejoicing to hear that so far they were standing firm in their faith (5).

Without directly expounding the nature of the Colossian heresy, Paul presents counterarguments against it that expose its weaknesses in contrast with the superiority of the Christian Gospel (6-23). Before attacking specific points, Paul sounds a methodological warning about the emptiness of the philosophical speculation upon which the false teaching was based (6-8). The Colossians had a solid foundation for their faith in adhering to the traditions that had been handed down to them concerning the lordship of Jesus Christ (6-7). In view of the stability of building upon Christ as one's foundation, they were to be especially wary of the grave potential for deception in basing their faith upon human speculation (8).

Paul now sets forth several points showing the all-sufficiency of Christ in contrast with the implicit inadequacy of the false teaching (9-15). Contrary to the false teachers, Paul asserts that the full embodiment of deity permanently resides in Christ, who has made believers complete in him (9-10). Through baptism, we have been united with Christ in both his death and his resurrection (11-12); any record of our sins has been thoroughly erased (13-14). Furthermore, Christ has publicly triumphed over all the spiritual powers that are hostile to us (15).

Because the believer's complete sufficiency is found in Christ, Paul warns the Colossians not to let the false teachers impose upon them the observance of rituals that were really only prophetic shadows pointing to their substance in Christ (16-17). He also warns the Colossians not to let themselves be demeaned by false teachers who conceitedly boasted about their private revelations but did not hold on to Christ (18-19). Finally, Paul warns that although the ascetic rigors which the false teachers demanded might seem spiritual, they were completely ineffective in restraining the sinful nature (20-23).

From his doctrinal exposition, Paul turns now to a practical section in which he presents some foundational principles of Christian living (3:1-17). The theological basis for our seeking to live the Christian life lies in our union with Christ in the heavenly realm (1-4), and the practical methodology by which our lives are to become more Christ-like is by dying to self (5-17). First, we must reckon ourselves dead to the sins that were a part of our former lives (5-7). Second, we need to remove the sins of the old self as we would strip off dirty clothing (8-11). Third, we need to follow through with the corresponding positive action of putting on the virtues of the new self (12-14); and finally, we need to let the word of Christ richly dwell within us, controlling our thoughts, words, deeds and emotions (15-17).

Since one of the most important spheres in which the Christian life needs to be worked out experientially is that of our interpersonal relationships, Paul lays down a simple code of reciprocal duties governing believers' relationships within a domestic setting (3:18–

4:1). Wives are to submit to their husbands (3:18), and husbands are to love their wives (19). Children are to obey their parents (20), and fathers are not to discourage their children by being unreasonable with them (21). Slaves are to obey their masters (22-25), and masters are to treat their slaves with justice and fairness (**4:1**).

Beyond these close relations to those within one's own household, believers are also to manifest the outworking of the Christian life in their more general relations to people outside the narrow circle of daily interaction (2-6). In particular, the Colossians are to pray for other Christians, including the Apostle Paul himself (2-4), and they are to behave themselves in an exemplary way towards non-Christians (5-6).

The epistle concludes with a few remarks related to people who either were with Paul at the time of writing or were known to the church at Colossae (7-18). Paul gives the Colossians words of commendation for Tychicus, who was probably carrying the letter to them, and Onesimus, a runaway slave who was returning home with a separate letter to his master, Philemon (7-9). Paul also sends the Colossians greetings from his fellow workers who were standing by him in his imprisonment (10-14). He exhorts those at Colossae to exchange letters with the neighbouring church at Laodicea and to encourage Archippus to fulfill his ministry (15-17); and he then appends a final greeting in his own hand (18).

OUTLINE OF COLOSSIANS

Philemon

OVERVIEW OF PHILEMON

Theme: Paul's plea for a runaway slave

Key verse: Philemon 10, 'I appeal to you for my child, whom I have begotten in my imprisonment, Onesimus' (NASB).

Was Onesimus Freed?

The most probable answer is yes. If Philemon had refused to release Onesimus, he likely would have suppressed this piece of private correspondence, but the letter's preservation serves as a monument to Paul's tactful persuasiveness and Philemon's gracious obedience, as well as a witness to Onesimus' freedom. According to early tradition, Onesimus became the bishop of Ephesus, and there is no compelling reason to doubt that this Onesimus is the same person. If Philemon's slave became a bishop, he may well have had a hand in ensuring that his letter was included when the Pauline corpus was gathered together for publication sometime in the latter part of the first century.

HISTORICAL BACKGROUND

Scholars have generally accepted Paul's authorship of the Epistle to Philemon. This little gem of the apostle's personal correspondence is a model in the art of gentle persuasion. It is addressed primarily to Philemon, a Christian slave-owner, but the greeting also includes Apphia, who was probably his wife, and Archippus, a leader in the church that met in their home at Colossae (Phile 2). Paul wrote this letter on behalf of one of his converts, Onesimus, a runaway slave who had ministered to him in his imprisonment; now that Onesimus had become a believer, Paul requested Philemon to accept him back as a brother in Christ. Apparently the epistle had a happy ending; otherwise it would not likely have been preserved. If he is the same person of whom Ignatius writes, Onesimus later became the bishop of Ephesus.

Paul wrote this letter under the same circumstances as Colossians, probably during his first Roman imprisonment (cf. Acts 28:16-31), which would date it at 60 or 61. He probably sent it by the hand of Tychicus, who would have carried the epistles to the Colossians and Ephesians along with it (cf. Col 4:7-8; Eph 6:21-22).

THE FLOW OF PHILEMON

The salutation of the Epistle to Philemon (1-3) identifies Paul as the writer, along with Timothy (1a), and names Philemon as the letter's recipient, along with Apphia, his wife, and Archippus, a leader of the church that met in Philemon's house (1b-2). To all of them Paul sends his customary greeting of grace and peace (3).

Before he addresses the real business of the letter, Paul offers a grateful prayer for Philemon (4-7). He gives thanks for Philemon's expression of love towards all the saints (4-5), and he intercedes that Philemon's faith will become effective in every good thing (6-7).

Having built up Philemon, Paul now makes a personal plea for Onesimus, Philemon's runaway slave (8-20). He appeals, first of all, to Philemon's compassion as a man of noble character (8-16). Paul cites three conditions which should move Philemon to compassion: his own pitiable condition in prison (8-9), Onesimus' personal worth to Paul in ministering to his needs (10-14), and Onesimus' spiritual relation to Philemon as a brother in Christ (15-16). Paul also appeals to Philemon's duty as his personal friend (17-20). On the basis of their relationship as partners in the Gospel, Paul requests Philemon to treat Onesimus as he would himself (17). Paul offers to pay compensation if Onesimus owes his master anything (18-19a), and the apostle reminds Philemon of his own indebtedness to him (19b-20).

Paul expresses confidence that Philemon will respond positively to his letter (21-22). He knew this man well enough to expect him to be even more generous than he had requested with regards to Onesimus (21) and at the same time to expect his hospitality upon his own release from prison (22).

In conclusion (23-25), Paul conveys the greetings of Epaphras, his fellow prisoner, and his co-workers (23-24). To their regards, he adds a closing benediction of grace (25).

OUTLINE OF PHILEMON

Ephesians

OVERVIEW OF EPHESIANS

Theme: The church, the body of Christ

Key verses: Ephesians 1:22-23, 'And He ... gave Him as head over all things to the church, which is His body ..." (NASB).

Introduction	1:1-2
I. Doctrinal exposition	1:3–3:21
A. God's eternal purpose for us: spiritual blessings	1:3-23
B. Our tremendous obstacle to God's purpose: sin	2:1-22
C. God's 'secret' program to realize his purpose: the church	3:1-21
II. Practical application	4:1–6:20
A. The walk of the Christian	4:1–6:9
1. A Christian's walk in relation to the body	4:1-16
2. A Christian's walk in contrast with the world's	4:17–5:14
3. A Christian's walk under the control of the Holy Spirit	5:15–6:9
B. The warfare of the church	6:10-20
Conclusion	6:21-24

HISTORICAL BACKGROUND

Ephesians is generally considered to be written by Paul, although some scholars have questioned its authenticity because of similarities to Colossians. The two epistles share over 75 similar expressions; but they often use the same phrase in slightly different contexts, and they also commonly express the same idea using different words. This fluid interchangeability of form and meaning suggests that, rather than one of the epistles being copied from the other, both of them were produced by the same mind writing at about the same time.

The words 'at Ephesus' are missing from some ancient manuscripts. This omission may be an indication that the epistle is a circular letter that was distributed beginning from Ephesus, the leading city of Asia Minor, to the surrounding churches. So that this epistle might instruct and edify the larger church, Paul glossed over any local problems that were peculiar to Ephesus. In fact, next to Romans, Ephesians comes the closest of his epistles to a systematic theological treatment. The general background of the recipients does come out, however, in Paul's extended exposition of the doctrine of the church, which was intended to inform the predominately Gentile Christians of Asia Minor of how they fit into the same body with Jewish believers.

Paul probably wrote from prison in Rome (cf. Acts 28:16-31) in A.D. 60 or 61 and sent the letter by Tychicus, who also bore Colossians and Philemon (Eph 6:21-22; cf. Col 4:7-8). We cannot be sure which came first, but rather than Colossians being an abridgement of Ephesians, it is more likely that the problems at Colossae called for an immediate response that Paul subsequently expanded and adapted for a more general audience.

Much of the historical background of Ephesians is found in the Book of Acts. Acts 18:19-21 records the first visit of Paul to Ephesus, which took place on his second missionary journey. In Acts 18:24–20:1, we find Apollos ministering at Ephesus for a short time; then Paul returns on his third missionary journey and stays at Ephesus for about three years. Acts 20:15–21:1 relates a final visit with the Ephesian elders, who met Paul at Miletus before he returned to Jerusalem at the close of his third missionary journey.

THE FLOW OF EPHESIANS

The introduction to this epistle (**1**:1-2) begins by identifying its author as the apostle Paul (1a) and its recipients as saints living at Ephesus (1b), although several important manuscripts omit mention of their geographic destination presumably because the epistle was intended to circulate among other Asian churches as well. The introduction follows with the typical Pauline greeting, 'grace to you and peace ...' (2).

In the first half of the epistle, Paul gives a doctrinal exposition of how God, in grace, overcame the fatal obstacle of sin so that he could richly bless all of redeemed humanity together in a new social order called the church, which is the visible expression of Christ's body (**1**:3–3:21). Paul begins by unfolding the great spiritual blessings that God eternally purposed for us (1:3-23). His description of God's blessings is organized around the special role that each member of the Trinity played in redemption (3-14). The Father took the initiative in planning redemption (3-6). He is the ultimate bestower of every spiritual blessing (3), but he was especially active in choosing us (4) and predestining us to be adopted as his sons (5-6). The Son effected redemption so that we might receive the blessings that the Father had planned for us (7-12). Our redemption comes through Christ's blood (7-8a). Through Christ, God's purpose for administering the entire universe will be accomplished (8b-10), and our inheritance will also be realized by virtue of our position in him (11-12). The Holy Spirit applies the blessings of redemption to us (13-14). He is the seal of God's promises (13) and the pledge of our inheritance that is yet to come (14).

Having expounded how God has richly blessed us, Paul turns to pray for the Ephesians, his heart breaking into thanksgiving because he had heard of their faith and love in response to the gospel message (15-16). He requests that they might have the spiritual perception to understand all that this glorious God has done, and can do, for them (17-19a). He explains that the power that is working in believers is the same supernatural power that God exercised when he raised Christ from the dead and seated him at his right hand in the supreme position of honour, with authority over all spiritual powers and headship over the church (19b-23).

But Paul is forced to pause – a tremendous obstacle stood in the way of our realizing the wonderful purpose that God had intended for us, namely our sin (2:1-22). Sin created an obstacle in two ways. First, it made us spiritually dead and unresponsive to God (1-10). After stating this serious problem (1-3), Paul resoundingly declares God's solution to save us from our spiritual stupor: God made us alive (4-10). Paul explains that the reason why God saved us was the richness of his mercy (4-7); the method by which he saved us was grace (8-9); and the purpose for which he saved us was good works (10).

Second, sin created an obstacle to the realization of God's purpose by alienating us from Christ (11-22). Again, Paul states the problem, focusing particularly upon Gentile alienation from covenant blessings (11-12), and then he explains the solution, which

---

The Temple Inscription

The 'barrier of the dividing wall' to which Paul refers in Ephesians 2:14 is probably the wall within the temple enclosure separating the Court of the Gentiles from the Court of the Women. Archaeologists have uncovered a large warning sign that was inscribed on this wall. It reads, 'Foreigners must not enter inside the balustrade or into the forecourt around the sanctuary. Whoever is caught will have himself to blame for his ensuing death.' Paul was well aware of this prohibition because he was nearly lynched by zealous Jews who mistakenly supposed that he had brought a Gentile into the temple (Acts 21:27-35). Normally, the Jews did not have the right to inflict capital punishment, but they were so zealous for the sanctity of their temple that, according to Josephus, they were granted an exception in the case of anyone who dared to go beyond the partition even though he should be a Roman.

(The inscription may be found in Jack Finegan, *The Archaeology of the New Testament: The Life of Jesus and the Beginning of the Early Church* [Princeton University Press, 1969], 197. See also the comments of Josephus, *Wars of the Jews*, 6.2 .4 [124-128]; Antiquities. 15.11.5 [410-420]).

---

comes in two parts (13-22). First, we were united with Christ (13-18). In this vital union, Christ brought us near to all of God's blessings (13). He joined Jews and Gentiles together in one body (14-16) and preached the message of peace to us (17-18). Second, we were incorporated into the church (19-22). Although we Gentiles were formerly aliens, we have been granted full membership in this holy society (19), which is built upon the solid foundation of apostolic doctrine (20) and is growing together into God's dwelling place (21-22).

From the obstacle that sin had created to God's eternal purpose to bless us spiritually, Paul moves to God's 'secret' program to realize this purpose: the church (**3**:1-21). Paul was about to pray a second time for the Ephesians but he had to pause momentarily to explain the stewardship of the mystery that God had entrusted to him on their behalf as Gentiles (1-13). This mystery was graciously made known to Paul by special revelation (1-4). Although it had not been known in previous generations, the Holy Spirit had now revealed it (5). To be specific, the mystery is that Gentiles are fellow heirs and fellow members with Jews in the body of Christ, the church (6-7). Even though Paul felt unworthy, God appointed him to preach this mystery (8-10), which was now being worked out in accordance with God's eternal purposes (11-12); consequently, Paul asks the Ephesians not to become discouraged by his sufferings for them (13).

Having explained the mystery of the church, Paul resumes his prayer for the Ephesians that he had started earlier (14-21). He brings his petitions for his readers reverently before the Father (14-19) requesting that the Spirit would strengthen them in their inner persons (14-16) and that Christ would permanently reside in their hearts through faith (17) so that they might be able to grasp the unbounded nature of grace (18) and know Christ's surpassing love (19a), in sum that they be filled up to God's fullness (19b). Paul concludes his prayer with a benediction of praise to God for his power that is at work within us to do far beyond anything that we could possibly imagine (20-21).

From his theological exposition of the church, Paul turns to apply this doctrine practically to the Ephesians (**4**:1–6:20). As

Christians, they are called to a new walk (4:1–6:9), which Paul describes first of all in relation to the body of Christ (4:1-16). He emphasizes the unity of the corporate body of which they are now a part (1-6). He exhorts them to demonstrate personal attitudes that will promote unity within the body (1-3), and he lists common objective factors upon which that unity has already been established (4-6).

Within the body, there is a diversity of individual gifts (7-16). The spiritual giftedness of each member is based upon the grace that Christ bestowed in celebration of his triumph over the grave and ascension to heaven (7-10). Paul explains the nature of spiritual gifts (11-13), first of all, in terms of the leadership capacities of apostles, prophets, evangelists, and pastor-teachers in which certain gifts are expressed (11). He also explains that these gifts were intended for the common purpose of equipping the saints for ministry unto the building up of the body (12) and that they would be needed until we reach full maturity (13). Finally, Paul explains that spiritual gifts are to be worked out by each member of the body doing its part in conjunction with the others so that we all may grow up in relation to Christ (14-16).

Paul also describes a Christian's walk in contrast with the world's lifestyle (4:17–5:14). He exhorts the Ephesians to a new walk (17-24), which is not to resemble the world (17-19) but Christ (20-24). In accordance with what they learned about Christ, they are to put off the old nature, which is being corrupted by its lusts (20-22), and to put on the new nature, which is patterned after God (23-24). Paul gives specific instructions concerning their new walk in pairs of contrasting positive and negative actions, although he occasionally leaves half of the contrast implicit (4:25–5:14). They are to speak truth instead of falsehood (4:25), to be angry without sinning (4:26-27), to labour instead of stealing (4:28), to speak edifying words rather than foul language (4:29), [to obey the Spirit] rather than grieving him (4:30), to be kind instead of being bitter (4:31-32), to be imitators of God [instead of the world] (5:1-2), [to be pure] instead of immoral (5:3-5), [to be separate] rather than partners with sinners (5:6-7), to walk in light instead of darkness (5:8-10), and to expose evil deeds rather than participating in them (5:11-14).

Paul asserts that the walk of a Christian is to be under the control of the Holy Spirit (5:15–6:9). His rationale for walking in the Spirit flows out of the desire to live in a wise and productive way in accordance with God's will (5:15-17). He commands the Ephesians to be filled constantly with the Spirit (5:18) and follows through by describing several expressions of the Spirit's fullness in their relationships to God and other people (5:19–6:9). Being filled with the Spirit is to be evidenced by their speaking to one another in psalms (5:19a), singing to the Lord in their hearts (5:19b), giving thanks to God for everything (5:20), and being subject to one another in Christ (5:21–6:4).

Paul explicates this last expression of the Spirit's fullness in terms of three social relationships which call for submission, the first of which is the relationship of wives to their husbands (5:21-33). As the reason why wives ought to submit to their husbands, he states that the husband is the head of the wife (21-24), but he balances the duty of wives by instructing husbands how they ought to love their wives (25-33). A husband is to love his wife in the same way that Christ loved the church, that is by sacrificing himself for her (25-27); and he is to love her in the same way that he loves himself, that is by nourishing and cherishing her (28-31). Paul summarizes his teaching on husbands and wives by repeating his analogy of Christ and the church (32-33).

Submission is also expected as an evidence of the fullness of the Spirit in the relationship of children to their parents (**6**:1-4). Children should obey their parents because doing so is proper and conducive to long life (1-3). Fathers, however, should bring up their children in a disciplined but considerate way (4).

The third social relationship in which the Spirit's fullness is evidenced by submission is that of slaves to masters (5-9). Slaves are to obey their masters whole-heartedly, as if they were serving the Lord (5-8); and masters, for their part, are to treat their slaves fairly, knowing that they are accountable to the Lord (9).

Paul's practical application now moves from the Christian's new walk to the church's spiritual warfare (10-20). The subject is introduced by a call to arms, which directs the attention of the Christian soldier to the divine power available in the Lord (10-

11). It is followed by a reminder of the spiritual nature of the enemy (12) and a description of the complete armor that God has provided for the battle (13-17). Paul refers comprehensively to the equipment that the Christian is to put on as the panoply of God (13), and then he lists the individual pieces of which it consists: the belt of truth (14a), the breastplate of righteousness (14b), the shoes of the preparation of the Gospel (15), the shield of faith (16), the helmet of salvation (17a), and the sword of the Spirit (17b). He draws his discussion of spiritual warfare to a fitting end by entreating the Ephesians to keep on the alert by praying for all the saints and especially for him that he would fight boldly (18-20).

Paul concludes the epistle with a comment about himself and a prayer for his readers (21-24). He promises that, along with the letter, Tychicus will convey personal information that will lessen their concern about him (21-22), and he offers a benediction of grace and peace for them (23-24).

OUTLINE OF EPHESIANS

Philippians

OVERVIEW OF PHILIPPIANS

Theme: An epistle of joy

Key verse: Philippians 4:4, 'Rejoice in the Lord always; again I will say, rejoice!' (NASB).

HISTORICAL BACKGROUND

Tradition uniformly attributes Philippians to the Apostle Paul, and scholars generally accepted that verdict. The unity of the letter has been questioned by a few who think they can detect interpolations from other Pauline materials in such places as Phil 3:1–4:1, but the various interpolation theories have not proven to be compelling because they are not supported by manuscript evidence and they demand greater consistency than what can be expected from a man like Paul, who is known for interrupting his train of thought.

This letter was sent to Philippi, the capital of Macedonia. Many of its inhabitants were Roman citizens or connected to the military as a result of its privileged status as a Roman colony. Paul founded the church there on his second missionary journey in response to his vision of a man from Macedonia calling him to come over and help them (Acts 16:9-40). Significantly, this was the first church to be planted in Europe, and it was composed predominately of Gentile converts since there were not enough Jews in Philippi to form a synagogue. Paul enjoyed a good relationship with this church, and he visited it again on his third missionary journey (Acts 20:1-2, 6).

The immediate occasion that prompted him to write was the arrival of a generous gift from the Philippians. He wanted to thank them and at the same time to relieve their anxiety concerning Epaphroditus, who had become ill and almost died after delivering their gift (Phil 2:25-30; 4:18). Paul also used this occasion to inform them of his own circumstances and to attend to his pastoral responsibilities with respect to the church.

When he wrote this letter, Paul was in prison (Phil 1:7, 17), most likely at Rome (Phil 1:13-14; 4:22; cf. Acts 28:16-31). A number of scholars argue for an Ephesian imprisonment and a few for the imprisonment at Caesarea, but they remain a minority. Assuming a Roman provenance, Philippians would have been written in A.D. 60 or 61. The order is not certain, but it was probably written after the other prison epistles and sent back with Epaphroditus, who had now recovered.

THE FLOW OF PHILIPPIANS

In the salutation to Philippians, its author, Paul, along with Timothy, greets the saints at Philippi with grace and peace (**1**:1-2). He follows the salutation with an extended introductory thanksgiving for the Philippians (3-11). Paul was especially grateful for their partnership with him in the Gospel (3-6), which made him feel very fond of them in his imprisonment (7-8) and led him to pray confidently for their further growth in Christian knowledge (9-11).

From his readers, Paul turns to explain his own personal circumstances in greater detail (12-26). He indicates that as a result of his imprisonment the Gospel had made progress among the guards and beyond the walls of his confinement (12-14). Even though some of his opponents were preaching the Gospel out of questionable motives, he rejoiced that at least it was being proclaimed (15-18a). Furthermore, he rejoiced because he believed the prospects for his release to be favourable (18b-26). He was

---

Carmen Christi, An Ancient Hymn to Christ?

The christological passage in Phil 2:6-11 has been thought by some to be another case of borrowing from an ancient hymn (cf. Col 1:15-20). There are lengthy debates, however, over whether this hymn was originally in Hebrew or Greek, or whether Paul composed it himself.

> [6]Who, being in very nature God,
> did not consider equality with God something to be grasped,
> [7] but made himself nothing,
> taking the very nature of a servant,
> being made in human likeness.
> [8]And being found in appearance as a man,
> he humbled himself and became obedient to death--
> even death on a cross!
> [9]Therefore God exalted him to the highest place
> and gave him the name that is above every name,
> [10]that at the name of Jesus every knee should bow,
> in heaven and on earth and under the earth,
> [11]and every tongue confess that Jesus Christ is Lord,
> to the glory of God the Father (NIV).

---

confident that he would be released, both because the Philippians had been praying for him (18b-19) and because he continued to be useful in ministering to them (20-26). He explained that Christ would be exalted, whether by his life or his death (20-21); he also felt a tension between the two alternatives (22) because being with Christ was advantageous for him (23) but remaining to serve was necessary for them (24-26).

In view of his expectation to continue in ministry, Paul exhorted the Philippians concerning a variety of matters (1:27–2:18). He encouraged them to be steadfast in suffering for Christ (1:27-30) and to be considerate of others (2:1-11). They were to show their consideration by being united in spirit (1-2) and humble in service (3-11). Paul's exhortation to humility (3-4) is based upon the example of Christ (5-11), who voluntarily humbled himself in order to serve us by dying on a shameful cross (5-8), and in return was publicly exalted to the highest position of glory in the universe (9-11). Paul goes on to exhort the Philippians to be faithful in working out their sanctification (12-13), to be blameless in their conduct before the world (14-16), and to be participants in his own joy in serving the Lord (17-18).

To facilitate their mutual exchange of rejoicing in view of his absence, Paul proposes to send two of his fellow workers, whom he warmly commends to the Philippians (19-30). First, he commends his trusted and sincere assistant, Timothy, whom he promises to send as soon as he knows the outcome of his trial (19-24). Next in order of writing but first in order of dispatch, he commends Epaphroditus, the Philippians' messenger to Paul, who was returning immediately now that he had recovered from a life-threatening illness (25-30).

Paul could have ended the letter at this point if he had not felt compelled to sound a vehement warning against some people at Philippi who were seriously threatening to nullify the Gospel (3:1–4:1). The section opens with a transitional verse, which summarizes Paul's theme of rejoicing thus far and introduces the reason for including the warning that is to follow (3:1). Apparently the danger threatened from two opposing fronts; on the first front stood the false teaching of Jewish legalists (2-16). Paul denounces them for basing one's religious acceptance on the external rite of circumcision (2-4a).

Finally, Farewell?

Several times Paul gives the impression that he is about to conclude before his Epistle to the Philippians actually reaches its end. Twice he appears to be embarking upon a concluding exhortation prematurely as he addresses his readers, 'Finally, (my) brethren...' (Phil 3:1; 4:8). Furthermore, the key word in this epistle, which is usually translated as a command, 'rejoice', or 'be glad', can be used as a salutation either upon meeting someone, 'greetings', or upon parting, 'farewell', which is how the New English Bible translates it in 3:1 and 4:4. The concurrence of the concluding address in 3:1, together with the possibility of a parting salutation and an abrupt shift in subject matter, has led some scholars to postulate that our letter to the Philippians was spliced together from two or more shorter epistles.

    The lack of any manuscript evidence suggesting a seam in this epistle, however, stands opposed to the various theories of interpolation. While it is true that the same verb urging rejoicing can be used as a salutation, this meaning is contextually awkward in 4:4 and unlikely in 3:1. The insertion of the word 'finally' before the letter is finished is not unusual if one considers that many preachers indicate that they are about to conclude long before they actually finish speaking. All the data suggesting a break in Philippians can be easily accounted for on the supposition that Paul was interrupted while he was in the process of writing and that he picked up his pen and finished at a later date.

By contrast, he argues that if anyone had personal grounds for confidence in the fulfillment of legalistic requirements, he should (4b-6); however, he completely rejected trusting in his former religious advantages (7-11), which he gave up as a dead loss (7-8c), in order to gain the surpassing value of knowing Christ on the basis of faith (8d-11). Instead of looking to the past, he reached forward towards the goal so that he might win the prize (12-14), and he exhorts the Philippians to adopt the same attitude in their pursuit of spiritual maturity (15-16).

    On the opposite front, the Gospel was threatened by the immoral life-style of some pagan antinomians who were probably claiming to be Christians although they lived as they pleased in complete disregard of the law (3:17–4:1). Paul warns that their dissolute deification of earthly indulgences will result in their destruction (17-19). In contrast, he reminds the Philippians that their ennobling anticipation of a heavenly Saviour who will transform their mortal bodies into glorious ones should motivate them to moral steadfastness (3:20–4:1).

With these warnings in place to safeguard the Philippians, Paul returns to give them a renewed set of exhortations (4:2-9). He urges two women in particular to settle their disagreement and live in harmony with each other (2-3). To all of the Philippians he gives the command to entrust their lives to the sovereignty of God (4-7). He explains that the way to attain incomprehensible peace is to rejoice in the Lord always (4), to be tolerant towards everyone (5), to be anxious about nothing (6a), but to pray about everything instead (6b-7). Finally, he commands them to fill their minds with noble thoughts (8-9).

As he is about to conclude, Paul gives thanks for the Philippians' financial assistance to him (10-20). He explains that he was not in need because he had learned the secret of contentment in everything (10-13); nevertheless, he was very grateful for the Philippians' generosity in giving to him on repeated occasions (14-18). In response to their generosity, he assures them that God will supply all of their needs (19-20).

In closing (21-23), Paul sends general greetings to the entire church from himself and the believers who are with him (21-22). He ends with a benediction of grace (23).

OUTLINE OF PHILIPPIANS

The Letter of Polycarp to the Philippians

Polycarp, the much loved bishop of Smyrna, also wrote an epistle to the Philippians c. A.D. 110. Along with many other scriptural allussions, it contrains a couple allusions to Paul's Epistle to the Philippians and to the apostle's work among them.

> ... in [your] midst the blessed Paul labored, and [you] were his letters of recommendation in the beginning. For he boasts about you in all the churches (cf. 2 Cor 3:2; Phil 4:15).
>
> I urge all of you, therefore, to obey the teaching about righteousness and to exercise unlimited endurance, like that which you saw with your own eyes not only in the blessed Ignatius and Zosimus and Rufus but also in others from your congregation and in Paul himself and the rest of the apostles; be assured that all these "did not run in vain" (cf. Phil 2:16) but in faith and righteousness, and that they are now in the place due them with the Lord, with whom they also suffered together.

Polycarp himself courageously faced martyrdom as an old man of eighty-six.

(Polycarp, Letter to the Philippians *11:3; 9:1-2; in* The Apostolic Fathers, *2nd ed. trans. J. B. Lightfoot and J. R. Harmer, ed and rev. by Michael W. Holmes [Grand Rapids: Baker Book House], 128, 127.)*

The Pastoral Epistles

1 Timothy

OVERVIEW OF 1 TIMOTHY

Theme: Instructions to a young pastor

Key verses: 1 Timothy 3:14-15, 'I am writing these things to you ... so that you may know how one ought to conduct himself in the household of God, which is the church ...' (NASB).

HISTORICAL BACKGROUND

The authorship of 1 Timothy, along with the other pastoral epistles, Titus and 2 Timothy, is disputed on the grounds of differences in vocabulary and style from the other recognized Pauline epistles. First Timothy, however, claims to have been written by Paul (1 Tim 1:1), which forces alternative theories to reckon with the unlikely assumption that the early church would have willingly accepted the pseudonymous work of a pious imitator into the canon. Paul's authorship of the epistle is defended by early church tradition and most conservative scholars, who generally account for the stylistic differences by the change in subject matter or the supposition that Paul employed a different amanuensis, such as Luke.

The letter is addressed to Timothy (1 Tim 1:2; 6:20; cf. Acts 16:1-3; 2 Tim 1:5; 3:15), but it was indirectly intended for the benefit of the entire church at Ephesus (1 Tim 1:3; cf. 1 Tim 6:21 where the customary second person singular pronoun changes to the plural). On the establishment of the church at Ephesus during Paul's second and third missionary journeys, see Acts 18:19-21; 18:24–20:1; 20:17-38. Paul was hoping to come to Ephesus soon, but in case he was unexpectedly delayed, he wrote this letter to encourage Timothy and authorize him for the task of appointing church leaders and dealing with false teachers during his absence (1 Tim 1:3-4; 3:14-15). Paul probably wrote from somewhere in Macedonia, which is where he was headed when he left Timothy at Ephesus (1 Tim 1:3). The most likely city would be Philippi (Phil 2:19, 23-24), although Paul could have continued on to other places by the time of writing (cf. Tit 3:12).

First Timothy does not fit into the chronology of Acts; therefore, it is generally thought to be have been written after Paul's release from the confinement mentioned in Acts 28:30. If that is the case, it would have been written sometime during A.D. 63 to 66, depending upon whether Paul made his projected journey to Spain before visiting the churches in the east. Titus would also have been written about the same time. Who bore the epistle is not known, but it could have been Zenas and Apollos, who travelled to Crete with a similar epistle for Titus (Tit 3:13).

THE FLOW OF 1 TIMOTHY

The salutation to 1 Timothy (**1**:1-2) identifies Paul as the writer of the epistle (1) and Timothy as its recipient (2a). Paul greets him with a threefold wish for grace, mercy and peace (2b).

Without going into other preliminaries, Paul immediately starts in by responding to the needs of the church at Ephesus (1:3–3:13). Apparently the most pressing need was to warn Timothy about the theological errors that were threatening the church (1:3-20). Paul reiterates his earlier directive to Timothy to silence the false teachers (3-11) who were foisting upon the church their futile genealogical speculations and ignorant distortion of the law (3-7). Paul counters these false teachers by declaring that the law was not intended as a legalistic imposition upon those who are righteous but as a standard for condemning those who violate it (8-11).

In contrast with their perversion of the Gospel, Paul thanks God for entrusting him with the true Gospel (12-17) even though he was unworthy of this honor (12-14). His conversion from his former notoriety as a persecutor of the church and the foremost of sinners proved to be a prime example of God's grace to encourage others who wished to be saved (15-16). Reflecting on his experience of grace causes Paul to burst into a spontaneous doxology of praise to God (17) before rounding out his theological warnings by reminding Timothy of his responsibility for maintaining orthodox doctrine in light of the disastrous consequences suffered by two prominent Ephesians who had rejected the faith (18-20).

After the warnings, the epistle's negative tone lifts considerably as Paul gives Timothy some important instructions in response to the church's need for order (**2**:1–3:13). First, he addresses the issue of propriety in public worship (2:1-15), starting with the content of public prayer (1-7). The scope of public prayer is to include everyone, but especially political authorities (1-2a). Its goal is that believers might live a peaceful and godly life (2b), and its rationale is that God's desire for everyone to be saved can be most fully realized under peaceful conditions (3-7).

As far as the form of public worship is concerned (8-15), Paul spells out what propriety means for men in terms of holiness and freedom from dissension (8). For women propriety means that (9-15) they keep their public demeanour modest (9-10) and remain in quiet subordination to men in keeping with the created order and the implications of the Fall (11-15).

The second major issue that Paul addresses with respect to order in the church is the selection of its leaders (**3**:1-13). He gives detailed instructions concerning two church offices, the first of which is the office of overseer (1-7). Since an overseer is held in great respect, anyone who aspires to this office (1) must meet high qualifications (2-7). His personal life must be marked by the appropriate qualities of (2-6) moral character (2-3), leadership ability (4-5) and spiritual maturity (6). In addition, his public image must command the respect of the non-Christian world (7).

The second church office which Paul addresses is that of deacon (8-13). He lays down similar, but less comprehensive, personal qualifications for deacons (8-9) and instructs that candidates for this office be tested before being allowed to serve (10). The text is not clear, but along with the qualifications for deacons, Paul specifies similar qualifications for women who either constitute a corresponding order of deaconesses or who are the wives of deacons (11). He then returns to the deacons to list certain domestic qualifications which would have a bearing upon their ability to function in the church (12). He closes the instructions about deacons with a word about the dignity of the office (13).

Having responded to the most pressing theological and organizational needs of the church at Ephesus, Paul now turns his attention to prescribing how his young assistant, Timothy, should conduct himself as a minister of that church (3:14–6:19). During his prolonged absence, this letter becomes the apostle's primary means of continuing to mentor Timothy in church leadership (3:14-16). This task is vitally important because the church is the foundational support for God's truth (14-15). Having mentioned the church's role in upholding the truth, Paul uses the words of what was probably an ancient Christian hymn to express the greatness of the truth that the church confesses, particularly with respect to the incarnation and ascension of Christ (16).

These introductory words about the important task for which Timothy was being trained underline Paul's elaboration of two professional responsibilities that Timothy needed to discharge as a good minister (4:1-16). The first of these responsibilities was to check the spread of apostasy (1-11) both by understanding the deceptive nature of the asceticism that the false teachers at Ephesus were advocating (1-5), and by teaching sound doctrine to the brethren (6-11). The second professional responsibility that Paul emphasized to Timothy was to win the respect of his congregation (12-16) by his moral example (12), his biblically-based public ministry (13), and his self-discipline (14-16).

In addition to his professional responsibilities, Paul gave Timothy prescriptions concerning his social relations to people within the church (5:1–6:2). He begins generally by defining the attitudes that should govern the interpersonal relations of a young minister with those under his pastoral care in terms of their age and sex (5:1-2); he then gives specific directives concerning what the church's policy should be regarding three social groups within the congregation that required special attention (5:3–6:2). The first of these three groups was widows (5:3-16). Paul sets forth some general principles for assessing society's moral duty to widows (3-8), and then he lays down specific criteria for enlisting the church's financial assistance on behalf of older widows (9-16). The second social group about which Paul gave directions was elders (17-25). He instructs the church to reward faithful elders generously (17-18), to indict elders suspected of wrongdoing judiciously (19-21), and to appoint new elders cautiously (22-25). Finally, he directs the church to teach that Christian slaves should fulfill their duties to their masters respectfully, especially if their masters are believers (6:1-2).

From social relations, Paul moves to Timothy's personal integrity as a godly man (3-19). He contrasts the pure motives of Timothy with the corrupt motives of the false teachers (3-10). The false teachers were conceited and greedy (3-5), but Timothy was to be content with the humble necessities of life (6-10). Paul also contrasts Timothy's eternal rewards with the temporal wealth of the rich (11-19). He encouraged Timothy with the hope that he would receive eternal rewards for serving faithfully (11-16), but he warned rich Christians that they had a responsibility for using their temporal wealth as a stewardship (17-19).

In conclusion (20-21), Paul appeals to Timothy to remain faithful in his pastoral duties (20-21a). He closes the letter with a brief benediction of grace (21b).

OUTLINE OF 1 TIMOTHY

Biographical Sketch of Timothy

Timothy came from the Lycaonian region of Southern Galatia. Although Acts 16:1 leaves open the possibility that he might have resided in either Lystra or Derbe, the good reputation that he enjoyed among the brethren at Lystra and Iconium (Acts 16:2) and the distinction that Acts 20:4 makes between him and Gaius of Derbe suggest that Lystra was more likely his hometown.

Even though his father was a Greek, Timothy had been instructed in the Scriptures as a young lad because both his mother, Eunice, and his grandmother, Lois, were devout Jewesses (Acts 16:1, 3; 2 Tim 1:5; 3:16). Apparently, Timothy joined them in placing his faith in Christ during Paul's first visit to Lystra, but some legalistic Jews fiercely opposed the Gospel and stoned Paul leaving him for dead. Paul miraculously recovered, however, and encouraged his new converts to stand firm (Acts 14:5-23).

On his second visit to Southern Galatia, Paul was distributing the decrees of the Jerusalem church council. He had recently split with Barnabas and John Mark and was travelling with Silas when he chose Timothy to accompany him (Acts 15:36—16:4). He had Timothy circumcised in acknowledgment of his Jewish heritage (Acts 16:2-3); whereas, he adamantly refused to have Titus circumcised to prevent the Gentiles from falling into legalism (Gal 2:3-5).

Although he was young (1 Tim 4:12; 2 Tim 2:22) and may have had a shy, retiring personality (1 Cor 16:10-11; 2 Tim 1:7-8), Timothy was evidently gifted and showed good promise for ministry. His induction into the ministry was confirmed by the laying on of hands of the elders and by specific prophecies about his ministry (1 Tim 1:18; 4:14; 2 Tim 1:6). Evidently he was a gifted teacher (2 Tim 2:22) and probably a capable evangelist as well, even though he may not have been an outgoing person (2 Tim 4:5). Along with his reserved personality came the character traits of kindness, patience, and gentleness that would later prove valuable in correcting false teachers (2 Tim 2:23-25). Timothy was best known and appreciated for his genuineness and sincerity in selflessly seeking the welfare of those to whom he ministered (Phil 2:20-22; 2 Tim 1:5). Paul proudly claimed him as his beloved and faithful son in the Lord (1 Cor 4:17; Phil 2:22; 1 Tim 1:2, 18; 2 Tim 2:1) and included him jointly in the salutation of many of his epistles (2 Cor 1:1; Phil 1:1; Col 1:1; 1 Thess 1:1; 2 Thess 1:1; Phile 1:1).

Timothy accompanied Paul throughout his remaining missionary travels except at those points where the apostle needed a capable and trustworthy delegate to stand in his place. When he could not personally attend to an important but difficult situation, Paul usually entrusted it to Timothy. When persecution forced Paul to leave Thessalonica, he left Timothy and Silas behind to strengthen and encourage the young church there (Act 17:14; 1 Thess 3:2). On another occasion, Paul sent Timothy ahead of him to deal with the problems at Corinth so that he would not have to interrupt his fruitful ministry at Ephesus (Acts 19:22; 1 Cor 4:17; 16:10-11). Timothy travelled with the delegation that accompanied the offering for the poor in Jerusalem (Acts 20:4; 2 Cor 9:2-5). He was with Paul during his house arrest at Rome, from where Paul hoped to send him to Philippi (Phil 2:19-23). After his release, Paul revisited Ephesus and left Timothy behind to combat the false teachers and appoint leaders in the church (1 Tim 1:3). When Paul was imprisoned in Rome a second time and awaiting martyrdom, he requested Timothy, his faithful friend, to come to him (2 Tim 4:9, 13).

Titus

OVERVIEW OF TITUS

Theme: The organization of the local church

Key verse: Titus 1:5, 'For this reason I left you in Crete, that you might set in order what remains, and appoint elders in every city as I directed you' (NASB).

Salutation	1:1-4
I. Instructions concerning Titus' task in Crete	1:5-16
II. Instructions concerning the church's conduct as a community	2:1-15
III. Instructions concerning the church's conduct before the world	3:1-11
Conclusion	3:12-15

HISTORICAL BACKGROUND

The Epistle to Titus claims to have been written by Paul (Tit 1:1), but its authorship has been disputed, along with the other pastoral epistles, on the grounds of differences in vocabulary and style from the other recognized Pauline epistles. Early church tradition and most conservative scholars, however, hold that it was written by Paul, although perhaps with the assistance of an amanuensis (see the notes on 1 Timothy). The letter is primarily addressed to Titus (Tit 1:4; cf. Gal 2:1-5), Paul's valued assistant (cf. 2 Cor 2:12-13; 7:5-7, 13-14; 8:6, 16-24; 2 Tim 4:10), and secondarily to the church at Crete (Tit 3:15), a large Mediterranean island south of Greece.

The forthcoming visit of Apollos and Zenas to Crete probably prompted Paul to send this letter (Tit 3:13) as a means of formally authorizing and instructing Titus concerning his work of organizing the churches of Crete, especially in the appointment of elders (Tit 1:5; 2:1, 7-8, 15; 3:9, 12-13). The letter could have been written from Nicopolis, on the west coast of Greece where Paul was planning to winter, but it seems that he had not arrived there yet (Tit 1:5; 3:12). If it was written from the same place as 1 Timothy, the location would be somewhere in Macedonia, perhaps Philippi. Other less likely suggestions are Corinth or Ephesus.

There is no mention of Crete in Acts, except for Paul's brief stop-over on the way to Rome (Acts 27:7-13, 21); therefore, Paul's visit to Crete mentioned in Titus 1:5 is generally thought to have followed the close of Acts. Titus would have been written sometime during A.D. 63 to 66, depending upon whether or not Paul made his projected journey to Spain before visiting the churches in the east, and 1 Timothy would have been written about the same time.

THE FLOW OF TITUS

The salutation to this epistle (**1**:1-4) identifies its writer as the Apostle Paul and gives an extended description of the message with which he was divinely commissioned (1-3). It addresses Titus as the letter's recipient (4a) and adds the typical Pauline greeting of grace and peace (4b).

The apostle's foremost concern was to instruct Titus regarding the twofold task for which he had been left behind at Crete (5-16). Paul provides Titus with a list of qualifications to guide him in the positive task of appointing church leaders in each city on the island (5-9), and he presents a series of damning indictments against the false teachers who were disrupting the church to lend weight to Titus in the negative task of silencing them (10-16).

Paul also gives Titus instructions concerning the church's conduct as a community (**2**:1-15). After a brief introduction in which he puts a pastoral charge to Titus (1), Paul spells out the admonitions that Titus is to deliver to various groups within the church (2-10). Older men are to be models of respectability (2). Older women are likewise to be worthy of reverence and to set a good example for younger women in their domestic affairs (3-5). Younger men are to be sensible and above reproach, especially in relation to unbelievers (6-8). Bond slaves are to be conscientious and respectful to their masters (9-10). Paul grounds the theological motivation behind each of these admonitions in God's manifestation of saving grace that teaches all believers to live in a godly manner, especially in view of Christ's imminent return (11-14). He concludes the section by repeating and amplifying the pastoral charge that he put to Titus earlier (15).

From the conduct of believers within the Christian community, Paul expands the scope to give further instructions concerning their conduct before the world (**3**:1-11). He defines the godly conduct that he expects of believers in terms of their submission to authorities and consideration for all people (1-2), and he contrasts this life-style with the pagan vices that characterized his readers' pre-conversion days (3). The reason he gives for living a godly life is that God graciously saved us according to his mercy rather than our works so that we might share eternal life with him (4-7). Because this teaching is true and beneficial for everyone, Paul urges Titus to cultivate good works in those under his pastoral care (8). At the same time, Titus is to reject false teaching because it is unprofitable and a waste of time (9-11).

In conclusion (12-15), Paul gives Titus some personal instructions regarding the comings and goings of fellow missionaries (12-14). He also conveys general greetings from himself and those who were with him to the believers on Crete (15a) before closing with a simple benediction of grace (15b).

OUTLINE OF TITUS

2 Timothy

OVERVIEW OF 2 TIMOTHY

Theme: Paul's farewell message

Key verses: 2 Timothy 4:7-8, 'I have fought the good fight, I have finished the race, I have kept the faith. Henceforth there is laid up for me the crown of righteousness, which the Lord, the righteous judge, will award to me on that Day, and not only to me but also to all who have loved his appearing' (RSV).

HISTORICAL BACKGROUND

The Second Epistle to Timothy claims to have been written by the Apostle Paul (2 Tim 1:1), but its authorship has been disputed along with the other pastoral epistles. Early church tradition and most conservative scholars, however, hold that Paul wrote it (see the notes on 1 Timothy). Although the letter is addressed to Timothy (2 Tim 1:2), the church is also included by a simple switch in the closing benediction from the second person singular to the plural (2 Tim 4:22). Paul presumably sent this epistle to the same place as 1 Timothy, i.e., Ephesus, but there is no clear indication of its destination. Tychicus may possibly have been its bearer (2 Tim 4:12).

Second Timothy is the last of Paul's epistles. It was written from prison at Rome shortly before the apostle's death. Paul had already had an initial hearing, at which time all of his friends deserted him (2 Tim 1:8, 16-17; 2:9; 4:16-17); but he was still awaiting the final hearing, which he expected to result in his martyrdom (2 Tim 4:6-8). Under such conditions of concern for the church and loneliness in the face of approaching death, but with his confidence still firmly resting in God, Paul was inspired to write this epistle. He intended it as a very personal valedictory address in which he could review his completed life's ministry and pass his mantle on to Timothy, but he also addresses some very practical concerns. He summons Timothy to come to him (2 Tim 1:4; 4:9, 21) bringing along John Mark (2 Tim 4:11), his heavy cloak, which he would need for the cold winter, and the books and parchments that he had left behind (2 Tim 4:13).

The imprisonment that forms the background for 2 Timothy does not match the one mentioned in Acts, from which Paul expected to be released; therefore, most scholars have concluded that Paul was imprisoned twice at Rome. The second time would have been during the reign of Nero. Second Timothy could, accordingly, be dated from A.D. 65 to early autumn of 67.

THE FLOW OF 2 TIMOTHY

In the salutation to 2 Timothy (**1**:1-2), the writer, who identifies himself as the Apostle Paul (1), addresses Timothy, the recipient of this epistle, as his dear son (2a) and greets him with the familiar Pauline wish for grace, mercy and peace (2b).

Drawing upon his own apostolic experience, Paul devotes the first major section of the epistle to exhorting Timothy concerning the ministry that he had delegated to him (3-18). He begins with personal words to Timothy (3-7), giving thanks for his sincere faith (3-5) and encouraging him to rekindle his spiritual gift (6-7). The tone becomes more serious, however, as the apostle charges Timothy (8-14) to join him in suffering (8-12) and to maintain sound teaching (13-14). Paul also exhorts Timothy implicitly to maintain his loyalty by reminding him of one co-worker who stood beside him in prison when everyone else deserted (15-18).

These exhortations, which tend to address general matters, give way to specific directions as the focus shifts from Paul's previous experience to Timothy's present ministry (**2**:1-26). With respect to his personal involvement in ministry (1-13), Paul directs Timothy to be strong (1-2), to endure hardship (3-7), and to remember Christ (8-13). As he points out, Christ is the compelling motivation that inspires us to endure suffering (8-10) and the reliable basis for the hope that our faithfulness will be rewarded (11-13). Concerning his public office as teacher (14-19), Paul directs Timothy to be a reliable exegete of Scripture (14-15) and to avoid false teaching, especially profane speculations that are destructive to faith (16-19). Concerning his personal conduct before the church (20-26), Paul directs Timothy to cleanse himself from sin so that he might be fit for honorable service (20-22) and to correct his misguided opponents with patient understanding so that they might possibly come to repentance (23-26).

From the present situation, Paul projects himself into the future to anticipate problems that Timothy can expect to encounter in his ministry (**3**:1–4:8). He warns Timothy that the last days, into which they had already entered, will be marked by apostasy (3:1-9). The ungodly apostates of whom he warns will be lacking in moral character (1-5) and will use deceitful methods to captivate their gullible victims (6-9).

In the midst of increasing persecution, Paul exhorts Timothy to remain steadfast (10-17). He presents his own steadfastness under persecution as an example that Timothy had already followed (10-12) in contrast with humanity's general progression in ungodliness (13); and he reminds Timothy of his equipment for continuing steadfastly in the faith (14-17). Most valuable among Timothy's endowments for facing the challenges that lay ahead were the heritage of godly parental instruction (14-15) and the practical wisdom of inspired Scripture (16-17).

In view of his strategic role in opposing the spread of apostasy, Paul gives Timothy a final charge concerning his ministry of the Word (**4**:1-8). He solemnly charges Timothy with the responsibility to preach the Word faithfully (1-2) because a time will come when people will be unwilling to endure sound doctrine (3-5). Paul makes his charge even more poignant by informing Timothy that he expects his own ministry to be brought to a close shortly by martyrdom (6-8).

This comment leads Paul into some remarks about his personal situation that he had reserved until now (9-15). He requests Timothy to come soon because all his co-workers, except for Luke, had left him for one reason or another (9-13); and he interjects a warning about a mutual enemy, Alexander the coppersmith (14-15). He reports that no one stood with him on his first defence; but he was rescued by the Lord, in whom he was still trusting to bring him safely into the heavenly kingdom (16-18).

Paul concludes the letter (19-22) with final greetings to, and from, various people whom Timothy would have known (19-21). In benediction, he wishes the Lord's presence upon Timothy and grace to the entire community (22).

OUTLINE OF 2 TIMOTHY

Salutation	1:1-2
A. The writer	1:1
B. The recipient	1:2a
C. The greeting	1:2b
I. Exhortations based upon Paul's previous experience	1:3-18
A. Personal words to Timothy	1:3-7
1. Thanksgiving for Timothy's sincere faith	1:3-5
2. An encouragement of Timothy's spiritual gift	1:6-7
B. Apostolic charges to Timothy	1:8-14
1. A charge to join Paul's suffering	1:8-12
2. A charge to maintain sound teaching	1:13-14
C. Personal reminders about co-workers	1:15-18
II. Directions concerning Timothy's present ministry	2:1-26
A. Concerning his personal involvement in ministry	2:1-13
1. To be strong	2:1-2
2. To endure hardship	2:3-7
3. To remember Christ	2:8-13
a. Christ: the motivation for our endurance	2:8-10
b. Christ: the hope of our reward	2:11-13
B. Concerning his public office as teacher	2:14-19
1. To be a reliable exegete	2:14-15
2. To avoid false teaching	2:16-19
C. Concerning his personal conduct before the church	2:20-26
1. To cleanse himself from sin	2:20-22
2. To correct others with patience	2:23-26

Nero's Persecutions

Paul was probably martyred under Nero some time after the fire of Rome in AD 64. The vivid description that Tacitus, the Roman historian, gives of that persecution probably does not apply directly to Paul, but it gives some insight into Nero's great cruelty.

But all human efforts, all the lavish gifts of the emperor [Nero], and all the propitiations of the gods, did not banish the sinister belief that the conflagration was the result of an order. Consequently, to get rid of the report, Nero fastened the guilt and inflicted the most exquisite tortures on a class hated for their abominations, called Christians by the populace. Christus, from whom the name had its origin, suffered the extreme penalty during the reign of Tiberius at the hands of one of our procurators, Pontius Pilatus, and a most mischievous superstition, thus checked for the moment, again broke out not only in Judea, the first source of the evil, but even in Rome, where all things hideous and shameful from every part of the world find their centre and become popular. Accordingly, an arrest was made of all who pleaded guilty; then, upon information, an immense multitude was convicted, not so much of the crime of firing the city, as of hatred against mankind. Mockery of every sort was added to their deaths. Covered with the skins of beasts, they were torn by dogs and perished, or were nailed to crosses, or were doomed to the flames and burnt, to serve as a nightly illumination, when daylight had expired.

Nero offered his gardens for the spectacle, and was exhibiting a show in the circus, while he mingled with the people in the dress of a charioteer or stood aloft on a car. Hence, even for criminals who deserved extreme and exemplary punishment, there arose a feeling of compassion; for it was not, as it seemed, for the public good, but to glut one man's cruelty, that they were being destroyed.

(Tacitus, *Annals*, 15.44, in *The Complete Works of Tacitus*, trans. Alfred John Church and William Jackson Brodribb, ed. Moses Hadas, The Modern Library [New York: Random House, 1942], 380-81.)

Hebrews

OVERVIEW OF HEBREWS

Theme: The folly of returning to Old Testament Judaism since Jesus is superior to that system in every way

Key verses: Hebrews 1:1-2a 'God, after He spoke long ago to the fathers in the prophets in many portions and in many ways, in these last days has spoken to us in His Son' (NASB).

I. The superiority of the Son to Old Testament Judaism	1:1–10:18
A. The superiority of the Son to the prophets	1:1-4
B. The superiority of the Son to the angels	1:5–2:18
FIRST WARNING: The peril of neglecting such a great salvation	2:1-4
C. The superiority of the Son to Moses	3:1–4:13
SECOND WARNING: The peril of copying the Israelites' example of unbelief	3:7–4:13
D. The superiority of the Son to Aaron	4:14–10:18
1. A better person	4:14–5:10
THIRD WARNING: The peril of remaining immature	5:11–6:20
2. A better priesthood	7:1-28
3. A better ministry	8:1–9:14
4. A better sacrifice	9:15–10:18
II. Practical applications of the Son's superiority for the Hebrews	10:19-13:17
A. Exhortation to embrace the new way	10:19-25
FOURTH WARNING: The peril of despising the new covenant	10:26-31
B. Encouragement to continue their previous example of endurance	10:32-39
C. Exhortation to follow the biblical heroes of faith	11:1–12:3
D. Exhortation to value the discipline of the Father	12:4-13
E. Command to pursue sanctification of heart and life	12:14-17
FIFTH WARNING: The peril of refusing the heavenly warning	12:18-29
F. Exhortation to conduct social and private life from a Christian perspective	13:1-6
F. Reminder to consider the leaders and privileges of New Testament Christianity	13:7-17
Conclusion	13:18-25

HISTORICAL BACKGROUND

Hebrews remains an enigma to many people. All that we can say with reasonable certainty about its anonymous author, is that he was a well educated Hellenistic Jew and second generation Christian (Heb 2:3-4) who was acquainted with Timothy (Heb 13:23). In order to safeguard the epistle's canonicity, of which they were convinced, the eastern church fathers generally held that Hebrews was written by Paul, but the western fathers, who were convinced the epistle was not Pauline, denied that it was canonical. Once Jerome and Augustine finally endorsed Pauline authorship, the medieval church as a whole followed their lead. The vast majority of modern scholars accept it as canonical but deny that it is Pauline. The epistle's lack of a salutation and differences in language, style, manner of quoting the Old Testament, and theological emphasises make it very doubtful that Paul was the author. Some of the more common suggestions are Apollos (cf. Acts 18:24, 28), Luke, Barnabas, or Priscilla and Aquila.

We do not know where the author was at the time of writing. Italy is one possibility that has been suggested by the closing greeting (Heb 13:24), but that is more likely to be the destination of the letter than its origin. In any case, he wrote to encourage and warn a weary, disheartened (Heb 12:3, 12) and spiritually sluggish (Heb 5:11) audience of the danger of apostatizing in order to avoid persecution (Heb 3:12; 10:23-29, 35-39; 13:9, 13). The common observation that Hebrews begins like a treatise, proceeds like a sermon, and concludes like an epistle, is probably to be explained by the supposition that the author wrote out the sermon that he would have given if he could have been present.

His readers were a specific group of second generation Christians (Heb 2:3-4) whom he knew well. In the past, they had endured persecution, which consisted of ridicule, verbal abuse, confiscation of their property (Heb 10:32-34), and possibly imprisonment for some (Heb 13:3), but so far no one had been martyred (Heb 12:4). Suggestions that they were Gentiles with Gnostic leanings are unlikely. Supposed links with the Dead Sea Scrolls have made it more common to suggest that the readers were an Essene community living in Palestine, or more particularly in Jerusalem (cf. Heb 7 and 11Q Melchizedek), but the correlations seem overdrawn and Hebrews' description of the recipients does not always fit the early history of the Palestinian church (Heb 2:3; 12:4). It is more likely that the readers were a group of Jewish Christians meeting in a house church at Rome (Heb 10:25; 13:24). If that is the case, the former persecution is probably related to the decree of Claudius expelling the Jews from Rome because of "riots instigated by one Chrestus," i.e. *Christos* (Suetonius, *Claudius*, 25:4; cf. Acts 18:2). After some time the Jews returned (Rom 16:3-5), but Jewish Christians were tempted to avoid renewed persecution by reverting to their former Judaism, which enjoyed state recognition as a *religio licita*.

Hebrews must have been written before A.D. 96 because 1 Clement quotes from it. It was also probably written before the destruction of the temple in AD 70, since it represents the sacrifices as ongoing (Heb 8:4, 13; 10:1-2 13:10) and their cessation would certainly have affected the epistle's argument. If it was written to Rome, the earliest it should be dated would be long enough after the decree of Claudius in A.D. 49 that the Jews could have returned. The latest would be sometime shortly before any of the readers were martyred in the Neronian persecution that broke out following the fire of Rome in A.D. 64.

Origen's Comments on the Authorship of Hebrews

The style of the Epistle with the title, 'To the Hebrews,' has not that vulgarity of diction which belongs to the apostle [Paul], who confesses that he is but common in speech.... But that this epistle is more pure Greek in the composition of its phrases, every one will confess who is able to discern the difference of style. Again, it will be obvious that the ideas of the epistle are admirable, and not inferior to any of the books acknowledged to be apostolic.... I would say, that the thoughts are the apostle's, but the diction and phraseology belong to some one who has recorded what the apostle said.... If then, any church considers this epistle as coming from Paul, let it be commended for this, for neither did those ancient men deliver it as such without cause. But who it was that really wrote the epistle, God only knows (As cited by Eusebius, *Ecclesiastical History*, 6.25.11-14, trans. Christian Frederick Cruse [Grand Rapids: Baker Book House, 1955], 246-47).

Scripture as the Living Word in Hebrews

The writer of Hebrews clearly believed that the Old Testament was a divinely inspired and authoritative revelation that was relevant to the needs of his contemporary audience (4:12). In keeping with the sermonic character of his work, he portrays Scripture as a living oracle in which God is still speaking today, rather than a dead record of the past. One way that he brings the word of God to life is by introducing his Old Testament citations with present tense verbs of speech. Methods of enumeration may vary, but we count nineteen uses of a present tense verb of speech to introduce a citation in Hebrews, as compared to five aorists and six perfects.

The writer characteristically attributes his citations to the Divine Author of Scripture and suppresses their human source. He represents all three members of the trinity as speaking the words of Scripture. He has the Holy Spirit uttering the warning of Psalm 95 to listen to God's voice today (3:7 ff.) and promising the blessings of the New Covenant (10:15). He lets the Father address the Son in the words of Scripture and speak about the subordinate role of angels (1:5 ff.; 5:5). He also allows the Son to speak through the words of Scripture expressing his willing obedience to the Father and his unashamed acknowledgment of believers as members of his family (2:12, 13; 10:5-7).

He only names the human author of Scripture in the case of two short statements attributed to Moses (9:20; 12:21) and perhaps a couple lines from Psalm 95 attributed to David, although here he is more likely referring to the canonical book of David, i.e., the Psalms, rather than naming the psalmist (4:7). Twice he obscures the human writer by a vague introductory formula, even though he was probably well aware of the human source of his citation. The vague formula in 4:4, 'he said somewhere' introduces a citation from Genesis 2:2 that would have been well known to the writer of Hebrews and his readers. An even more vague formula, 'someone has testified somewhere, saying,' is used in 2:6 to introduce the quotation from Psalm 8:4-6. Here the quotation could not be attributed to God because it refers to him in the second person. That the quotation is contained in Scripture was more important for the writer of Hebrews than the identification of its human author. Since he regarded all of Scripture as a divinely inspired oracle, he did not need to attach the name of the human author to a particular passage for it to be authoritative.

THE FLOW OF HEBREWS

The primary theological point to be driven home repeatedly by the Epistle to the Hebrews is that the Son, who has inaugurated a new means of access to God, is superior to the Old Testament system of Judaism (**1**:1–10:18). Since this skillfully crafted work of biblical exposition was probably originally composed as a written homily, its writer omits the salutation that would characteristically begin a first-century epistle and commences directly with a majestic christological confession that unabashedly declares the Son's superiority to the prophets and introduces key points that will be developed later (1:1-4).

From his very brief mention of the prophets, the writer moves into an extended discussion of the superiority of the Son to the angels (1:5–2:18). To support this point he sets forth a chain of Old Testament quotations in which the Son is addressed with three titles that are much more highly exalted than anything ever said to angels (1:5-14). The first title has already been mentioned; now it is grounded in Scripture. From the Father's decree in Psalm 2:7 and 2 Samuel 7:14 declaring the Messiah to be his *Son* today, the writer of Hebrews contrasts Jesus' divine adoption as God's Son with the angels' worship of him (5-6). From the words addressed to the davidic king in Psalm 45:6-7, 'Your throne, O *God*, is for ever and ever,' he contrasts Jesus' permanent reign as deity with the angels' transitory nature (7-9); and from Psalm 102:25-26, which in the Septuagint[1] has God addressing another person who created the heavens and earth as *LORD*, he contrasts Jesus' creation of the universe with the angels' service to believers, noting in closing that angels were never asked to sit at God's right hand as Psalm 110:1, the epistle's most foundational Old Testament text,[2] invites Jesus to do (10-14).

At this point, the writer of Hebrews pauses to insert the first of five warnings, which he places on a track parallel to his expository development so that he can constantly call his readers back to the

---

1. LXX Psalm 101:26-28.
2. Psalm 110:1 is also quoted or alluded to in Hebrews 1:13; 8:1; 10:12, 13; 12:2.

The Use of Inclusion as a Structural Clue in Hebrews

The writer of Hebrews often marks off a section of his text by a literary device known as an *inclusio*. This device uses a repeated phrase at, or near, the beginning and end of a section to mark its boundaries. There are differences of opinion concerning how many times this device is used in Hebrews because it is not always clear if the phrase is being intentionally repeated or if similar wording occurs naturally in different places, but a few of the clearer cases are listed below.

The section in 1:5-14, which uses a series of Old Testament quotations to show the superiority of the Son to the angels, begins and ends with the formula, 'to which of the angels did (has) he ever say (said),' followed by a quotation (1:5, 13). The section in 4:3-13 discussing the readers' prospects of entering into God's rest begins with the affirmation that 'we who have believed enter that rest' (4:3). It closes with the exhortation, 'Let us therefore be diligent to enter that rest,' followed by a brief reason for the urgency of this exhortation (4:12-13). The section in 4:14–10:18 arguing for the superiority of the Son to Aaron begins with a reason introduced by the words, 'since we have...,' and a double exhortation, 'Let us hold fast our confession,' and, 'Let us therefore draw near with confidence' (4:14-16). The next section (10:19–13:17), which makes application from the first part of the book, begins with a reason introduced by the same formula, 'since we have...,' and essentially the same double exhortation in reverse order, 'Let us draw near with a sincere heart,' and, 'Let us hold fast the confession of our hope' (10:19-23). Chapter 11:1 introduces the list of Old Testament exemplars of faith (11:4-38) with the assertion that by faith 'the men of old gained approval.' Following that list, a similar phrase looks back in retrospect on those people who 'gained approval through their faith' (11:39) and introduces Jesus as the supreme example of faith (12:1-3).

---

immediate relevance of the theological points he is making. Building upon his exposition of the Son's superiority to the angels, he warns that if all those who rejected the word spoken though angels were justly punished, those who reject such a great salvation as announced by the Son stand in much greater peril of judgment (**2**:1-4).

Hebrews' Quotations from the Old Testament

The book of Hebrews illustrates the breadth and variety of the New Testament's use of the Old Testament than any other New Testament book. In addition to making numerous allusions, the writer of Hebrews quotes from about thirty different Old Testament texts and repeats several of these texts, for a total of thirty-nine citations. Twenty-one of these texts are not cited elsewhere in the New Testament.[1] Although his choice of citations shows freedom and originality, the writer of Hebrews maintains general continuity with his inspired colleagues in his interpretation of the Old Testament.

He draws more heavily upon the Psalms than other parts of the Old Testament, perhaps because the early church's use of the Psalter as a hymnbook guaranteed that his readers would have been familiar with these quotations. In total, he cites eighteen times from eleven texts in the Psalms, twelve times from the Pentateuch, seven times from five prophetic texts, once from a historical book, and once from Proverbs. His christology tends to come from the Psalms and his lessons in redemptive history from the Pentateuch.

Often he uses the Psalms to work backwards to other parts of the Old Testament. YHWH's decree of sonship in Psalm 2:7, for example, takes him back to the Davidic covenant in 2 Samuel 7:14 (Heb 1:5). He probably links the promise of Psalm 110:1, that the enemies of the one invited to sit at YHWH's right hand will be made into a footstool for his feet (Heb 1:13), with the subjection of all things under the feet of man in his quotation from Psalm 8:4-6 (Heb 2:6-8), which alludes to the creation mandate given to Adam in Genesis 1:26-30. The reference in Psalm 95:7-11 to the curse brought upon the Israelites for testing and provoking God takes him back by way of allusion to their refusal to enter the promised land in Numbers 14 (Heb 3:7-19), and the prospect that Psalm 95:11 holds for our entering God's rest leads him back to God's rest at the completion of creation (Gen 2:2; Heb 4:3-5). From Psalm 110:1, which is the most frequently quoted text from the Old Testament in the New

---

[1]The only texts that he cites in common with other New Testament writers are Genesis 21:12; Exodus 25:40; Deuteronomy 32:35; 2 Samuel 7:14; Psalms 2:7; 8:6; 110:1; Jeremiah 31:31; and Habakkuk 2:4.

Testament and the most fundamental text for the writer of Hebrews, he works back to Psalm 110:4 on the assumption that the person seated at YHWH's right hand is the same one who is decreed to be 'a priest forever according to the order of Melchizedek' (Heb 5:6; 8:1; 10:12-13); and the mention of Melchizedek naturally takes him back to the historical account of Abraham's encounter with this mysterious king-priest in Genesis 14:18-20 (Heb 6:20–7:10).

Rather than depending upon a series of minor proof texts, the argument of Hebrews for the superiority of the Son to the Old Testament system of Judaism rests on a limited number of core citations. These core citations and the discussion that follows from them determine the structure of the book. All other citations are ancillary to them and explain, illustrate, or apply points that they make.

The christological confession of Hebrews 1:1-4, which claims that Jesus possesses a superior name to that of angels, is followed by a supporting catena of quotations in which the Father addresses Jesus with three divine titles. The first title, *Son*, is drawn from Psalm 2:7, 'You are my Son, today I have begotten you,' and 2 Samuel 7:14, 'I will be a Father to him, and he will be a Son to me' (Heb 1:5). The second title, *God*, comes from Psalm 45:6-7, 'Your throne, O God, is forever and ever' (Heb 1:8-9). The third title is no less striking. The Septuagint translation of Psalm 102:25-27 (LXX Ps 101) is used in a context where the Hebrew text refers to YHWH to address Jesus as the *Lord* who created the heavens and the earth.

The quotation from Psalm 8:4-6, which follows the warning passage in Hebrews 2:1-4, controls the discussion of Hebrews 2:5-18. It shows that Jesus is superior to angels because he identifies with humanity as the ideal man.

Psalm 95:7-11 is central to the section from Hebrews 3:1 to 4:13. This section introduces Moses as a model servant so that his faithfulness in that role, which is still inferior to Christ's faithfulness as a Son (Heb 3:1-6), may contrast the disobedience of the Israelites whom he led out of Egypt, about whom Psalm 95 was written. The entire quotation is given first (Heb 3:7-11), and parts of it are repeated or expounded later to warn of the danger of missing God's promised rest by falling into the same error of disobedience as the Israelites in the wilderness.

Psalm 110:4 is the key text undergirding the argument of Hebrews 4:14–7:28 for the superiority of the Son to Aaron in regards to his person and priesthood. The quotation is formally stated in Hebrews 5:6 in connection with the superiority of the Son as a person (Heb 4:14–5:10), and an allusion to this text in Hebrews 5:10 introduces the superiority of his priesthood. The immaturity of the readers forces a postponement of that discussion, however, until they can be warned of the peril of remaining in their present condition (Heb 5:11–6:20). In Hebrews 6:20 a second allusion to Psalm 110:4 reintroduces the superiority of the Son's priesthood, which is shown by its eternal perfection in typological fulfillment of the Melchizedekian priesthood and its contrasting lack of the temporal weaknesses inherent in the Levitical order (Heb 7:1-28, with further allusions or quotations in verses 3, 17 and 21).

The promise of a new covenant in Jeremiah 31:31-3, which is quoted fully in Hebrews 8:8-12 and summarized in 10:16-17, controls the discussion from 8:1 to 10:18. Although a lengthy quotation from Psalm 40:6-7 intervenes in Hebrews 10:5-7, with parts of it repeated in verses 8 and 9, the summary of the new covenant at the conclusion of the section shows that Jeremiah 31 is still the primary text. This text was particularly valuable to the argument of Hebrews because it contains an admission from the Old Testament itself that the old covenant was inadequate and needed to be replaced. From this text, the writer of Hebrews argues that Jesus' heavenly ministry is better than Aaron's earthly ministry because it is founded upon this superior covenant, which provides immediate access into the presence of God (Heb 8:1–9:14), and he goes on to argue that the single sacrifice of Jesus' own blood, which inaugurated this new covenant, is superior to Aaron's repeated sacrifices of bulls and goats because it removes sin once and for all (Heb 9:15–10:18). Upon this note of finality, Hebrews' exegetical argument for the superiority of the Son to the Old Testament system of Judaism is complete, and the writer takes up practical implications of the Son's superiority for his readers.

He then returns to the point where he left off to show how the superiority of the Son to the angels was revealed through his humanity (5-18). The glory of having everything subject to the Son in the world to come, as Psalm 8:4-6 promises,[3] was temporarily concealed by his becoming human so that he could suffer and die for us, which made him 'for a little while lower than the angels' (5-9). But by suffering as a human, the Son was able to identify with us in our suffering as a 'merciful and faithful high priest'[4] and bring many other sons along with him to glory (10-18).

The Son is also superior to Old Testament Judaism in that he is superior to Moses, whose name was virtually synonymous with that system (3:1–4:13). Although both Jesus and Moses are set forth as positive examples of faithfulness, Jesus' superiority to Moses is likened to that of a builder over a building he has constructed (3:1-4) and to that of a son over a servant who works in his house (5-6).

These examples of faithfulness lead into a warning about the peril of copying the Israelites' negative example of unbelief (3:7–4:13). The writer of Hebrews reminds his readers that all of the Israelites whom Moses led out of Egypt failed to enter rest in the promised land because of their unbelief (3:7-19). After quoting from Psalm 95, in which the Holy Spirit warns the generation of that day not to copy the Israelites' failure (7-11), he applies the same lesson to his own generation (12-19). He then faces his readers with their present danger of failing to enter God's promised rest, which by now clearly has connotations extending beyond occupation of the physical land (4:1-2); he also sets before them the prospects of entering into this rest today (3-11). By linking God's rest from which the wilderness generation was excluded

---

3. The promise in Psalm 8 goes back to the glory and dominion given to Adam at creation, which the writer of Hebrews believes is yet to be fully realized in Jesus as the representative of the human race. The verbal similarity between Psalm 110:1, 'until I make your enemies a footstool for your feet,' which was quoted earlier in Hebrews 1:13, and Psalm 8:6, 'you have put all things in subjection under his feet,' probably suggested the appropriateness of this quotation to our writer.

4. Hebrews 2:17 f. Jesus' role as a merciful and faithful high priest will be developed later in Hebrews, point by point. The faithfulness of Jesus is highlighted in Hebrews 3:1-6, his mercifulness as a high priest in 5:1-10, and his high priestly office in 7:1–10:18.

with God's rest on the seventh day of creation, he concludes that a day of rest into which the faithful could have entered has existed since creation (3-5). Because the promise of rest still remained unfulfilled at the time when David wrote Psalm 95, God set a new day of opportunity (6-8); consequently, a rest similar to God's Sabbath rest must still remain for the people of God to realize (9-10). The writer of Hebrews exhorts his readers to be diligent to enter into this rest (11) because the word of God can penetrate the hidden intentions of their hearts (12-13).

From this warning about rest, which, as we have seen, flowed from the comparison between Jesus and Moses, the writer of Hebrews turns his attention to the superiority of the Son to Aaron, the archetypical high priest of Old Testament Judaism (4:14–10:18). The superiority of the Son to Aaron is seen first of all in the superiority of his person (4:14–5:10). As a high priest, Jesus is a superior mediator (4:14–5:3) because his endurance of testing without sinning encourages us to draw near with confidence that he will be merciful[5] and can help us in our need (4:14-16). By contrast, Aaron and his successors were limited in their ability to mediate between men and God because, although they could be sympathetic with human weaknesses, they had to offer sacrifices for their own sins (5:1-3). Even though both Christ and Aaron were appointed to the priestly office by God, Christ's appointment is superior in that God formally decreed Christ to be not only his Son, but also 'a priest forever according to the order of Melchizedek' (4-6).[6] Christ is also a superior person to Aaron in that he has a greater maturity, having been perfected through his suffering (7-10).

Although the writer of Hebrews would have liked to discuss Melchizedek in greater detail,[7] he felt compelled by the spiritual

---

5. Cf. Hebrews 2:17.

6. The quotation from Psalm 110:4, which controls the section on the superiority of the Son to Aaron (Heb. 4:14–10:18) and is repeated or alluded to in Hebrews 5:6, 10; 6:20; 7:3, 11, 15, 17, 21, 24, 28, is likely joined here with the decree of sonship from Psalm 2:7, which was quoted earlier in Hebrews 1:5, because of similarities between Psalm 110:1, which speaks about making the Messiah's enemies a footstool for his feet (Heb. 1:13; cf. Ps. 8:6; Heb. 2:8), and the subjugation of the Son's enemies in Psalm 2:8-9.

7. He will return to Melchizedek in Hebrews 7:1-28.

sluggishness of his readers to interject a warning about the peril of their remaining immature (5:11–6:20). After presenting a case that they truly are immature (5:11-14) and need to progress beyond their understanding of elementary doctrines (6:1-3), he lays out the irreversible consequences of enlightened apostasy (4-8). Based upon their previous conduct, however, he anticipates that they will continue to persevere (9-12); and he assures them that from God's side the promise that anchors their souls is absolutely certain since God, himself, confirmed it with an oath (13-20).

Having sounded this necessary warning, the writer of Hebrews returns to his interrupted discussion of Melchizedek to show that the Son possesses a better priesthood than Aaron because he is a perpetual high priest in the order of Melchizedek, as Psalm 110:4 declares (7:1-28). Working backwards from this psalm to its historical context in Genesis,[8] the writer of Hebrews shows how Melchizedek typifies the superiority of the priestly order that he founded (1-10). The glaring omission of any record in the biblical narrative concerning either Melchizedek's ancestry, which would have been of vital importance for a Levitical priest, or his death, allowed the writer of Hebrews to conclude by way of typological comparison to the Son of God that Melchizedek holds his priestly office in perpetuity (1-3). Furthermore, the fact that Melchizedek collected tithes from Abraham long before Levi was born, when viewed from the Semitic perspective of corporate solidarity, implied that Melchizedek received tithes from Levi after a figurative manner of speaking (4-10).

After etching this mysterious Old Testament figure upon his readers' historical memories, the writer of Hebrews allows Melchizedek to recede gradually into the background so that the perfection attained by Jesus, the greater and final priest in his order, can come to the fore (11-28). He argues that through Jesus the Melchizedekian priesthood legally superseded the Levitical priesthood (11-22) upon the basis of, first, the power of Jesus' indestructible life rather than a requirement of physical generation (11-19) and, second, God's declaration of an oath appointing Jesus to the office of high priest forever, in contrast with the Levitical

---

8. Genesis 14:18-20.

priests, who were admitted without any oath (20-22). Moreover, Jesus guaranteed that the Melchizedekian priesthood could function permanently because he lives forever, whereas death prevented the Levitical priests from continuing in office and necessitated their replacement from time to time (23-25). By his sinless life, Jesus also conferred moral perfection upon the Melchizedekian priesthood that the Levitical priesthood could not attain (26-28).[9]

In addition to holding a better priesthood in the order of Melchizedek, Jesus offers us a better ministry (**8**:1–9:14), which he conducts in the heavenly sanctuary (8:1-6). The writer of Hebrews provides a transition into this new section by summarizing his main point thus far: we have the kind of perfect high priest we require in Jesus (1-2); he also adds a note to the effect that Christ's ministry is superior to that of Aaron because it is performed in the true heavenly sanctuary rather than an earthly copy (3-6). Christ's ministry is also superior because it is founded upon the new covenant of Jeremiah 31, which has made the former covenant obsolete (7-13). Furthermore, Christ's ministry attained immediate access into the presence of God in the heavenly Holy of Holies (**9**:1-14). Whereas access into the earthly Holy of Holies was restricted in the Old Testament to the high priest, who could only enter once a year carrying blood for his own sins and those of the people (1-10), Christ obtained eternal redemption for us by his personal appearance in heaven (11-14).

God's Son, Jesus Christ, is also superior to Aaron in that he has offered a better sacrifice for us (9:15–10:18). The writer of Hebrews begins to build his case upon the general principle that the death of a testator must take place before his will can be executed (15-22). From this principle, he argues that Christ inaugurated the new covenant by sacrificing himself so that we might inherit what was promised (15-17)[10] in the same way that Moses inaugurated the former covenant by sprinkling the people and the tabernacle with the blood of animals (18-22). His next point is that, although animal

---

9. Cf. Hebrews 5:1-3.

10. The same Greek word for a will is also used for a covenant, which might not require the death of the one who made it to be brought into effect, but here death is necessitated by the mention of our inheritance in verse 15.

THE TABERNACLE

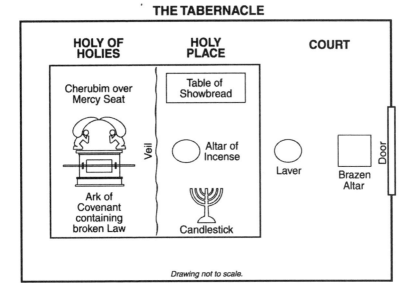

blood might have been sufficient for ceremonial cleansing, a superior sacrifice was necessary to remove sin (9:23–10:4). By a single sacrifice of himself, Christ cleansed the heavenly sanctuary (9:23-28), but the repeated animal sacrifices offered by the Levitical priests were not able to cleanse the human conscience permanently (**10**:1-4). Because these sacrifices were ineffective, Christ volunteered to come to do God's will, as it was written about him in Psalm 40 (5-10). We can be assured that the sacrifice of Christ is efficacious to forgive sin forever (11-18) because his session at the Father's right hand indicates that his redemptive work, unlike that of the Levitical priests, is finished (11-14), and because the Holy Spirit guarantees the truthfulness of the new covenant, which provides for the complete forgiveness of sin (15-18).

Having concluded that the Son is superior to Judaism because his sacrifice removes sin completely, the writer of Hebrews has brought his theological exposition to its climax, and so he turns to draw practical applications out of this truth for his readers (10:19–13:17). On the basis of all that we have in Jesus, he urges his readers with a series of first person plural exhortations to embrace wholeheartedly the new and living way that Christ has inaugurated for us (19-25). Alongside this encouragement, he adds a warning that if those who rejected the law of Moses were punished without mercy, those who despise the new covenant instituted by the Son's blood will be punished much more severely (26-31). The writer follows through with an encouragement for his readers to continue their previous example of endurance (32-39). He takes note of their heroic endurance of suffering in the past (32-34) and urges them to continue to endure so that they might receive their reward and not God's displeasure when he comes in just a little while (35-39).[11]

As a means of encouraging his readers to endure, the writer of Hebrews exhorts them to follow the example of the biblical heroes of faith (**11:1–12:3**). He begins this extended exhortation with an introduction describing the confident and forward-looking nature of faith with regard to invisible realities for which the Old Testament heroes were commended, in implicit contrast to the unbelief for which the Israelites who were mentioned in chapter three fell in the wilderness (11:1-3). He then illustrates this faith by a long list of Old Testament exemplars drawn from across the course of redemptive history (4-38) beginning with the faith of three antediluvians (4-7): Abel (4), Enoch (5-6), and Noah (7).

Next in the historical progression, the writer of Hebrews pays special attention to the faith of Abraham (8-19). Both the obedience of Abraham to God's call to go to a land that he would receive as an inheritance (8-10) and his belief in God's promise that his descendants would be as numerous as the stars (11-12) are cited as prime examples of faith. For a moment, the progression of historical events is held back so that the writer can comment on the distant perspective of Abraham, whose faith reached beyond the promise of an earthly inheritance, which he did not receive in his own lifetime, to the anticipation of a better heavenly country (13-16). The faith of Abraham climaxes with the offering of his only son, Isaac, whom he received back from the dead figuratively speaking, even

---

11. The quote in verse 37-38 is from Habakkuk 2:3-4. Here the need to do the will of God by persevering so that he might not be displeased with the Hebrews when he comes is subtly contrasted with the earlier quote from Psalm 40:6-8 in Hebrews 10:5-7 where God did not take pleasure in burnt offerings so Jesus came to do his will.

as God the Father would receive back his Son literally (17-19). The eschatological orientation of Abraham's faith is confirmed by the faith of the other patriarchs (20-22), Isaac (20), Jacob (21), and Joseph (22), who all looked beyond their own lives to the fulfillment of the promise.

Moses, the next exemplar of faith, looked past the temporal wealth of Egypt to the unseen, eternal reward for identifying with God's people in suffering and delivering them from bondage (23-28). The Israelites of his and the succeeding generation also exemplified faith in their crossing of the Red Sea and their conquest of the land (29-31). Since time would fail the writer of Hebrews to tell of each one individually, he groups together an innumerable host of Jewish heroes whose faith enabled some of them to perform heroic feats or miraculous acts and others to suffer persecution, ridicule, or even martyrdom (32-38).

To this long list of illustrations of faith, he appends a comment that although God commended all of these Old Testament heroes for their faith, none of them received the promise because they had to wait to be perfected together with us (39-40). In view of their testimony to the possibility of a life of faith and in view of the supreme example of faith shown by Jesus, who brought faith to its perfect end by enduring the worst suffering imaginable, the writer of Hebrews concludes this exhortation by urging his readers to run with endurance the race that God had set before them (**12**:1-3).

He follows with a closely related exhortation urging them to value the discipline of the Father (4-13). After setting up the exhortation with a quotation from Proverbs (4-6),[12] he argues that they should highly esteem the Father's discipline, even though it might be painful, because it is a loving and necessary means of helping any son reach the enjoyable rewards of maturity (7-11). With this goal in mind, he calls upon his weary readers, who are drooping from fatigue, to straighten up and accept the discipline of running the race (12-13). Using the negative example of Esau, who lost out because he did not value his sonship very highly, the writer of Hebrews adds a general exhortation commanding his readers to pursue sanctification of both heart and life (14-17).

---

12. Proverbs 3:11-12.

As he is preparing to draw the epistle to a close, the writer of Hebrews sounds a final warning about the peril of refusing the warning from heaven (18-29). He contrasts the Israelites' approach to Mount Sinai, where God's voice thundered out the law amid a terrifying blaze of fire, darkness, whirlwind and the blast of a trumpet, with his readers' approach to God's glorious habitation on Mount Zion, where Jesus, the mediator of the new covenant, has assembled with myriads of angels and the perfected spirits of the saints (18-24). Building upon this contrast, he warns that if those who rejected God when they were warned on earth could not escape, those who reject him when he warns from heaven will most certainly suffer an even more terrifying judgment that will shake not only the earth but also the very foundations of the heavens themselves (25-29).

Having made his main point as forcefully as possible, the writer now strings together a series of general ethical admonitions concerning the need to conduct one's social and private life from a Christian perspective (**13**:1-6). He also reminds his readers in closing to consider their leaders and the privileges of New Testament Christianity (7-17). Because Jesus Christ does not change, they are to maintain theological and moral continuity with their leaders who taught them in the past (7-8) and not to relinquish their privilege of partaking of the food sacrificed on the heavenly altar (9-10). Since Jesus was sacrificed outside the gates of the holy city in typological fulfillment of the regulations for the sacrifices on the Day of Atonement, the readers ought to bear his disgrace willingly by going outside the sanctioning walls of ritualistic Judaism to share his alienation (11-16). With respect to these exhortations in particular, they were to submit to the spiritual authority that God had entrusted to their current leaders for the watchcare of their souls (17).

In conclusion (18-25), the writer appends a personal postscript in which he requests his readers to pray for him along with their prayers for other leaders so that he might be restored to them (18-19). His pastoral concerns for his readers lead into a magnificent benediction wishing upon them God's equipping grace for every good work through the blood of the great Shepherd of the sheep,

Jesus Christ (20-21). Final greetings to and from acquaintances on both ends close the epistle, which its writer stylizes as a brief word of exhortation (22-25).

The Literary Genre of Hebrews

It has been said that Hebrews opens like a treatise, proceeds like a sermon, and concludes like a letter. Skipping the customary epistolary introduction identifying the writer and readers, the book begins like a formal treatise with a majestic confessional statement extolling the superiority of Christ. Its rhetorical structure unfolds logically as its anonymous author argues from the Old Testament, point by point, that the present revelation in God's Son is superior to the outmoded system of Judaism in every respect. Behind this biblical exposition lies an urgent pastoral concern that compels the person who penned it to pause periodically along the way to warn his readers to pay attention to the good news that they had heard and not give up their faith under threat of persecution. At the end of each warning section, the writer returns to the point where he left off, unlike Paul, and picks up the argument again.

He describes his communication as a 'word of exhortation' (13:22). In more current terminology, we would call it a homily, or a written sermon. Undoubtedly, he would have preferred to have delivered his exhortation in person, but circumstances forced him to send it in writing. Even though he was absent, he skillfully maintains a sense of presence by avoiding references to the written medium and describing his communication in terms of speech (cf. 2:5; 5:11; 6:9; 8:1; 9:5; 11:32). The book closes, as a letter would, with personal comments and greetings (13:18-19, 23-25).

OUTLINE OF THE EPISTLE TO THE HEBREWS

The General Epistles

The Value of Hebrews and the General Epistles

If our New Testament did not contain Hebrews and the General Epistles, the Christian church would be greatly impoverished. These books show that early Christianity was not limited to the creative genius of any one person for its leadership and theological development. It possessed a rich variety of capable leaders who have left us a literary heritage: besides Paul, we have two of Jesus= closest disciples, Peter and John; our Lord's half-brothers, James and Jude; and the brilliant but anonymous writer of Hebrews. They offer us a different perspective from what we find in the Gospels and Paul's epistles, all within a grand theological unity that allows for differences of emphasis while still remaining self-consistent.

Practical Lessons from the General Epistles

1 From the Epistle of James, we learn the importance of demonstrating our faith by translating it into visible actions.

2 From Peter's First Epistle, we learn how to face suffering as a Christian maturely in the context of an unfriendly world.

3 From the Second Epistle of Peter and the Epistle of Jude, we learn the importance of maintaining orthodox doctrine and upright behaviour in a world characterized by heresy and immorality.

4 From John's First Epistle, we learn to grow in fellowship with God as we walk in the light and love the brethren in practical ways.

5 From Second John, we learn the importance of walking according to Christ's commandment to love one another and of abiding in Christ's teaching about the incarnation.

6 From Third John, we learn the importance of carrying out Christian ministry with an attitude of hospitality and humility.

James

OVERVIEW OF JAMES

Theme: Faith in action

Key verse: James 2:26b, 'Faith without works is dead' (NASB).

Salutation	1:1
I. Faith tested by various trials	1:2-18
II. Faith exercised in practical actions	1:19–3:12
A. Practising true religion	1:19-27
B. Avoiding social prejudice	2:1-13
C. Performing good works	2:14-26
D. Controlling the tongue	3:1-12
III. Faith opposed to worldly principles	3:13–5:6
A. Worldly wisdom	3:13-18
B. Selfish strife	4:1-12
C. Presumptuous planning	4:13-17
D. Economic exploitation	5:1-6
IV. Faith strengthened by divine means	5:7-20
A. The promise of judgment	5:7-12
B. The power of prayer	5:13-18
C. The restoration of sinners	5:19-20

HISTORICAL BACKGROUND

The James who wrote this epistle (Jas 1:1) was probably the half-brother of Jesus (Matt 13:55; cf. John 7:5) and the leader of the early Jerusalem church (Acts 15:13; 21:18; 1 Cor 15:7; Gal 2:9, 12). Most likely he wrote from his home in Jerusalem.

The title by which he addresses his readers, 'the twelve tribes who are scattered abroad' (Jas 1:1), could refer to either the Jewish diaspora in general or the scattering of the early Christians in Jerusalem by persecution (Acts 8:2). In either case, they would have been Hellenistic Jewish Christians whom he wished to instruct and encourage in practical and ethical behaviour.

This epistle lacks any specific details that would make precise dating possible, but assuming the traditional view of authorship, it must have been written before James' martyrdom c. A.D. 62. Its strong Jewish flavour and its primitive theology, with an emphasis on practical ethics rather than doctrinal formulations, suggest that it could be as early as the mid 40s. If that is the case, it could be the earliest book in all of the New Testament.

THE FLOW OF JAMES

In the salutation to his epistle, James introduces himself as a bond-servant of God and sends his greetings to the twelve tribes of Israel who are scattered abroad (**1:1**). He begins to develop his theme of faith in action by considering how his readers should respond to the various trials that will sooner or later test their faith (2-18). He radiates great confidence, however, that it is possible to be joyful in the midst of trials because they produce endurance and maturity (2-4). He assures those who do not know how to cope with trials that God will grant the needed wisdom to anyone who asks in faith (5-8). To lessen their pain, he reminds his readers that both the trials of the poor and the ease of the rich have a limited duration when viewed from the end of life (9-11); and he promises that those whose character has been proven by testing will be crowned with life as their reward (12). He guards his readers against failure by explaining that temptation, which is the negative side of testing,[1] seeks to use trials to destroy them rather than to prove their character (13-15). The source of temptation (13-14) is certainly not God (13); rather, it is our own fallen human desires (14). The consequences of yielding to temptation are sin, at first, and, ultimately, death (15). From the finality of this solemn warning, James returns his discussion of testing to its opening positive note by affirming that only good things come from God, which implies that God must be gracious in allowing trials for good ends (16-18).

After preparing his readers for the inevitability of testing, James exhorts them to exercise their faith in practical actions (1:19–3:12). The first of these is practising true religion (1:19-27), by which James means giving expression to one's faith by being considerate of other people (19-20), by obeying the Word of God rather than merely listening to it (21-25), by controlling one's tongue (26), and by visiting the destitute in their need (27).

---

1. Unlike English, Greek uses the same word for both the positive idea of testing and the negative idea of temptation, but in this context James clearly distinguishes between the two meanings.

The Martyrdom of James

But after Paul...had been sent to Rome by Festus, the Jews, being frustrated in their hope of entrapping him...turned against James, the brother of the Lord, to whom the episcopal seat at Jerusalem had been entrusted by the apostles.... Leading him into their midst they demanded of him that he should renounce faith in Christ in the presence of all the people. But...with a clear voice...he spoke out before the whole multitude and confessed that our Savior and Lord Jesus is the Son of God. But they were unable to bear longer the testimony of the man who, on account of the excellence of ascetic virtue and of piety which he exhibited in his life, was esteemed by all as the most just of men, and consequently they slew him. ...Clement...records that he was thrown from the pinnacle of the temple, and was beaten to death with a club. But Hegesippus, who lived immediately after the apostles,...writes as follows: 'James, the brother of the Lord, succeeded to the government of the Church in conjunction with the apostles. He has been called the Just by all from the time of our Savior to the present day. ...he was in the habit of entering alone into the temple, and was frequently found upon his knees begging forgiveness for the people, so that his knees became hard like those of a camel.... Now some of the...sects...asked him, "What is the gate of Jesus?" and he replied that he was the Savior. On account of these words some believed that Jesus is the Christ.... The Jews and Scribes and Pharisees,...coming therefore in a body to James...said, "We entreat thee, restrain the people; for they are gone astray in regard to Jesus, as if he were the Christ.... Stand therefore upon the pinnacle of the temple, that... thou mayest be clearly seen, and that thy words may be readily heard by all the people...." [They]...therefore placed James upon the pinnacle of the temple, and cried out to him...: "Thou just one...declare to us, what is the gate of Jesus." And he answered with a loud voice, 'Why do ye ask me concerning Jesus, the Son of Man? He himself sitteth in heaven at the right hand of the great Power, and is about to come upon the clouds of heaven." And when many were fully convinced..., these same Scribes and Pharisees said again to one another, 'We have done badly in supplying such testimony to Jesus...." So they went up and threw down the just man, and...they began to stone him, for he was not killed by the fall; but he turned and knelt down and said, "I entreat thee, Lord God our Father, forgive them, for they know not what they do...." '

James was so admirable a man and so celebrated among all for his justice, that the more sensible even of the Jews were of the opinion that this was the cause of the siege of Jerusalem, which happened to them immediately after his martyrdom.... (Eusebius, *Church History*, 2.23.1-19; cf. Josephus, *Antiquities*, 20.9.2).

Another practical action in which faith needs to be exercised is avoiding social prejudice (**2**:1-13). As a vivid example of showing favoritism, James contrasts the royal treatment that a rich man who visits their assembly receives with the disrespect that is shown to the poor (1-4). He then argues for acting impartially on the practical grounds that God has chosen the poor of this world to inherit his kingdom, whereas those who are rich by the world's standards often oppress believers and blaspheme the Lord's name (5-7). To this argument, James adds an exposition of the Scriptural basis for acting impartially (8-13). The Mosaic law is consistent in judging those who violate it, whether they are guilty of adultery, murder, or failing to love their neighbor as themselves (8-11); therefore, we who are under the higher law of liberty should be consistent in showing mercy to everyone (12-13).

Faith also needs to be exercised practically in performing good works (14-26). James contends that faith without works is dead (14-19). To support this contention he gives two illustrations: the first is of unhelpful Christians who wish a destitute brother or sister well but do nothing to alleviate their need (14-17); the second is of condemned demons who intellectually acknowledge the *Shema*, the orthodox creed of Jewish monotheism, but shudder in fear of God's judgment (18-19). Conversely, James contends that faith is manifested by works (20-26). Again he supports his point with two illustrations: the first is Abraham's manifestation of faith in offering up Isaac, for which Israel's greatest patriarch was reckoned righteous (20-24); the second is a Gentile prostitute's manifestation of faith in protecting the spies who came to Jericho, for which Rahab was spared her life (25-26).

Finally, faith needs to be exercised by controlling one's tongue (**3**:1-12). James shows that controlling the tongue is crucially important because its dominant position in the body makes controlling the tongue the key to controlling the whole person (1-5a). First, James sets forth this principle in the human realm, focusing upon teachers in particular (1-2); and then he illustrates it in impersonal realms (3-5a). Even though the tongue is relatively small, it controls a person's whole body in the same way that a bit controls a horse's movements (3) or a rudder steers a large ship (4-

5a). James also shows that controlling the tongue is important because this small instrument can produce harmful effects far out of proportion to its size, just as a tiny spark can destroy a great forest (5b-6). Although James strongly advocates the importance of controlling the tongue, he was also well aware of the difficulty – or as he puts it somewhat hyperbolically, the impossibility – of taming the tongue, which he laments is more restless than any wild animal (7-8). He easily finds evidence of the unruliness of the tongue in the curses that flow from it, but the inconsistency of cursing one's fellow man with the same tongue that blesses God strengthens James' resolve to see it brought under control (9-12).

As well as being exercised in good works, faith takes a stand in opposing worldly principles, whether they are followed by unbelievers, as one might expect, or by believers who act inconsistently with their profession (3:13–5:6). Faith opposes the worldly wisdom of jealousy and selfish ambition that can easily creep into a Christian's life and promotes instead the heavenly wisdom of righteousness (3:13-18). It also opposes selfish strife among brothers (4:1-12), which, as James points out, has its source in one's sinful desires (1-3). Selfish strife is opposed to the exclusive claim that God makes upon our loyalty (4-6) and can be cured by humbly submitting one's self to him (7-10). As one example of selfish striving, James singles out slandering one's neighbour, and he reminds his readers that this behaviour is condemned by the law (11-12). Faith opposes the presumptuous planning of arrogant Christians who, in their greedy haste to make money, forget their dependence upon God for life and breath (13-17); it also opposes the economic exploitation of poor and innocent people by rich unbelievers (5:1-6).

James reassures his readers that even though many of them were suffering economic injustices or other hardships, their faith could be strengthened by divine means (7-20). Those who were being exploited he encourages to be patient because the promise of judgment at the Lord's coming is not far away (5:7-12), and those who were physically ill he encourages to avail themselves of the power of prayer (13-18). In response to their immediate physical needs, he gives explicit instructions on how to appropriate the prayer of faith through the elders of the church (13-16a), and drawing upon Israel's ancient history he recalls to mind the power of Elijah's prayer (16b-18). Finally, he encourages those who see a brother falling into error to become the means themselves of restoring him back to the truth (19-20).

OUTLINE OF JAMES

1 Peter

OVERVIEW OF 1 PETER

Theme: Facing suffering as a Christian

Key verse: 1 Peter 4:16, 'If anyone suffers as a Christian, let him not feel ashamed, but in that name let him glorify God' (NASB).

HISTORICAL BACKGROUND

This epistle claims to be written by Peter (1 Pet 1:1; cf. 5:1), although he probably wrote with the assistance of Silvanus as an amanuensis (1 Pet 5:12). Assuming that 1 Pet 5:13 refers to spiritual, rather than geographic, Babylon, Peter would have written from Rome. He addresses his readers as 'the elect who reside as aliens, scattered throughout Pontus, Galatia, Cappadocia, Asia, and Bithynia' (1 Pet 1:1). A number of his references to his readers suggest that they were primarily Gentile converts (cf. 1 Pet 1:14, 18; 2:9-10; 3:6; 4:3-4), although there were probably some Jewish Christians among their number. Peter wrote to help them face the suffering that they were experiencing for their stand as Christians.

The date of the epistle depends upon the identification of the persecution that forms its background. If the persecution is to be identified with an official imperial persecution under Domitian (81-96) or Trajan (98-117), who declared refusing to renounce Christianity a capital offense (cf. his letter to Pliny and 1 Pet 4:16), the epistle must be dated late, and it could not have been written by Peter. But if the persecution came from individual pagan neighbours or local officials, as is more likely the case (1 Pet 2:12-17; 3:16; 4:12; 4:15-17; 5:9), no serious objection to Petrine authorship remains, and the epistle should be dated sometime between Peter's arrival in Rome (c. 60) and the apostle's martyrdom by Nero (67 or 68). The most likely date would be around, or shortly before, the outbreak of the Neronian persecutions in 64. At that time there was a growing anti-Christian mood in Rome that could have spilled over to Asia Minor.

Biographical Sketch of Peter

Simon, or more properly Simeon, the son of Jonas (or John) came from the village of Bethsaida at the northern end of the Sea of Galilee (Matt 16:17; John 1:42-44; Acts 15:14). He was married, and early in the Gospels we find him living in the neighbouring town of Capernaum where Jesus healed his mother-in-law of a fever (Mark 1:29; 1 Cor 9:5). He and his brother, Andrew, were fishermen in partnership with James and John, the two sons of Zebedee (Luke 5:10). Andrew, who was initially a disciple of John the Baptist, introduced Simon to Jesus (John 1:40-42), and Jesus, in prophetic anticipation of what Simon would become, changed his name to Cephas, which means a rock. Paul retains the Aramaic name, Cephas, but the other New Testament writers prefer either the Greek equivalent, Peter or the compound, Simon Peter. After the imprisonment of John the Baptist, Jesus called Simon Peter and his partners to follow him (Mark 1:14-20; Matt 4:12, 18-22), and he repeated this call after a miraculous catch of fish that helped Peter to grasp the implications of Jesus' supernatural identity for his own change of occupation (Luke 5:3-11).

Peter was a member of the inner circle of disciples, together with James and John, and sometimes Andrew. This smaller group was privileged to be with Jesus on the most private occasions in his ministry including his raising of Jarius' daughter (Mark 5:37; Luke 8:51), his transfiguration (Matt 17:1; Mark 9:2; Luke 9:28), his discourse on the Mount of Olives (Mark 13:3), and his prayers in the Garden of Gethsemane (Matt 26:37; Mark 14:33). .

Peter is always listed first in the enumeration of the disciples (Matt 10:2; Mark 3:16; Luke 6:14). His readiness to speak and act made him their natural leader and spokesman. When, for example, the crowds were turning away and Jesus asked the twelve if they wanted to leave as well, Peter instantly replied, 'Lord, to whom shall we go?' (John 6:68). When Jesus came to the disciples by night walking on the Sea of Galilee, Peter unthinkingly jumped out of the boat to meet him (Matt 14:29). When Jesus asked the disciples, 'Who do you say that I am?' Peter did not hesitate to confess, 'You are the Christ' (Mark 8:29; Matt 16:16; Luke 9:20).

The meaning of Jesus' reply, 'You are Peter (Petros), and upon this rock (petra) I will build my church' (Matt 16:18), has been much debated. From the mention of Peter in the context, one might suppose that he is the rock, but the change in Greek from the masculine (*petros*, a piece of rock, or stone) to the feminine (*petra*, a mass of rock, or a crag) signals a disjunction between Peter and this rock. Grammatically, it is more likely that Jesus promised to build the church either upon Peter's confession or upon himself. In the same context, Jesus promised to give Peter 'the keys of the kingdom' and assured him that whatever he bound on earth would already have been bound in heaven (Matt 16:19). Later on, Jesus extended the authority to bind and loose to all of the apostles, and even to the church as a gathered body (Matt 18:18; John 20:23), but 'the keys of the kingdom' were granted uniquely to Peter.

Unfortunately, the impetuous personality that made Peter a natural leader got him into trouble on more than one occasion. Right after making his great confession, Peter tried to dissuade Jesus from going to the cross, for which he received Jesus' harshest rebuke (Matt 16:21-23; Mark 8:31-33). When Peter realized that he had stepped out of the boat and was walking on water in the midst of a fierce storm, he began to sink (Matt 14:30). Peter spoke rashly on the mount of transfiguration because he was so terrified that he didn't know what to say (Mark 9:6; Luke 9:33). When Jesus warned Peter that his adamant refusal to let him wash his feet would exclude him from fellowship, Peter immediately wanted his hands and head washed as well, which the Lord had to point out was unnecessary (John 13:5-10). When the armed mob came to arrest Jesus in the garden, Peter instinctively drew his sword and swung it at the head of the nearest assailant (John 18:10). Jesus had to heal the ear that Peter had lopped off (Luke 22:51) and remind him that the cross was part of the Father's plan (John 18:11). When Jesus predicted that Peter would deny him, he strenuously insisted that he would follow to death (Mark 14:29, 31; Matt 26:33, 35; Luke 22:31; John 13:36-37), but when the moment of testing arrived Peter denied three times that he knew the Lord (Matt 26:69-75; Mark 14:66-72; Luke 22:54-62; John 18:15-18; 25-27).

Even though he failed, or possibly because he needed to be restored, Peter is singled out as a witness of the resurrection. Of all the disciples, he is the only one mentioned by name in the women's reports of the empty tomb (Mark 16:7; John 20:2). Although John outran him to the tomb, Peter was the first to step inside (John 20:2-6; Luke 24:12) and the first of the disciples to see the risen Lord (1 Cor 15:5).

Some weeks later, Jesus appeared by the Sea of Galilee to a group of disciples who had gone back to fishing with Peter. They had caught nothing all night, but Jesus granted them a miraculous catch of fish (John 20:1-8). After serving the disciples breakfast (John 20:6-14), Jesus commissioned Peter three times for his coming ministry (John 21:15-17) and warned that he would die as a martyr (John 21:18-19).

After Jesus' ascension, Peter assumes leadership at the most critical junctures in the establishment of the early church throughout the first twelve chapters of Acts. He immediately takes the initiative in choosing a replacement for Judas (Acts 1:15-26). On the day of Pentecost, Peter stands up and declares the significance of the events that had recently taken place to the Jewish pilgrims who had assembled from around the world (Acts 2:14-40). When the first Samaritans are converted, Peter and John go as representatives of the church in Jerusalem to welcome this despised race of mixed Jewish and Gentile extraction into the fellowship of believers (Acts 8:14-17). After having his prejudices broken down by a special vision, Peter takes the unprecedented step of entering Cornelius' house and introducing the Gospel to complete Gentiles (Acts 10:1-48), and he successfully defends their inclusion in the church before the Jewish believers in Jerusalem, who were scandalized that he would eat ceremonially unclean food (Acts 11:1-18). Peter's opening of the Gospel to these three ethnic groups follows the general progression of the Gospel in Acts from Jerusalem to the ends of the earth and can be reasonably interpreted as Peter's use of the keys of the kingdom.

By the Holy Spirit's heightening of his natural abilities and tempering of his weaknesses, the unstable and impulsive Peter of the Gospels is transformed in Acts into a fearless and dynamic apostle who exhibits the qualities of a rock. Even after being imprisoned twice, he boldly proclaimed the Gospel and confidently stood before the high priest and Sanhedrin defying their injunction to be silent (Acts 4:1-22; 5:17-42). On a third occasion, he was imprisoned by Herod, who intended to execute him as he had James the brother of John, but an angel released Peter from prison by night (Acts 12:1-19). Peter was also bold in confronting sin, whether it was in a Christian couple who lied about the amount of their offering and dropped dead at his feet (Acts 5:1-11) or a pagan magician who attempted to buy the Holy Spirit's power for personal gain (Acts 8:18-24).

One way that Peter gained a hearing for the Gospel was by healing the sick. Included among the more notable miracles attributed to him in Acts are the healing of a man born lame (Acts 3:1-10), the restoration of another who had been paralyzed for eight years (Acts 8:32-35), and the raising of a dead woman (Acts 9:36-42). The reputation of Peter as a miracle worker grew so great that people even carried their sick out into the streets in hopes that his passing shadow might fall on them (Acts 5:15).

In keeping with the expansion of the early church from Jerusalem to the ends of the earth, the focus of Acts gradually shifts away from Peter, the apostle to the Jews, to Paul, the apostle to the Gentiles (Gal 2:7-8; 1 Tim 2:7). Peter was personally acquainted with Paul (Gal 1:18) and affirmed Paul's refusal to impose Jewish ceremonial law upon Gentile converts (Gal 2:9), but under pressure from orthodox Jews, he withdrew from eating with Gentile believers, implicitly placing them back under obligation to keep the law in order to be accepted (Gal 2:12-13). For his inconsistency, Peter received a sharp rebuke from Paul (Gal 2:11, 14), but he apparently accepted it with humility. At the Jerusalem church council, we find Peter arguing against the imposition of legalistic restrictions upon Gentile converts (Acts 15:7-11), and, in his later life, he refers to Paul as a 'beloved brother' (2 Pet 3:15).

Although Peter is better known from Acts for his early ministry in Palestine, his apostleship carried him far abroad. He probably traversed northern Asia Minor evangelizing and ministering to the scattered group of predominantly Gentile believers to whom his canonical epistles were later sent (1 Pet 1:1). He probably also ministered at Corinth long enough for a factious Petrine party to form there upon his departure (1 Cor 1:12; 3:22). Tradition strongly associates the last years of his life with Rome. It was probably during his stay there that John Mark reworked Peter's recollections of Jesus' earthly ministry into the earliest Gospel and that Silvanus served as an amanuensis for the writing of 1 Peter, in which Peter cryptically refers to the imperial capital as Babylon (1 Pet 5:12-13). In keeping with Jesus' prediction (John 21:18-19), Peter died a martyr's death under Nero following the great fire of Rome. According to legend he was crucified upside down, but the sources from which this legend grew are historically suspect.

THE FLOW OF 1 PETER

Peter opens his first epistle with a salutation in which he conveys a Trinitarian blessing to his readers, who resided as aliens throughout northern Asia Minor (**1**:1-2). He begins to address the situation in which they were suffering for their Christianity by highlighting the importance of hope in times of suffering (1:3-2:10). He notes that the Christian's hope of salvation has great value for transcending the suffering that must be faced in the present (1:3-12). This hope was provided for us in Jesus Christ (3-9). It is a living hope (3-5) that has not yet been fully realized but will have a glorious outcome when Jesus is revealed (6-9). As we hope for what is yet to come, so the Old Testament prophets anticipated, but did not fully understand, many aspects of the salvation that has now come to us in Christ (10-12).

Peter also affirms that our hope of final salvation can have great significance for effecting sanctification in practical ways (1:13–2:10). He explains that, first of all, hope motivates us to holiness (1:13-21). In view of the gloriousness of the salvation we will receive when Jesus is revealed, Peter reiterates God's command for us to be holy (13-16); and in view of the costliness of our redemption together with the impartiality of God's judgment, he reasons that we should be fearful of not being holy (17-21). Second, hope sanctifies us by stabilizing our love for our fellow Christians (22-25). Third, it encourages us to grow (**2**:1-10) both personally (1-3) and corporately (4-10). As believers, we are growing corporately into a spiritual edifice (4-8) that is being built with living stones (4-5) aligned with the precious cornerstone, Jesus Christ (6-8). To change the metaphor, we are growing within a special people whom God has chosen to be a royal priesthood (9-10).

Having built a bridge of hope so that his readers can reach beyond and be effective in their present situation, Peter alerts them to their further need of Christian character in order to withstand the pressures of suffering (2:11–4:11). He begins to address this need by specifying some contexts in which they might need to

---

Peter's Old Testament Stone Imagery

In 1 Peter 2:4-8, Peter draws upon several Old Testament texts to develop the image of a spiritual edifice composed of believers as living stones, with Jesus Christ being the chief corner stone. Although this stone was rejected by the original builders of the temple and many people stumbled over it, it became the corner stone and a precious source of faith, stability, and direction to believers. In his messianic interpretation of these stone texts, Peter is following a well established tradition that may be traced back to Jesus himself.

1 Peter 2:6 and Isaiah 28:16: 'Therefore thus says the Lord God, "Behold, I am laying in Zion a stone, a tested stone, a costly cornerstone [for] the foundation, firmly placed. He who believes [in it] will not be disturbed' (cf. Rom 9:32-33 where it is linked with Isaiah 8:14-15; see also Romans 10:11; 1 Corinthians 3:11 ff.; Ephesians 3:20).

1 Peter 2:7 (cf. v 4) and Psalm 118:22: 'The stone which the builders rejected has become the chief corner [stone].' (In the parable of the vineyard, Jesus identified himself as this stone, which he links with the stone in Isaiah 8:14-15 and perhaps Daniel 2:34 [Matt 21:42, 44; Luke 20:17-18]. Peter also identifies this stone as Jesus in Acts 4:11. The crowd at the triumphal entry quoted verses 25-26 of Psalm 118 messianically [Matt 21:9], and Jesus applied verse 26 to himself [Matt 23:39]).

1 Peter 2:8 and Isaiah 8:14 (cf. v 15): 'Then He shall become a sanctuary; but to both the houses of Israel, a stone to strike and a rock to stumble over, [and] a snare and a trap for the inhabitants of Jerusalem' (NASB). (Paul identifies Jesus as the stumbling stone in Romans 9:32-33, and Simeon may be alluding to it in Luke 2:34).

---

suffer as Christians (2:11–3:12). They might have to experience verbal abuse from their pagan neighbors (2:11-12) or accept ill treatment from civil authorities (13-17), to whom they are instructed to submit (13-15) while exercising their Christian freedom (16) and showing proper respect to everyone (17). They might also need to endure a beating from an unjust master (18-25), to whom they are likewise commanded to submit (18-20) in imitation of the example of Christ, who entrusted himself to God when he was unjustly crucified for our sins (21-25). They might also need to put up with an unsympathetic spouse (**3**:1-7). In such cases where a husband rejects the Gospel, the wife is still ordered to submit to him so that he may be won by her exemplary behavior (1-6); and Christian husbands in particular are reminded of their obligation to treat their wives with gentle understanding and respect (7). In case he has missed some human source of suffering, Peter sums up the list of possibilities by advising his readers that they are to be magnanimous towards whatever sort of unpleasant people they encounter (8-12).

Not expecting them to accept suffering blindly, however, Peter states three good reasons why they might need to suffer as Christians (3:13–4:6). First, suffering for righteousness provides a valuable opportunity for witnessing to unbelievers (3:13-17). Second, it copies the example of Christ who suffered unjustly so that he might bring us to God (3:18-22); and third, it has a valuable

---

The Correspondence between Pliny the Younger, and Trajan (c. AD 112)

The persecution that the readers of 1 Peter were facing has sometimes been identified with Pliny's official persecution of those who refused to renounce Christ's name, but if that is the case, Peter, who was martyred in 67 or 68, could not have written this epistle. It is more likely that Peter addressed an informal persecution of individual Christians from pagan neighbours or local officials that developed later into the imperial policy of persecuting anyone who named the name of Christ.

Pliny, the Governor of Bithynia, wrote the following letter to the Emperor, Trajan, asking his advice on how to deal with the Christians:

It is my rule, Sire, to refer to you in matters where I am uncertain.... I was never present at any trial of Christians; therefore, I do not know what are the customary penalties or investigations.... I have hesitated a great deal on the question whether... those who recant should be pardoned, or...whether the name [Christian] itself, even if [a person is] innocent of crime, should be punished, or only crimes attaching to that name.

Meanwhile, this is the course that I have adopted in the case of those brought before me as Christians. I ask them if they are Christians. If they admit it I repeat the question a second and third time, threatening capital punishment; if they persist I sentence them to death.... All who

---

effect against sin (**4**:1-6), both on the sufferer, in whom sin is put to death (1-2), and on the observers, who have the Gospel proclaimed to them (3-6).

Now that Peter has made his readers aware of the contexts in which they might have to suffer and the reasons why they should accept suffering, he describes three attitudes that should characterize Christians who are undergoing this experience (7-11). The first is serious prayer (7), the second, fervent love for one another (8-9), and the third is wholehearted service for one another (10-11).

In all of their suffering, Peter helps his readers to stand fast by placing them within a wide circle of sympathetic Christian fellowship, which he then breaks down into several smaller categories (4:12–5:11). He reminds them that many ordinary Christians share in suffering similar injustices (12-19). One should

---

denied that they were or had been Christians I considered should be discharged....

But they declared that the sum of their guilt or error had amounted only to this, that on an appointed day they had been accustomed to meet before daybreak, and to recite a hymn antiphonally to Christ, as to a god, and to bind themselves by an oath, not for the commission of any crime, but to abstain from theft, robbery, adultery and breach of faith, and not to deny a deposit when it was claimed. After the conclusion of this ceremony it was their custom to depart and meet again to take food....

The contagion of this superstition has spread not only in the cities, but in the villages and rural districts as well; yet it seems capable of being checked and set right (*Epp.* 96.1-79).

Trajan replied:

You have taken the right line, my dear Pliny, in examining the cases of those denounced to you as Christians, for no hard and fast rule can be laid down of universal application. They are not to be sought out; if they are informed against, and the charge is proved, they are to be punished, with this reservation – that if any one denies that he is a Christian, and actually proves it, that is by worshipping our gods, he shall be pardoned as a result of his recantation....(*Epp.* 97.1-2)

(Henry Bettenson, ed. *Documents of the Christian Church*, 2nd ed. [London: Oxford University Press, 1963], 3-4)

naturally expect to suffer for Christ (12-13) and consider it to be an honourable experience (14-16). Since everyone must stand before God's righteous judgment sooner or later, those who are suffering for Christ now should be thankful that their present trials are much less severe than the dreadful punishment from which the ungodly will not be able to escape (17-19). Those who are suffering for Christ can look for encouragement to their spiritual leaders, whom Peter exhorts to follow him in sharing Christ's sufferings so that they might be a positive example to the flock and also share in the glory that is to be revealed (5:1-4). Beyond the human sphere, those who are suffering can entrust themselves to an understanding God who graciously sustains humble Christians (5-7). Finally, Peter reminds his suffering readers that they belong to a worldwide fellowship of Christians who face a common adversary (8-11), namely the devil (8-9), over whom God will grant them a common victory after they have suffered for a little while (10-11).

Peter ends with an epistolary conclusion in which he acknowledges the assistance of Silvanus and conveys personal greetings to his readers along with a benediction of peace (12-14).

OUTLINE OF 1 PETER

2 Peter

OVERVIEW OF 2 PETER

Theme: True knowledge as foundational to various aspects of Christianity

Key Verse: 2 Peter 2:3 'His divine power has given us everything we need for life and godliness through our knowledge of him who called us by his own goodness and glory' (NIV).

HISTORICAL BACKGROUND

Second Peter claims to be written by Peter (2 Pet 1:1, 17-18; 3:1), but it is the most disputed New Testament book on the question of authorship because its literary style differs significantly from that of 1 Peter. These differences are reconcilable, however, if Peter employed Silvanus as an amanuensis for his first epistle (1 Pet 5:12) but wrote the second one without his assistance.

Peter was probably still at Rome at the time of writing, and his readers were presumably the same broad audience living in the same geographic area as those addressed in 1 Peter (2 Pet 3:1; cf. 1 Pet 1:1). Peter wrote this epistle in light of his imminent death (2 Pet 1:14) to warn about the coming of false teachers, who were probably of a primitive gnostic variety, and to encourage his readers to grow in the grace and knowledge of Christ (1 Pet 3:18).

The subject matter of 2 Peter has parallels in Jude at many spots. These correspondences have generated much debate about the literary relationship between the two epistles, but 2 Peter is more likely to be an expansion upon Jude than Jude a condensation of it. Second Peter should be dated after 1 Peter and before the apostle's death, which would place it some time between A.D. 64 and 68.

THE FLOW OF 2 PETER

Peter opens his second epistle with a general greeting wishing multiplied grace and peace in the true knowledge of God to those of like faith (1:1-2). He then proceeds to develop the theme of true knowledge in its foundational relationship to Christian vitality (3-21). He begins by portraying knowledge as a valuable means of growing in Christ (3-11). God's provision of divine power to live a godly life is granted through knowledge (3-4). Our progression up the staircase of virtues that he lists is accomplished through knowledge (5-7). Our production of fruit is cultivated in the sphere of knowledge (8-9), and the assurance of our election is mediated through knowledge (10-11).

Peter also shows how knowledge is a foundational basis for confirming the Gospel (12-21). The truthfulness of the theological and ethical reminder that he gives to his readers in view of his own imminent death is confirmed by facts that they already knew (12-15). To be specific, Jesus' transfiguration was confirmed by the eyewitness testimony of himself and other apostles (16-18), and the inspiration of the Old Testament prophets under the direction of the Holy Spirit is confirmed by the fulfillment of Scripture in Jesus (19-21).

As true knowledge is foundational for Christianity, so, conversely, it is the point from which false teachers depart (2:1-22). Peter predicts the infiltration of false teachers (1-3), but he assures his readers that these false teachers will be included in God's judgment that will eventually fall upon all unrighteous beings (4-10a). In support of this assertion, he cites several examples of God's judgment and deliverance in the past (4-10a). God judged the angels who sinned (4) and the entire antediluvian world, with the exception of Noah and his family (5).

He also judged the cities of Sodom and Gomorrah (6) but delivered righteous Lot (7-8). From these examples, Peter formally concludes that false teachers will be judged but the godly will be spared (9-10a).

He then describes the error of the false teachers more precisely

(10b-22). Their life style is characterized by (10b-16) arrogance (10b-11), irrationality (12-13a), and immorality following the pattern of Balaam (13b-17). Their teaching will have the twin effects of (18-22) enslaving both themselves and their followers to moral corruption (18-19) and of causing them to fall backwards into worse filth than that which they knew before they rejected the truth (20-22).

Peter has already stated in a different connection that the false teachers will be judged,[1] but now he concentrates on guaranteeing the certainty of the final judgment (3:1-18a). Before he develops his argument, however, he pauses to remind his readers that the purpose of his writing is to secure their reliance upon what the other inspired prophets and apostles have already said (1-2). First, he refutes the opposing position of the scoffers who deny that Christ will return (3-7). He predicts the arrival of such scoffers, who will deny Christ's coming on the grounds that God has not intervened in judgment upon the world since creation (3-4). The flaw in their reasoning, as Peter points out, is that God has intervened in the past, most notably by deluging the entire ancient world with water; therefore, it is reasonable to believe that in the future he will judge the heavens and the earth by fire, as the prophets have foretold (5-7).

Having discredited the scoffers' agnosticism, Peter presents Christ's return in judgment as an event that is certain to happen (8-10). The real reason for the delay of judgment is that God, in his patience, is mercifully allowing everyone opportunity to repent (8-9); but that opportunity will end suddenly and without warning when the universe dissolves under the intense heat of God's judgment (10).

Since Christ's return is certain, Peters draws out some implications from it for the conduct of his readers (11-18a). They should live in eager expectation of that day because it will be the beginning of a new heavens and new earth, in which righteousness will find a home (11-13). They should also be diligent in purifying their lives (14) and should consider the Lord's patience as an opportunity for salvation (15-16). On one hand, they should guard

---

1. 2 Peter 2:3b-10a, 12b, 17.

against the charlatans who would deceive them (17), and on the other hand, they should grow in grace and the knowledge of our Lord and Savior Jesus Christ (18a). To him Peter ascribes a doxology of eternal praise (18b).

OUTLINE OF 2 PETER

Jude

OVERVIEW OF JUDE

Theme: Contending for the faith

Key verses: Jude 3-4, 'Beloved, ... I felt the necessity to write to you appealing that you contend earnestly for the faith which was once for all delivered to the saints.... For certain persons have crept in unnoticed ... who turn the grace of our God into licentiousness and deny our only Master and Lord, Jesus Christ' (NASB).

HISTORICAL BACKGROUND

This little epistle claims to be written by Jude, a brother of James and bond-servant of Jesus Christ (Jude 1). Its author was probably a half brother of Jesus (Matt 13:55; Mark 6:3). Jude wrote to exhort a local community of believers to contend for the purity of the faith in light of false teachers who had infiltrated their numbers (Jude 3-4). We know neither the place of writing nor the destination of the epistle.

There are many parallels in subject matter between Jude and 2 Peter. Although the literary relationship between the two epistles is much debated, it is more likely that 2 Peter used Jude than it is that Jude condensed 2 Peter. It is less likely that both epistles are dependant upon a source that they shared in common. If 2 Peter used Jude, Jude would have to be dated before AD 68; if 2 Peter did not use Jude, Jude could possibly be as late as AD 80.

THE FLOW OF JUDE

The introduction to the Epistle of Jude (1-4) comes in two parts. First, a personal salutation (1-2) serves to identify the writer (1a), remind the readers of their high spiritual status (1b), and offer a prayer-wish for their spiritual well-being (2). An epistolary introduction, which follows (3-4), begins by formally stating the altered purpose of the letter (3). Originally Jude had intended to write about the salvation that he shared in common with his readers (3a), but he felt compelled instead to address their pressing need to contend for their unchanging faith (3b). The epistolary part of the introduction goes on to explain the undetected seriousness of the situation (4). Some false teachers had surreptitiously intruded into the ranks of Jude's readers (4a). Predictions of their intrusion, Jude says, were written long ago (4b), and he does not hesitate to characterize these false teachers (4c) as godless (4ca), debauched (4cb), and blasphemous (4cc).

The main body of the letter is concerned, first of all, with warnings of the judgment coming on these false teachers (5-16). Jude presents a case for their judgment by arguing from historical examples of judgment on similar people (5-13).

In the past, God judged apostates (5-10), of whom Jude gives three well-known examples (5-7): unbelieving Israel (5), fallen angels (6), and perverted Sodom and Gomorrah (7). Jude seals these historical examples by making contemporary application to the false teachers (8), and then he sets them in contrast with the archangel Michael, who, although much greater in rank, was more humble in his demeanour (9-10).

God also judged ungodly people (11-13), and Jude presents three well-known, historical examples here as well (11). God judged Cain for his disobedience (11a), Balaam for his corruption (11b), and Korah for his rebellion (11c). Jude then describes the false teachers by a series of vivid metaphors that clearly place them in the same ungodly company (12-13). They are submerged rocks (12a), waterless clouds (12b), barren trees (12c), frothing waves (13a), and wandering stars (13b).

From historical examples, Jude turns now to a prophetic warning of judgment on such people (14-16). The particular prophecy that Jude selects to argue his case is from Enoch (14-15). Jude identifies the prophet to whom he is referring (14a) and repeats the contents of his prophecy (14b-15),[1] which affirms the public nature (14b) and judicial purpose of the Lord's return (15). Again, Jude makes application to the false prophets infecting his readers (16).

The last part of the letter proper concentrates on exhorting its readers to be vigilant in light of these false prophets (17-23). Jude alerts his readers to the problem by reminding them of the predicted rise of scoffers in the last days (17-19). He appeals to the prophetic warning of Christ's apostles as the authority for this prediction (17-18), and then he makes a contemporary application to local schismatics (19).

The solution comes in two exhortations to the faithful (20-23). First, they are to keep themselves in God's love (20-21) by building themselves up in the faith (20a), by praying in the Spirit (20b), and by waiting for the Lord's return (21). Second, they are to rescue the lost from self-destruction (22-23). Those who need to be rescued are grouped into three categories: the doubting who need mercy (22), the perishing who need immediate action (23a), and the polluted who require caution (23b).

Jude concludes his epistle with a doxology (24-25). Because of God's ability to preserve the readers from stumbling (24) and because of God's uniqueness as the only Saviour (25a), Jude attributes everlasting praise to God (25b).

---

1. 1 Enoch 1:9.

OUTLINE OF JUDE

1 John

OVERVIEW OF 1 JOHN

Theme: Our assurance of fellowship with God

Key Verse: 1 John 1:7, 'If we walk in the light as He Himself is in the light, we have fellowship with one another, and the blood of Jesus His Son cleanses us from all sin' (NASB).

Introduction: John's assurance concerning the Word of life 1:1-4

I. Our fellowship with God, who is light 1:5–2:29
A. Conditions of fellowship 1:5–2:11

B. Sharers in fellowship 2:12-14

C. Opposition to fellowship 2:15-29

D. An exhortation to fellowship 2:28-29

II. Our fellowship with God, who is love 3:1–4:21
A. God's love manifested in God's making us children 3:1-2

B. Our love manifested in our practicing righteousness 3:3-10

C. Our love manifested in our loving the brethren 3:11-18

D. Our mutual love manifested in our asking with confidence 3:19-24

E. God's abiding in us manifested in our possessing the true
    Spirit 4:1-6

F. Our abiding in God manifested by our reciprocating love 4:7-21

III. Our fellowship with God, who is life 5:1-21
A. Evidences that we have been born of God 5:1-5

B. Witnesses that we have life in the Son 5:6-12

C. Benefits that we derive from our relationship to God 5:13-17

D. Three conclusions that we may assert with certainty 5:18-21

HISTORICAL BACKGROUND

First John was written by an eyewitness of Jesus' earthly life (1 John 1:1-3), who has traditionally been identified as the Apostle John. This epistle bears close stylistic and verbal similarities to the Gospel of John, which argue strongly that the person who wrote the Gospel is also the one who wrote the epistle.

John probably wrote from Ephesus to a group of churches in Asia Minor over which he exercised oversight (cf. Rev 1:4, 11; 2:1–3:22). His aim was to assure the believers in these churches of their fellowship with God, contrary to the claims of a troublesome group of proto-gnostic teachers who thought that they had a corner on divine enlightenment even though they were living immorally and denied Christ's physical nature. The most probable date for the epistle is near the end of John's life, c. A.D. 90 to 95.

The Purpose of 1 John and the Gospel of John

Both 1 John and the Gospel of John offer clear statements of purpose that nicely complement each other. The Gospel is evangelistic; it was written primarily to help people come to faith so that they might enter eternal life. Near the end of his Gospel, John states that 'these [signs] have been written that you may believe that Jesus is the Christ, the Son of God, and that by believing you may have life in his name' (John 20:30-31). The First Epistle of John is pastoral; it was written to believers, who were being troubled by false teachers (1 John 2:26), in order to instruct and assure them concerning the eternal life they already possessed. First John 1:4 gives a general statement of purpose, 'these things we write, so that our joy may be made complete', but 1 John 5:13 is more explicit: 'These things I have written in order that you who believe in the name of the Son of God may know that you have eternal life.'

Similar Wording in 1 John and the Gospel of John

There are numerous cases of similar wording between 1 John and the Gospel of John. The freedom with which slight variations in wording can occur while still retaining the underlying thought suggests it is more likely that these similarities arose spontaneously from a single mind that was steeped in the ideas common to both books than that they were imposed artificially by a conscious attempt at imitation.

1 John 1:1 **What was from** the beginning, what we have heard . . . concerning **the Word** of life
John 1:1 ***In*** the beginning *was* the Word

1 John 1:4 **that *our* joy may be made full**
John 16:24 **that *your* joy may be made full**

1 John 2:8 **I am *writing* a new commandment to you**
John 13:34 **a new commandment I *give* to you**

1 John 2:11 the one who hates his brother . . . **walks in the darkness**, and **does not know where he is going**
John 12:35 he who **walks in the darkness does not know where he goes** (cf. 8:12)

1 John 2:24 **if *what you heard from the beginning* abides in you**
John 15:7 **if . . . *My words* abide in you**

1 John 3:1 that we ***should be called* children of God**
John 1:12 he gave them the right *to become* **children of God**

1 John 3:5 that one appeared that He might **take away sin**
John 1:29 who **takes away the sin** of the world

1 John 3:8 **the devil *has sinned* from the beginning**
John 8:44 **he [the devil] *was a murderer* from the beginning**

1 John 3:13 *do not marvel* . . . **if the world hates you**
John 15:18 **if the world hates you,** *you know that it has hated me first*

| 1 John 3:14 | *we have* passed out of death into life |
| John 5:24 | *he has* passed out of death into life |

| 1 John 3:16 | he laid down His life for *us* |
| John 10:11 | he lays down His life for *the sheep* (cf. v. 15) |

| 1 John 4:6 | *We are from God*; he who *knows* God *listens to us*; *he who is not from* God does not *listen* to us |
| John 8:47 | He who *is from* God *hears the words of God*; for this reason *you* do not *hear* them, because *you are* not *of* God. |

| 1 John 4:9 | God *sent* his one and only Son into the world so that *we* might live *through him*. |
| John 3:16 | God so loved the world, that he *gave* his one and only Son that *whoever believes in him* . . . might have *eternal* life (cf. 1:14, 18, 3:18) |

| 1 John 4:12 | no one has *beheld* God at any time |
| John 1:18 | no one has *seen* God at any time |

| 1 John 5:3 | *this is the* love *of God*, that *we* keep *his* commandments |
| John 14:15 | *If you* love *me*, *you will* keep *my* commandments |

| 1 John 5:5 | *who is the one who* overcomes the world? (cf. v. 4) |
| John 16:33 | *I have* overcome the world |

| 1 John 5:13 | in order that *you may know that you* have eternal life |
| John 3:15 | in order that *whoever believes in him* may have eternal life |

| 1 John 5:14 | if we ask anything *according to his will* he *hears us* |
| John 16:23 | if you ask *the Father* anything *in my name*, he *will give it to you* |

THE FLOW OF 1 JOHN

The introduction to the First Epistle of John commences in a way that is similar to the prologue of John's Gospel: both start from the beginning with the eternal Word, in whom life exists, only in the epistle the elder apostle reaches beyond the incarnation of the Word to assure his troubled readers of the objective existence and theological significance of this living Word (1:1-4). John attests to the reality of the Word of life from his own empirical interaction

The Literary Structure of 1 John

The literary structure of 1 John is notoriously difficult to follow because it lacks hard and fast boundaries. Rather than treating one topic and then moving on to the next, the author weaves several important themes together, developing and contrasting them as he goes. What he says appears to be very important, but the order in which he says it seems to be of little consequence. Contrary to initial appearances, however, Robert Law argues that 1 John has a carefully thought-out structure but that it comes in a unique artistic form rather than a logical progression:

> The word that...might best describe St. John's mode of thinking and writing in this Epistle is 'spiral'. The course of thought does not move from point to point in a straight line. It is like a winding staircase – always revolving around the same centre, always recurring to the same topics, but at a higher level. Or, to borrow a term from music, one might describe the method as contrapuntal. The Epistle works with a comparitively small number of themes, which are introduced many times, and are brought into every possible realtion to one another. As some master-builder of music takes two or three melodious phrases and, introducing them in due order, in diverse modes and keys, rears up from them an edifice of stately harmonies; so the Apostle weaves together a few leading ideas into a majestic fuge in which unity of material and variety of tone and effect are wonderfully blended (Robert Law, *The Tests of Life*, 3rd ed. [Edinburgh: T. & T. CLARK, 1914], 5; cf. 1-2).

with it (1), and he affirms that it became visibly manifested (2). Furthermore, he now publicly proclaims this life (3-4) as the basis for his readers' fellowship with him (3) and the source of his overflowing joy (4).

Like a skillful contrapuntal composer, John develops his overarching theme of our assurance of fellowship with God in relation to three interwoven melodic lines: light, life and love. All of them play against each other simultaneously, but each takes its turn at leading, beginning with our fellowship with God, who is light (1:5–2:29). In his fatherly way, John lays down three conditions of our enjoying fellowship with God as light (1:5–2:11). The first is walking in the light (5-7). God is light (5); therefore, one's claim to have fellowship with him will be judged by truth (6). If we really are walking in the light, we are assured that we have fellowship with God and are promised the ongoing cleansing of Jesus' blood (7).

The second condition of fellowship with a God of light is confessing our sins (1:8–2:2). If we deny that we have sin, we only deceive ourselves (8), but if we confess our sins, we are forgiven (9). If we deny that we have sinned, our claim is inconsistent with what God says about us in his word (10). The ideal objective is that we might not sin (2:1a), but John assures his readers that if we do, we have forgiveness through Jesus Christ (1b-2), who is our advocate before the Father (1b) and the propitiation not only for our own sins, but also for those of the whole world (2).

The third condition of fellowship with God is keeping his commandments (3-11). Keeping God's commandments is a proof that we know God personally (3-4). For emphasis, John states this point both positively (3) and negatively (4) before he adds that keeping God's commandments is also a proof that we have been perfected by the love of God (5a), that we genuinely abide in him (5b-6), and that we are walking on a well-lighted pathway (7-11).

John elaborates upon this last point by somewhat cryptically specifying the keeping of one commandment in particular that proves our pathway has been clearly illuminated (7-8). This commandment, he says, is familiar to his readers (7), but it is just now starting to be understood fully in light of the dawning age (8). John then applies the commandment to love one another (9-11), negatively, to hating one's brother as a proof that one is walking in the darkness (9) and, positively, to loving one's brother as a proof that one is walking in the light (10). He also spells out the causal relationship between hatred and walking in darkness (11).

Now that he has laid down these conditions of fellowship, John addresses three groups of readers who share in his fellowship with God (12-14). He writes to the children in God's family (12, 13c) because their sins are forgiven (12) and they know the Father (13c). He writes to the young men (13b, 14b) because they have overcome the evil one (13b, 14b), they are strong (14b), and they know the word of God (14b). He writes to the fathers because they know him who has been from the beginning (13a, 14a).

John realized, however, that his readers would face strong opposition to their ongoing experience of fellowship with God (15-29). This opposition would come, first of all, internally from the love of the world (15-17), which is incompatible with loving God (15). John defines the love of the world (16) in terms of the lust of the flesh (16a), the lust of the eyes (16b), and the pride of life (16), and he remarks that everything that rivals our love for God is transitory (17).

He warns his readers that opposition to their fellowship with God would also come externally from the spirit of antichrist (18-27). He predicts that the appearance of the final antichrist would be a logical extension of the rising up of many lesser antichrists (18-19) in the last hour, which had already begun (18). These antichrists had started to operate within the Johannine churches but had left because they didn't belong to the company of true believers (19). John assures true believers that they are safeguarded against the spirit of antichrist (20-21) by the anointing of the Holy Spirit (20) and by their knowledge of the truth (21). He identifies the error that the antichrist was propagating (22-23) as a denial that Jesus is the Christ (22a), which is a distortion of the Trinity (22b-23). By contrast, John asserts that orthodoxy, which his readers should hold dear (24-27), is rooted in the historical traditions they had received (24a); it will keep them in close relationship to

---

Light, Life, and Love in 1 John

The concepts light, love, and life bear special prominence in 1 John. All the members of this trio flow throughout the epistle, but each one of them is assigned a section in which its voice is heard more clearly: light predominates in 1:5–2:29, love in 3:1–4:2, and life in 5:1-21. If we separate each of these themes and place them in a logical, rather than a symphonic arrangement, we can summarize John's essential message fairly simply.

John writes to those who have believed in the Son of God that they may be assured that they have the eternal life which was visibly manifested in Jesus Christ and experientially received by them through faith. John wants them to be convinced of the reality of this life and to enjoy its privileges.

Since this life is the very life of God, himself, God requires its recipients to walk in the light as he is in the light so that they might have fellowship with him. John always contrasts light with darkness. God is pure light, and in him there is no darkness at all; therefore those who walk in darkness cannot abide in his presence. The light exposes their evil deeds, which must be confessed and forgiven. But the light also reveals the righteous deeds of those who walk in it; thus, walking in the light is both a condition of fellowship with God and an evidence that fellowship exists.

God supremely manifested his love for us by sending his one and only Son to be the propitiation for our sins so that we might be forgiven and come into his light. Only those who have received God's love are capable of expressing it to others, and they have a moral obligation to love all of mankind, and especially God's children, with the same kind of love that they have experienced.

---

the Trinity (24b). Furthermore, it contains the promise of eternal life (25). To protect his readers from the antichrist's attempt at deception (26), John assures them, once again, that they will learn orthodoxy from the Spirit's anointing, so they have no need to listen to false teachers (27).

Having stated these necessary warnings and instructions, John now affectionately exhorts his spiritual children to maintain their fellowship with God (28-29). He motivates them to this end by setting before them the desirability of their being confident at Christ's return (28) and the promise of their bearing a resemblance to God's righteousness (29).

John continues his development of our fellowship with God by shifting the spotlight onto the love that God has for us and which we, in turn, give back to him and one another (**3:1–4:21**). God manifested his love for us by making us his children (3:1-2). We are quite properly called his children (1a) even though the world fails to recognize our true identity (1b-2a), but when God appears we will be gloriously transformed into his likeness (2b).

Our love for God will be manifested in our practicing righteousness in imitation of him (3-10). John contrasts the motivation for practicing righteousness with the basis for sinning (3-4). The hope of our glorious transformation into God's likeness is a compelling motivation for our practicing righteousness (3), and the practice of lawlessness is the basis of all sinning (4). John

---

Gnosticism

Gnosticism proved to be the most troublesome heresy to affect the early church. Its syncretistic nature and refusal to be tied to a clearly defined set of beliefs enabled it to attach itself readily to various religions. Although Gnosticism did not become a fully developed system until the second century, an incipient form of it lies behind several New Testament books, most notably 1 John and Colossians, and to a lesser extent Ephesians, the Pastoral Epistles, and Corinthians. One should not assume that the error being counteracted in each of these books is identical, but, at the risk of oversimplification, we can summarize the most basic beliefs that characterized the system.

Underlying Gnosticism was a dualistic philosophy that viewed spirit as good and matter as evil. The highest god was pure spirit. Gnostics generally held that a series of emanations proceeded from this supreme god in staircase fashion, each one progressively lower, until a lesser deity known as the Demi-urge could create a physical universe; finally, at the bottom of the ladder came Christ, who was sufficiently evil to actually come in contact with physical matter.

The incarnation presented a great difficulty for Gnostics who wished to merge their teaching with Christianity; for them it was inconceivable that God could take on a human body. They handled the problem in one of two ways. The Docetics held that Jesus did not really have a human body but only appeared to have one, hence their

---

locates the power to be righteous (5-6) in Christ's removal of our sin (5) and our abiding in Christ (6). He also contrasts the source of righteousness with the source of sin (7-10). God is the source of righteousness (7, 8b-9), and the devil is the source of sin (8a, 10).

Our love for God will also be manifested in our loving the brethren (11-18). From the beginning God commanded that we should love one another (11), but Cain left us a negative example of hatred (12). The natural attitude of the world is to hate us (13), but for us hatred is spiritually incompatible with our transformation from death to life (14-15). The supreme example of love is Christ's dying for us (16), and, following that example, we ought to demonstrate our love for one another in practical ways (17-18).

The mutuality of love between God and us is manifested in our

name from the Greek *dokeō*, to seem. Cerinthus, however, made a distinction between Jesus, who was human, and Christ, who was a spirit. He taught that Christ descended upon Jesus at his baptism but departed again before the crucifixion and left Jesus to suffer alone (cf. Irenaeus, *Against Heresies*, 1.26.1).

The dualistic idea that matter was evil had an important effect on morals in one of two opposite ways: on one hand it lead to asceticism in an attempt to subdue the body by rigorous discipline; on the other hand it lead to indulgence of the fleshly appetites on the assumption that what one did with the body did not matter and the only important thing was the spirit.

The way to salvation came through direct knowledge (Greek, *gnōsis*), which only a privileged few received in a special enlightenment. This enlightenment developed into a secret initiation rite in the second century mystery cults.

Neither John nor Paul engage in a point-by-point debate with the Gnostics; rather they simply reaffirm the orthodox position where the two systems clash, sometimes borrowing their opponents terminology and standing it on its head or flatly contradicting the most basic Gnostic assumptions. Conceding nothing, the apostles restore the true deity and humanity of Christ, the goodness of all creation under his dominion, the importance of living righteously without becoming legalistic, and the believer's possession of true knowledge and eternal life in Christ without recourse to the false teachers.

The Apostle John's Encounter with Cerinthus, the False Teacher

It is hard to confirm the historicity of the following story of John's encounter with the Gnostic teacher Cerinthus, but it comes to us on the good authority of Irenaeus, who attributes it to Polycarp, one of John's disciples:

> There are also those who heard from [Polycarp] that John, the disciple of the Lord, going to bathe at Ephesus, and perceiving Cerinthus within, rushed out of the bath-house without bathing, exclaiming, 'Let us fly, lest even the bath-house fall down, because Cerinthus, the enemy of the truth, is within.'

(Irenaeus, *Against Heresies*, 3.3.3, in *The Ante-Nicene Fathers*, Alexander Roberts et al., eds. vol 1: *The Apostolic Fathers*, trans. A. Cleveland Coxe (Grand Rapids: Wm. B. Eerdmans Pub. Co., 1975), 1:416; cf. Eusebius, *Church History*, 3.28).

---

bringing our requests to him with confidence that he will answer (19-24). We may be reticent to ask God for something if we have a guilty conscience (19-20); but if we have a clear conscience before him, as we certainly may, we can ask with confidence (21). The reason why God is willing to answer us is that we keep his twofold commandment (22-23) to believe in Jesus (22, 23a) and to love our fellow believers (22, 23b). The evidence of our mutual abiding in each other, from the human side, is that we keep God's commandments and, from the divine side, is that God has given us his Spirit (24).

John elaborates on the evidence of our mutual abiding, starting first with the reception of the Spirit. God's abiding in us is manifested in our possessing the true Spirit, in contrast with the world's possession of false spirits (4:1-6). John provides a specific test for identifying the many false spirits who have invaded the world: anyone who denies that Jesus Christ has come in the flesh is not of God (4:1-3), but the elder apostle lovingly reassures his readers that God's children have no reason to fear these false spirits because we have already won the victory through God's Spirit who lives in us (4). John explains the present polarization of public opinion over the gospel message by the simple phenomenon that people of the world willingly receive false spirits (5), but those who are of God receive his Spirit (6).

Having developed the possession of the Spirit negatively as an evidence that the world does not abide in God, John returns to the keeping of God's commandments,[1] and particularly the command to reciprocate God's love, as an evidence that we abide in God (7-21). Whatever love we have received (7-10) has its ultimate source in God (7-8) and finds its supreme manifestation in the Father's sending the Son so that we might live (9-10).

Having been loved by God, we should now show love to others (11-21). We have a moral obligation to love one another because God loved us (11). As a result of loving one another, we will be assured that we abide in God (12a, 13-16) and God's love will be perfected in us (12b, 17-18). John concludes his encouragement to love one another by reiterating the two primary reasons why we should love (19-21): God loved us (19-20),[2] and he commanded us to love others (21).[3]

From love, John moves smoothly into life as the featured characteristic of our fellowship with God (5:1-21). That we have been born of God is evident (1-5) from our believing his Son (1a), loving his children (1b-2), keeping his commandments (3), and overcoming this world (4-5).

That we have life in God's Son is attested by multiple witnesses (6-12). The first of these witnesses is historical and came in three parts (6-8): the Spirit (7, 8), the water (6, 8), and the blood (6, 8). The second witness is authoritative because it is the witness of God himself (9), and the third witness is an internal witness within the believer (10-12).

John sets forth two benefits that we who believe derive from our relationship to God as life (13-17). First, we can be sure that we possess eternal life; in fact, the apostle's stated purpose for writing this epistle is to impart this assurance to its readers (13). The second benefit follows from the first: we can have the

---

1. 1 John 3:24.
2. 1 John 4:11.
3. 1 John 3:11, 23

confidence to petition God for anything according to his will (14-17). John expounds upon this benefit by stating the general principle (14-15) with respect to our boldness in requesting (14) and our assurance of receiving (15); and he makes specific application to interceding for a brother whose sin does not lead to death (16-17).

John draws his epistle to a close by stating three conclusions that we may assert with certainty (18-21). First, we can state categorically that God's children do not practice sin as a way of life (18). Second, we can be certain that we are God's children (19); third, it is possible to distinguish true religion from idolatry (20-21) because God's Son has imparted the necessary understanding to us (20); accordingly, we are obliged to guard vigilantly against religious distortions of the truth (21).

'Little Children, Love One Another'

Jerome relates a touching story of the Apostle John in his extreme old age: 'He used to be carried into the congregation in the arms of his disciples and was unable to say anything except "little children, love one another." At last wearied that he always spoke the same words, they asked: "Master, why do you always say this?" "Because," he replied, "it is the Lord's command, and if only this is done, it is enough" ' (Jerome, *Commentary on the Epistle to the Galatians* in *Patrologia Latina,* ed. J. P. Minge [Paris: Garnier Fratres, 1884], 26:462; English translation in John R. W. Stott, *The Epistles of John,* Tyndale New Testament Commentaries [Grand Rapids: Wm. B. Eerdmans Pub. Co., 1964], 49.)

OUTLINE OF 1 JOHN

2 John

OVERVIEW OF 2 JOHN

Theme: Walking in truth and love

Key verses: 2 John 6a, 7a 'And this is love, that we walk according to His commandments.... For many deceivers have gone out into the world who do not confess Jesus Christ as coming in the flesh' (NKJV).

HISTORICAL BACKGROUND

The author of this letter refers to himself as 'the elder' (2 John 1; cf. 3 John 1). Tradition identifies him as the Apostle John, but some scholars argue that the Elder John and the Apostle John were two different people. That disjunction, however, originally arose from a questionable attempt to deny the apostolic authorship of Revelation and is by no means necessary. Furthermore, Second John bears close stylistic and verbal similarities to John's Gospel and the other Johannine epistles, which argues that the same person wrote them all.

John probably wrote from Ephesus, the center of his ministry in Asia Minor. He addresses his epistle to 'the chosen lady and her children' (2 John 2). This address is more likely a figurative reference to a local church with its members, but it could possibly be a reference to a literal lady along with the church that she hosted in her home. In either case, he was probably writing to one of the churches in Asia Minor under his spiritual oversight (cf. Rev 1:4, 11; 2:1–3:22). His general purpose in writing was to combat an incipient form of Gnosticism that denied Christ's physical nature, and his specific objective was to warn against offering hospitality to the false teachers who propagated this heresy. The letter should probably be dated near the end of John's life at c. AD 90 to 95.

John the Elder Versus John the Disciple

On the basis of the following statement by Papias, Eusebius concluded that there were two Johns, John the Elder and John the Disciple:

'I shall not hesitate...to put down for you along with my interpretation whatsoever things I have at any time learned carefully from the elders and carefully remembered, guaranteeing their truth. For I did not...take pleasure in those that speak much, but in those that teach the truth.... If, then, any one came, who had been a follower of the elders, I questioned him in regard to the words of the elders, – what Andrew or what Peter said, or what was said by Philip, or by Thomas or by James, or by John, or by Matthew or by any other of the disciples of the Lord, and what things Aristion and the presbyter John, the disciples of the Lord, say. For I did not think that what was to be gotten from the books would profit me as much as what came from the living and abiding voice.'

It is quite possible, however, that Papias mentions John twice because he was both an apostle and a living witness. Note the change from the past tense 'said' to the present tense 'say'.

(Eusebius, *Church History*, 3:39.3-4; trans. Arthur Cushman McGiffert, in *The Nicene and Post-Nicene Fathers*, 2nd Series, Philip Schaff, ed., vol. 1: Eusebius, *Church History* (Grand Rapids: Wm. B. Eerdmans Pub. Co., 1976), 1:170-71; cf. 'Fragments of Papias,' in *The Ante-Nicene Fathers*, Alexander Roberts et al., eds. vol 1: *The Apostolic Fathers*, trans. A. Cleveland Coxe [Grand Rapids: Wm. B. Eerdmans Pub. Co., 1975], 153).

THE FLOW OF 2 JOHN

The Second Epistle of John opens with a salutation (1-3) identifying its writer simply as 'the elder' (1a) and its readers as the chosen lady together with her children (1b-2). The standard epistolary greeting contains a wish for grace, mercy and peace (3).

This epistle has a simple, two-fold message (4-11). First, the writer, who is presumably the Apostle John, requests his readers to walk in love (4-6). He makes this practical request in a setting where some of them were walking faithfully in accordance with the truth (4). Rather than invoking his own authority, he founds this request upon Christ's command (5-6).

The second part of the epistle's message is an appeal to remain in the truth (7-11). John sets this theological appeal against the backdrop of certain deceivers who where propagating a heresy denying the physical nature of Christ (7). The motivation given for being aware of deviant theology is the loss of rewards that following it entails (8). John alerts his readers that because the Godhead is a unity, the false teachers' defective christology implicitly denied the Father as well as the Son (9). He cautions that allegiance to the truth precludes his readers from indirectly supporting or endorsing the false teachers by offering them hospitality (10-11).

John concludes (12-13) by acknowledging the letter's brevity (12a) and announcing an intended visit that will make up for this deficiency (12b). He closes with a greeting from the children of his readers' chosen sister (13).

OUTLINE OF 2 JOHN

I. Salutation	1-3
A. The writer: the elder	1a
B. The readers: the chosen lady and her children	1b-2
C. The greeting: grace, mercy and peace	3
II. The message	4-11
A. A request to walk in love	4-6
1. Its setting in the faithfulness of some children	4
2. Its foundation in the command of Christ	5-6
B. An appeal to remain in the truth	7-11
1. Its setting in the heresy of deceivers	7
2. Its motivation in the loss of rewards	8
3. Its implications for the unity of the Godhead	9
4. Its application to the welcoming of false teachers	10-11
III. Conclusion	12-13
A. An acknowledgement of the letter's brevity	12a
B. An announcement of the elder's intended visit	12b
C. A greeting from the chosen sister's children	13

3 John

OVERVIEW OF 3 JOHN

Theme: Ministering with an attitude of hospitality and humility

Key Verses: 3 John 5, 'Beloved, you are acting faithfully in whatever you accomplish for the brethren, and especially when they are strangers' (NASB).

HISTORICAL BACKGROUND

As is the case with 2 John, the author of this letter refers to himself as 'the elder' (3 John 1; cf. 2 John 1). Tradition identifies him as the Apostle John, but some scholars argue that the Elder John and the Apostle John were two different people. That disjunction, however, originally arose from a questionable attempt to deny the apostolic authorship of Revelation and is by no means necessary. Furthermore, Third John bears close stylistic and verbal similarities to John's Gospel and the other Johannine epistles, which argues that the same person wrote them all.

John was probably at Ephesus when he wrote this letter to Gaius, a leader in one of the churches under his supervision. The church in which Gaius served could well have been one of the seven churches of Asia Minor that are mentioned in Revelation (Rev 1:4, 11; 2:1–3:22). John's purpose in writing was to encourage the church to support itinerant missionaries who proclaimed the true Gospel and to censure Diotrephes, who was ostracising genuine co-workers. The date of the letter would be near the end of John's life, sometime between AD 90 and 95. The letter could have been carried by Demetrius.

THE FLOW OF 3 JOHN

The salutation of John's Third Epistle (1-4) contains a superscription (1) that designates its writer as 'the elder' (1a) and its addressee as Gaius (1b). It also includes a blessing on Gaius (2) and a brief thanksgiving for him (3-4).

The message of the epistle has two main points that are opposite sides of the same coin (5-12). The positive side is an appeal to Gaius to accommodate itinerant missionaries who proclaim the true Gospel (5-8). John, the elder, commends Gaius for his hospitality to the missionaries who were working in his neighbourhood (5-6a), and he encourages Gaius to offer further assistance to them (6b). As a rationale for supporting these missionaries, John argues that those who assist them are co-workers with the truth (7-8).

The epistle's negative side is an appeal not to imitate arrogant leaders who ostracise genuine co-workers for the Gospel (9-12). John had one particular example in mind, a certain Diotrephes, whom he denounces openly (9-10). Since Diotrephes had arrogantly rejected John's letter to the church (9), John had determined that when he came he would expose Diotrephes' malicious actions against the brethren (10). Specifically, he charges Diotrephes with accusing church leaders, including himself, without just cause (10a-b), with refusing hospitality to Christian missionaries (10c), and excommunicating believers out of personal vindictiveness (10d). John then applies Diotrephes' bad example of leadership to Gaius by warning him not to copy it (11). On a more positive note, John adds his endorsement to the church's unanimous approval of Demetrius as a model to be emulated (12).

In conclusion (13-15), John offers a polite explanation of the letter's brevity (13-14). He pronounces a personal benediction on Gaius (15a)[1] and exchanges mutual greetings between friends (15b).

---

1. Verse 15a and b is verse 14b and c in most English translations.

OUTLINE OF 3 JOHN

---

1. Verse 15a and b is verse 14b and c in most English translations.

Prophecy

John's Return from Exile after Domitian's Death

At that time the apostle and evangelist John, the one whom Jesus loved, was still living in Asia, and governing the churches of that region, having returned after the death of Domitian from his exile on the island. And that he was still alive at that time may be established by the testimony of two witnesses. Irenaeus...in the second book of his work *Against Heresies*, writes as follows: 'And all the elders that associated with John the disciple of the Lord in Asia bear witness that John delivered it to them. For he remained among them until the time of Trajan.' And in the third book of the same work he attests the same thing in the following words: 'But the church in Ephesus also, which was founded by Paul, and where John remained until the time of Trajan, is a faithful witness of the apostolic tradition.' Clement likewise... indicates the time,...

(Eusebius, *Church History*, 3:23.1-5; trans. Arthur Cushman McGiffert, in *The Nicene and Post-Nicene Fathers*, 2nd Series, Philip Schaff, ed., vol. 1).

Reigns of Major First-Century Roman Emperors

Augustus	30 BC - AD 14
Tiberius	AD 14-37
Caligula	37-41
Claudius	41-54
Nero	54-68
Vespasian	69-74
Titus	79-81
Domitian	81-96
Nerva	96-98
Trajan	98-117

Revelation

OVERVIEW OF REVELATION

Theme: The revelation of Jesus Christ as the King of kings and Lord of lords

Key verse: Revelation 1:7, 'Behold, He is coming with the clouds, and every eye will see Him' (NASB).

---

1. Verse 18 of the Greek text is verse 17b in most modern English translations.

HISTORICAL BACKGROUND

Revelation claims to have been written by a person called John (Rev 1:1, 4, 9; 22:8), who was apparently well known to his readers. The early church fathers widely held he was the Apostle John, but some scholars argue on the basis of an ambiguous statement by Papias (cited in Eusebius, *Ecclesiastical History*, 3:39) that he is a different John, the Elder (cf. 2 John 1; 3 John 1). Still others hold that he is an unknown John. There is no agreement among those who distinguish between different Johns as to which one wrote which of the Johannine compositions, although tradition strongly attributes the Fourth Gospel, three epistles, and the Apocalypse all to the Apostle John.

The recipients of this letter were seven churches in Asia Minor over which John exercised oversight: the church at Ephesus, Smyrna, Pergamum, Thyatira, Sardis, Philadelphia, and Laodicea (Rev 1:4, 11; 2:1–3:22). John wrote to encourage and strengthen these churches for the persecution that they were undergoing, or about to experience, by unfolding to them his visions of God's final victory over evil.

Revelation contains features of three different genres: apocalypse (Rev 1:1), epistle (Rev 1:4, 11), and prophecy (Rev 1:3; 22:7, 10, 18, 19). Grammatically it is rougher than the Fourth Gospel or the Johannine epistles, but it is still closer to these writings stylistically than any other body of literature. It was more likely written under the persecution of Domitian (81-96), who instituted emperor worship, than during the earlier persecutions of Nero (54-68). John probably wrote from the Island of Patmos, where he was exiled because of his witness for Christ (Rev 1:9), but he could possibly have worked his draft into final literary form at some other place shortly after his release, c. AD 96. By this time the aged apostle was nearing the end of his life.

The Central Message of the Mysterious Book of Revelation

Revelation is a mysterious and intriguing book. When a slain lamb, who is a lion, breaks its seals, seven angels blast upon their trumpets and pour out golden bowls of plagues and pestilence upon the earth amid flashes of lightning and peals of thunder. Mounted horsemen prepare to charge forth into battle. An old, red dragon engages the forces of heaven in mortal combat until an archangel throws him down to earth. A grotesque beast with horns and multiple heads emerges from the sea; another beast comes up out of the ground. Together they command the worship of the world and control its finance. Upon the first beast, rides a drunken woman who has amassed the world's wealth by prostituting herself with the kings of the earth. But suddenly the beast turns upon her and devastates her world-wide commercial empire in a single hour. As the smoke from her immoral city ascends to heaven, the saints rejoice. Confidently and deliberately, the King of kings and Lord of lords mounts his white horse for war. All the vultures flock together to feast upon the corpses of those slain in the decisive victory over the beast. A new city made of pure gold slowly descends to earth from heaven. The lamb, resplendent in glory, takes up his residence in the middle of the city, and righteousness reigns forever.

What are we to make of this obscure book with all of its strange imagery? Revelation has been marked by such a variety of divergent interpretations that one might think it was purposely designed to conceal rather than reveal, contrary to what its name suggests. One point, however, is abundantly clear. Throughout the book we find heaven and earth worshipping and singing praises to the one who sits on the throne and to the lamb. We ought to join in their worship because Jesus Christ is the King of kings and Lord of lords who will ultimately triumph over evil.

THE FLOW OF REVELATION

The account of the Revelation of Jesus Christ that was given to John opens with a prologue containing three parts (1:1-8). First, it has a superscription (1-3) setting forth the unique character of the writing (1-2) and pronouncing a blessing upon those who heed its message (3).[1] Following the superscription, we find a typical epistolary salutation (4-5a) introducing the writer, John (4a), and the letter's recipients, seven churches in Asia Minor, whom he greets with a Trinitarian benediction of grace and peace (4b-5a)[2] before bursting into an unexpected doxology of praise to God (5b-6). To round out the prologue, John conveniently states his prophetic theme, which concerns the visible return of Jesus Christ (7), and he guarantees the truthfulness of what he writes by appending a personal endorsement from the Lord God Almighty, who is the Alpha and Omega (8).[3]

On the macro level, the book is structured around four visions that John received. These visions are classified topically into three groups: 'the things which you have seen,...the things which are, and the things which shall take place after these things'; but this threefold division does not strictly set the structural lines of the book and is a less reliable clue to its literary structure than it is to the interpretation of these visions.[4]

In the first vision, John sees the exalted Christ speaking to the seven churches (1:9–3:22). Before we learn what Christ has to say, his authority over the churches is graphically portrayed in an awesome representation of him standing in the midst of seven

---

1. Verse 3 is the first of seven blessings in Revelation; cf. 14:13; 16:15; 19:9; 20:6; 22:7, 14.

2. Cf. the closing benediction in Revelation 22:21.

3. This opening speech of the Alpha and Omega is parallelled by two concluding declarations from him in Revelation 21:6 and 22:13.

4. Revelation 1:19. 'The things which you have seen' probably refers to the vision that John saw of Christ standing in the midst of the seven lampstands (Rev 1:9-20). 'The things which are' refers to the seven churches of Asia Minor that Christ addresses individually in the second part of this vision (Rev 2:1–3:22), and 'the things which shall take place after these things' refers to the following visions concerning the future (Rev 4:1–22:5).

lampstands (1:9-20). John paints the setting for this vision by informing his readers that while he was in exile on the Island of Patmos for testifying about Jesus, he heard a loud voice speaking to him from behind (9-11). When he turned around, his gaze quickly fixed upon the spot in the middle of seven lampstands where an imposing figure resembling Daniel's Son of Man (Dan. 7:13) stood dressed in the attire of the high priest radiating a blaze of power and glory (12-16). This terrifying heavenly figure, who identified himself as the First and the Last, who was dead but lives for evermore, commissioned John to write down the vision for the seven churches that were represented by the seven lampstands (17-20).

The Literary Composition of the Seven Letters

Revelation contains seven "letters" within a larger letter. All of them are constructed after the same pattern:

1.) a superscription to the church addressed
   - 'To the angel of the church in _____ write:'

2.) a description of the divine author
   - Usually it employs a descriptive phrase from the vision of chapter 1.

3.) an account of the spiritual condition of the church
   - 'I know...'
   - With each church except Laodicea (3:15) and perhaps Sardis (3:2), the Lord finds something positive to say.

4.) a message of praise or censure
   - Two churches, Smyrna and Philadelphia, receive only praise. There is nothing good to say about two churches, Sardis and Laodicea, only blame. Three churches, Ephesus, Pergamum, and Thyatira, receive a mixture of praise and blame. Usually the censure comes with the formula, 'But I have this against you....'

5.) an exhortation in view of the church's special need
   - 'Remember, repent, and do' (2:5); 'Do not fear, be faithful' (2:10); 'Repent' (2:16); 'hold fast' (2:25); 'Wake up, strengthen,

---

This heavenly figure gives each of these seven churches a personalized message of commendation, where that is possible, along with a warning, where that is necessary, to correct its failures before he comes to judge it (2:1–3:22). He commends the church at Ephesus for opposing false teachers but reproves it for letting its first love grow cold (2:1-7). He finds no fault with the church at Smyrna, but he exhorts it to remain steadfast under the persecution that it would soon suffer (8-11). He commends the church at Pergamum for holding fast his name even under the real threat of martyrdom, but he rebukes it for tolerating false teachers who were advocating moral compromise (12-17). He acknowledges the good

remember, keep, repent' (3:2-3); 'hold fast' (3:11); 'be zealous and repent' (3:19).

■ An allusion to the Lord's coming is usually appended to the exhortation as a motivation to ensure that it is heeded seriously.[2]

6.) a promise to him who overcomes
■ 'I will grant to eat of the tree of life' (2:7); 'He shall not be hurt by the second death' (2:11); 'I will give [some] hidden manna...and a white stone...' (2:17); 'I will give authority over the nations' (2:26); 'He...shall be clothed in white...' (3:5); 'I will make him a pillar' (3:12); 'I will grant to him to sit down with Me on My throne' (3:21)

7.) a command to pay attention to the voice of the Spirit
■ 'He who has an ear, let him hear what the Spirit says to the churches.'[3]

1. (1) Ephesus 2:1 cf. 1:12, 16; (2) Smyrna 2:8 cf. 1:17, 18; (3) Pergamum 2:12 cf. 1:16; (4) Thyatira 2:18 cf. 1:14-15; (5) Sardis 3:1 cf. 1:16; (6) Philadelpha 3:7 cf. 1:18; (7) Laodicea 3:14 cf. 1:5.

2. "I am coming" (3:5); [none]; "I am coming to you quickly" (2:16); "until I come" (2:25); "I will come like a thief" (3:3); "I am coming to you quickly" (3:11); "I stand at the door" (3:20).

3. With the last four churches, Thyatira (2:29), Sardis (3:6), Philadelphia (3:13), and Laodicea (3:22), the exhortation to hear is placed last; with the first three, Ephesus (2:7), Smyrna (2:11), and Pergamum (2:17), it precedes the promise to the overcomer.

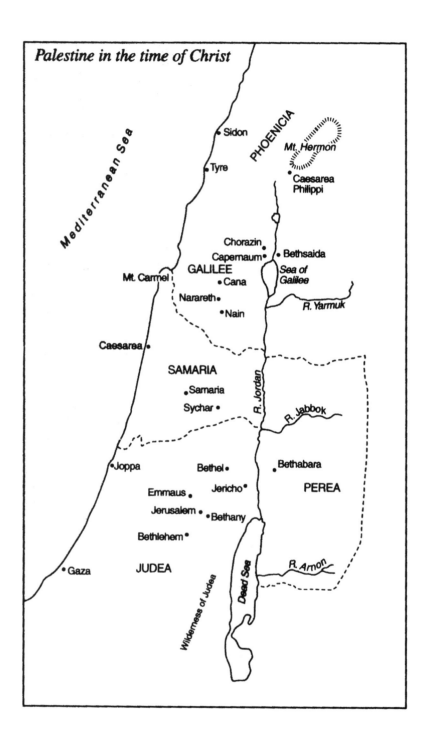

deeds of the church at Thyatira but faults the church for tolerating a self-appointed prophetess, who, like Jezebel in the Old Testament, was leading God's children into idolatry and immorality (18-29). He has nothing good to say about the church at Sardis; although it had a reputation for being a lively church, he charges that most of its members were, in fact, spiritually dead (3:1-6). He has nothing but praise for the church at Philadelphia for its perseverance under testing, and he encourages it to keep holding fast (7-13). Although the church at Laodicea prided itself on being prosperous and healthy, he condemns it for its spiritual lukewarmness and calls it to awaken to the miserable reality of its blindness and destitution (14-22).

After seeing these things,[5] John is caught up in the spirit from earth to heaven where he sees a second vision containing three series of judgments (4:1–16:21). As a prelude to these judgments, he is ushered into the throne room of heaven (4:1–5:14), where he sees the majestic glory of the One sitting on the throne, whose sovereignty does not show the slightest sign of being threatened by the turmoil that will shortly break out upon the earth (4:1-11). The heavenly throne was encircled by a rainbow of light (4:1-3). Seated in an outer circle around the throne were twenty-four elders dressed in white with golden crowns on their heads (4). While John looked upon this scene, thunder and lightning proceeded from the throne (5-6a). Immediately surrounding the throne were four living creatures, the first like a lion, the second like an ox, the third like a man, and the fourth like a flying eagle; these living creatures were occupied day and night with praising the One seated on the throne, while the twenty-four elders joined in worship (6b-11).

For a moment, the awesomeness of this sight is forgotten as everyone's attention is drawn towards an enigmatic book with seven seals in the right hand of the One seated on the throne (5:1-14). A search went out throughout heaven and earth, but, much to John's distress, no one was found who could open the book (1-5) until a

---

5. Cf. Revelation 1:19 and note 1 above. As was the case in John's Gospel, some form of the phrase 'after these things' or 'after this' is often used in Revelation to mark a transition to a new section (Rev 4:1; 7:1, 9; 9:12;15:5; 18:1; 19:1; 20:3).

Lamb that looked as if he had been slain stepped forward to take it (6-7). In response, all of creation united their voices in praise to the Lamb (8-14). First, the four living creatures and the twenty-four elders who surrounded the throne spontaneously burst into a new song proclaiming the worthiness of the Lamb to open the book (8-10). Countless angels added their voices on the second verse (11-12); finally, all created beings in heaven and on earth

---

Numbers in Revelation

Numbers play an important part in the apocalyptic imagery of Revelation. Many of these numbers have symbolic meaning, others are intended to be taken literally, and sometimes a literal number has symbolic significance. Context and the broader biblical background from which many of these numbers arose must be our guide in interpreting them correctly. A number that is used with a good connotation often has an evil counterpart as well.

Jesus is the first and the last the alpha and omega. No one but the slain lamb can open the sealed book. The ten kings have one purpose and reign with the beast for one hour. Judgment comes upon Babylon in one day, and in one hour she is destroyed. While Satan is bound in the abyss, Jesus will reign for one thousand years.

A two-edged sword proceeds from Christ's mouth. There are two witnesses and two olive trees. The beast out of the earth has two horns like a lamb.

Revelation contains three woes, and three series of judgments. In the first series, a fourth of the earth is killed. The second series of judgments harms or destroys a third of the earth, the trees, the sea, the creatures in it, the ships, and the fresh waters. A third of the stars were swept out of heaven by the red dragon.

John had four visions. He saw four living creatures and an altar in heaven with four horns. Riders on four horses bring the first four judgments, and four angels stand at the four corners of the earth holding back the four winds.

The number of the beast is 666.

John writes to seven churches that are represented by seven lampstands. In his hand, Christ holds seven stars, which are the seven angels, or messengers, of these churches. The book of Revelation contains seven benedictions. The lamb has seven horns and seven eyes, which are the seven Spirits of God. The judgements are unfolded

---

joined in a mass choir singing praise to the one sitting on the throne and to the Lamb (13-14).

From this heavenly vantage point, the first in a series of three judgments unfolds as the Lamb breaks the book's seven seals (**6:1– 8:1**). The breaking of the first seal discloses the first of four horses, a white charger bent on conquest (6:1-2). With the breaking of the second seal, a red horse goes out to war (3-4). A black horse

in groups of seven: there are seven seals, seven trumpets blown by seven angels, and seven bowls of plagues poured out by seven angels. The announcement of a mighty angel is echoed by seven peals of thunder. Seven thousand people are killed in an earthquake when the two witnesses ascend to heaven.

The great red dragon has seven heads, with seven crowns, and ten horns. The beast on which the woman sits also has seven heads and ten horns. The seven heads are described as seven kings and seven mountains. The ten horns, which are crowned with ten crowns, are also ten kings.

Several different ways are used to describe a period lasting for half of seven years. The beast is given authority for forty-two months, and the holy city is trodden under foot by the Gentiles for forty-two months. The woman who bore the male child is protected from the dragon for a time and times and half a time, or for 1,260 days, and the two witnesses prophesy for 1,260 days. As well as seven years being divided in half, we also find seven days divided in half in the case of the two witnesses, who are killed by the beast, and whose bodies lie in the street for three and a half days.

Twelve is a popular number. The woman who bore the male child wears a crown of twelve stars. The new Jerusalem has twelve gates, each made of a solid pearl. The gates are guarded by twelve angels and inscribed with the names of the twelve tribes of Israel. The city also has twelve foundations stones bearing the twelve names of the twelve apostles. The tree of life, which bears every month of the year, produces twelve kinds of fruit.

Multiples of twelve are also common. Twelve times two yields twenty-four thrones and twenty four elders. The new Jerusalem is a perfect cube, twelve thousand stadia in length, width, and height. The wall of the city is one hundred and forty cubits, or twelve cubits squared. Twelve thousand are sealed from each of the twelve tribes of Israel for a total of 144,000.

representing famine appears when the third seal is broken (5-6); and the last horse, looking the sickly pale color of death, follows upon the breaking of the fourth seal 7-8).

The fifth seal moves beyond the equestrian imagery to reveal the souls of the martyrs who were standing under the altar and praying for God's vengeance (9-11). The sixth seal unleashes a powerful earthquake that announces the arrival of the great day of God's wrath (12-17).

Before the breaking of the seventh seal, an interlude allows the reader a breathing space to prepare for its devastating impact (7:1-17). Four angels stand poised to release judgment upon the earth, but they are held back until 144,000 of God's servants can be sealed, 12,000 from each tribe of Israel (1-8). Following their sealing, John sees an innumerable multitude of people from every race and language standing before the throne in heaven (9-17). They are all dressed in white and lead the other creatures around the throne in praise to God (9-12). One of the elders informs John that these people dressed in white are saints who have come out of the great tribulation (13-17).

When the seventh seal is broken, heaven is silent for about half an hour (**8**:1). This seventh seal has no content of its own but unfolds the second series of judgments, which is represented by seven trumpets (8:2–11:19). Another brief delay precedes the sounding of the trumpets (8:2-6). An angel mixes incense with the prayers of the saints and throws his fire-filled censer to the earth (2-5); then the seven angels prepare to blow (6).

The first trumpet unleashes a mixture of hail, fire and blood upon the earth, burning a third of it (7). At the second trumpet, a giant volcano erupts in the sea and destroys a third of all marine life and ships (8-9). When the third trumpet sounds, a falling star strikes a third of the fresh waters and makes them bitter (10-11). With the sounding of the fourth trumpet, the sun, moon and stars are darkened so that a third of their light is extinguished (12).

The last three trumpets are set off from the first four by the announcement of a flying eagle that three woes are coming upon the ungodly inhabitants of the earth (13). The fifth trumpet, which corresponds to the first woe, sees the bottomless pit opened to release a demonic plague of locusts upon those who are not sealed by God (**9**:1-11). John reports the torments that come upon those who are not sealed (1-6), and then he describes the fierceness of the demonic locusts that afflict these unbelievers (7-11). A transitional sentence announces that the first woe is over and warns that two more are coming (12).

When the sixth trumpet sounds, four angels who had been bound are released so that they might slaughter a third of mankind (13-21). In a similar manner to the unfolding of the preceding trumpet, John recounts the onslaught of warring hordes of cavalry who, along with the four angels, had been held back at the Euphrates River (13-16); he then describes the power of the horses and riders who do the slaughtering by emitting plagues of fire, smoke and burning sulphur from their mouths (17-19). To this trumpet, John adds a comment about the impenitence of those who survive (20-21).

Just as an interlude precedes the breaking of the last seal, so a corresponding interlude comes before the sounding of the seventh trumpet (**10**:1–11:13). During this interlude, a mighty angel, who was holding a little book in his hand and standing with one foot on the sea and the other on the land, makes preparations for the impending consummation of God's purposes (10:1-11). This angel gives a loud shout that is followed by seven thunderclaps, the meaning of which John was commanded to conceal from his readers (1-4). The angel then announces that God's purposes will be completed without further delay (5-7). He presents John with the little book (8-11) upon the apostle's request (8-9). When John eats it, as he is instructed, he discovers that at first it tastes sweet in his mouth but later becomes bitter in his stomach (10-11).

The interlude before the seventh trumpet also includes John's symbolic action of measuring the temple along with those who worship in it at a time when the city is subject to Gentile occupation (**11**:1-2). During this period, which lasts for twelve hundred and sixty days, two witnesses give powerful testimony for the Lord (3-13). These witnesses are given authority to prophesy and perform miracles like Elijah (3-6), but they are martyred by the beast, much to the rejoicing of the inhabitants of the earth (7-10). After three

The Beasts in Daniel

Image 2:31-45	Four Beasts 7:3-8, 17-28	Two Animals with horns Dan 8:3-27	Antagonistic Kings 11:2-45
Head of gold	Lion		
Breast and arms of silver	Bear raised on one side	Ram with two unequal horns	three more kings in Persia plus a fourth
Belly and thighs of bronze	Leopard 4 wings 4 heads	Male goat Large goat 4 horns Little horn	Mighty king of Greece Kingdom divided in four Contemptible person King of South
Legs of iron	Peaceful beast		End-time King
Feet of iron and clay	10 horns little horn		

The Beasts in Revelation

Beast out of the Sea 13:1-10, 18 (11:7)	Beast carrying harlot 17:3, 7-18	Beast out of the earth 13:11-17	Red dragon 12:1-17
Mouth like a lion			
Feet like a bear			
Like a leopard			
Receives worship Blasphemes	Destroys harlot Blasphemous names	two horns like a lamb Speaks like a dragon Causes worship of first beast	Persecutes woman with child
Wages war with saints	Wages war with Lamb		War with Michael
666			
seven heads one slain and healed	seven heads – seven mountains		= Serpent, Devil, Satan
ten horns	ten horns – ten kings		seven heads ten horns

and a half days, however, they return to life and are caught up to heaven (11-13).

A transitional sentence marks the end of the second woe and the coming of the third one (14). The sounding of the seventh trumpet is accompanied by an announcement from heaven of God's reign over the kingdom of the world (15-19).

Before the next series of judgments is unveiled, another interlude takes the readers behind the heavenly curtain, as it were, to give us special insight into the spiritual conflict between the cosmic forces of good and evil (**12**:1–14:20). John uses several images to depict this great conflict, the first of which is a fierce battle with a dragon (12:1-18). He sets the stage by introducing the major characters in this battle (1-6). A pregnant woman wearing a crown with twelve stars appears on the stage of heaven (1-2). A great red dragon with seven heads and ten horns, who had already swept a third of the stars down from heaven with his tail, stands poised in front of her, ready to devour her child the moment it is born (3-4). The woman gives birth to a male child who is destined to rule all the nations, and she flees to the wilderness for twelve hundred and sixty days after her child is caught up to God's throne (5-6).

With this backdrop in place, John describes the war in heaven (7-12). Michael and his angels overpower the dragon, who is identified as Satan, and hurl him down to earth along with his evil angels (7-9). A joyful victory celebration breaks out in heaven (10-12), but the dragon directs his remaining energy against the woman, who remains on the earth but is kept beyond his grasp for three and a half years (13-18).

In addition to war with the dragon, the conflict of good against evil includes opposition to the two beasts (**13**:1–18). The first beast, who derives his power and authority from the dragon, rises up out of the sea (1-10). He possesses the most fearsome characteristics of a leopard, bear, and lion combined; and, like the dragon, he also has ten horns and seven heads, one of which had been healed from a fatal wound (1-3a). The people of the whole world worship him because his recovery seemed miraculous and to fight against him seemed impossible (3b-4). For forty-two months, the beast arrogantly blasphemes God and wages war against the saints (5-

8). As an aside, John concludes his prophetic vision of this beast by warning his readers of their need for vigilance (9-10).

The second beast, who exercises his authority on behalf of the first beast, rises up out of the earth (11-18). By performing deceptive signs, this beast persuades the inhabitants of the earth to erect an image of the first beast (11-14). He is so powerful that he can make the image of the beast come to life and can prevent anyone who does not bear his mark from buying or selling (15-17). In another aside, John reveals in cryptic symbolism that the number of the beast is 666 (18).

Now that the forces of evil in this great conflict have been presented, John introduces the good side in a contrasting revelation of the Lamb along with 144,000 celibate men who follow him singing his praises (**14**:1-5). Following this jubilant revelation, three angels announce the coming victory of righteousness (6-12). The first angel announces the imminent approach of judgment (6-7). The second announces the fall of Babylon (8), and the third predicts the doom of those who worship the beast (9-12).

When the three angels have spoken, a voice from heaven pronounces a blessing on those who are about to die in the Lord (13).[6] The assurance of their blessedness prepares the earth for harvesting (14-20). A heavenly figure who resembles a son of man reaps the grain with a sickle (14-16), and then he gathers the clusters of grapes and throws them into a great wine press where God's wrath is trodden out (17-20).

Following this extended interlude, the third series of judgments, which consists of seven bowls, is poured out (**15**:1–16:21), but before these terrible judgments fall, the reader is mentally prepared for them in three ways (15:1–16:1). An introductory statement declares that their objective is to bring God's wrath to its completion (15:1). A hymn sung by the saints who have been victorious over the beast reveals God's righteousness in executing these judgments (2-4), and the appearance of the administering angels in the heavenly temple, where one of the living creatures hands them seven bowls containing God's wrath, demonstrates that these

---

6. This blessing is the second of seven in Rev.; cf. note on 1:3.

judgments are authorized by God (15:5-16:1).

The first angel pours out his bowl upon the earth, and it causes malignant sores on those who worship the beast (16:2). The second angel pours out his bowl on the sea, and it turns to blood (3). The third angel pours out his bowl on the fresh waters, which also turn to blood as a fitting punishment on those who have poured out the blood of the saints (4-7). The fourth angel pours out his bowl on the sun, and it scorches people with intense heat (8-9). The fifth angel pours out his bowl on the throne of the beast, and darkness falls upon his kingdom (10-11). The sixth angel pours out his bowl on the Euphrates River, and it is dried up so that all the armies of the world might gather together for the great battle of Armageddon (12-16). Embedded in this section is a blessing on those who are watchful (15). The seventh angel pours out his bowl on the air, and a great earthquake causes all the cities of the nations to collapse (17-21).

As was the case with the seals and the trumpets, where the seventh in each series opens up the following set of judgments, so in a similar way, the seventh bowl judgment, which sees the fall of all cities, leads into the third vision in Revelation, which expands upon the fall of the greatest pagan city, Babylon, and the establishment of God's universal reign (**17**:1-21:8). So that he might see this vision, John is translated to heaven by one of the angels who had the seven bowls (17:1-3a). First, he sees the fall of Babylon (17:3b–18:24) portrayed symbolically as the fall of a great harlot (3b-18). John gives us a description of her appearance and the beast upon which she sits (3b-6a), and he confesses that he was utterly amazed at the vision (6b-7). To help him understand, the angel interprets the key elements of the vision (8-18) including: the destiny of the beast upon which the woman sits (8), the identity of its seven heads (9-11) and ten horns (12-14), and also of the waters upon which the woman sits (15). He explains the hatred of the ten horns and the beast for the woman, which leads to her demise (16-17); and, finally, he identifies the woman herself as a great city (18).

The vision then expands upon this identification of the harlot by portraying Babylon's fall in more literal language as the fall of a great commercial center (**18**:1-24). An angel with great authority, who is distinguished from the interpreting angel of chapter seventeen, announces Babylon's fall (1-3), and a voice answers from heaven disclosing the divine attitude towards the city's demise (4-8). This voice both warns God's people to flee the city (4-5) and cries for God's judgment upon it (6-8). Humans respond to Babylon's fall in two very different ways (9-20): the city's commercial patrons lament greatly (9-19), but the saints rejoice (20). To depict the violence with which Babylon will be overthrown, a strong angel symbolically enacts its fall by heaving a boulder the size of a large millstone into the sea (21-24).

The fall of Babylon makes way for the establishment of God's universal reign (**19**:1–21:8). John reports that he heard a vast crowd in heaven singing a hymn of rejoicing over Babylon's fall (19:1-5) and preparing to celebrate the marriage of the Lamb (6-10). Those who are invited to the marriage supper are noted parenthetically in this section in a fourth blessing (9). At this point, Jesus Christ appears mounted on a white horse, ready for battle (11-16). The war against the beast is very brief and decisive (17-21). An angel calls all the vultures together to feast upon the flesh of kings and soldiers, great and small (17-18), and the beast is seized along with his false prophet and thrown into the lake of fire while his entire army is put to death by the sword of the rider on the white horse (19-21). The dragon, who is Satan, is also bound and thrown into the abyss for one thousand years (**20**:1-3).

With Satan's binding begins the millennial reign of Christ (**20**:4-6). The righteous who had died during the tribulation are raised to reign with Christ (4-5), and a blessing is pronounced upon them (6). After the thousand years, Satan is released from his prison and gathers the nations together to make war against the saints, but his armies are destroyed and he is thrown into the lake of fire, where he is tormented forever (7-10). At that time the dead are raised to life and stand before God's great white throne to be judged (11-15).

As a transition to the eternal age, John introduces the arrival of the new heaven and new earth before zeroing in on a particular aspect of them (**21**:1-8). With the coming of the new heaven and earth, the presence of God among his people is realized (1-4), and his purposes are completed for those who overcome to inherit, while the unbelievers are thrown into the lake of fire (5-8).

The fourth vision in Revelation is introduced, once again,[7] by one of the seven angels who had the golden bowls carrying John away to see the vision, which, this time, concerns the new Jerusalem (21:9–22:5). He describes the glorious descent of the city (21:9-14) in terms of its heavenly origin, as the bride of the Lamb coming down from heaven (9-11), and its solid foundations with its twelve gates being named after the twelve tribes of Israel and its twelve foundation stones named after the twelve apostles (12-14). Using symbolic language, John also describes the physical construction of the city (15-21). It is a city of magnificent proportions both in its immense size and its layout as a perfect cube (15-17); it is built of pure gold and precious stones (18-21). The city has no temple and no sun or moon because it is illumined by the presence of God and the Lamb (22-27). From God's throne flows a crystal clear river that gives life to all of the city (22:1-5).

The book closes with an epilogue (6-21). In this epilogue, which in some ways parallels the prologue, the angel who had shown John the vision endorses the book's trustworthiness (6), and Jesus blesses those who heed the book's message (7).[8] The angel instructs John (8-11) not to worship him because he is John's fellow servant (8-9)[9] and not to seal the book because the time of its fulfillment is so near that neither the righteous nor the unrighteous will change their behaviour (10-11).

The epilogue also contains Jesus' final message to the churches (12-16). Speaking as the Alpha and Omega, Jesus warns that his coming in judgment is imminent (12-13).[10] He pronounces a seventh, and final, blessing on the redeemed in the new Jerusalem (14) and sounds a contrasting warning to the ungodly, who will be excluded from the city (15). He also adds a personal testimony stating that he has authorized the angelic messenger to reveal the contents of the book (16).

---

7. Cf. Revelation 17:1.
8. This blessing is the sixth in Revelation; cf. the similar blessing in Rev 1:3.
9. He had given a similar warning to John in Revelation 19:10.
10. Cf. Revelation 1:8.

The Spirit and the bride of the Lamb invite the readers of the book to accept its offer of life (17), and John gives a few concluding words to them (18-21). He sternly warns them not to tamper with the book's wording (18-19) and affirms his wish for Jesus' speedy return (20). Finally, he concludes the book as he began with a benediction of grace (21).[11]

---

11. Cf. the opening benediction of grace and peace in 1:4-5a.

OUTLINE OF REVELATION

---

1. Cf. Revelation 14:13; 16:15; 19:9; 20:6; 22:7, 14.

---

2. If the first woe is the fifth trumpet (9:1-11) and the second woe the sixth trumpet (9:13-21), one would expect the third woe, which is not explicitly identified, to be the seventh trumpet (11:15-19), which unfolds the seven bowl judgments (15:1–16:21).

3. Verse 18 of the Greek text is verse 17b in most English translations (NASB, NIV, RSV), with the notable exception of the KJV which makes it 13:1. The NLT follows the Greek text in its versification.

Dale Leschert is a young Canadian scholar whose studies and teaching have taken him to Bible colleges and seminaries all across western Canada, down the west coast of the United States and across to the east coast. He earned his Ph. D. at Fuller Theological Seminary on Hermeneutical Foundations of Hebrews, which has been published in a distinguished series sponsored by the National Association of Baptist Professors of Religion. He holds professional memberships in the Evangelical Theological Society and the Society of Biblical Literature and is also an active member of First Baptist Church in Vancouver, British Columbia. His spare time is usually spent hiking the scenic mountains of the west coast or training for another marathon.